Commendations for *Mission in Motion: Speaking Frankly*

A new generation of mission mobilisers are emerging fron[...] giving life, meaning, and definition to what is known as Polycer[...] timely to fan the flame of that which God is already doing. [...] around the complexity of mission mobilisation, but also clears the pathway for new and fresh methodologies to be applied in raising an army of mission practitioners. I gladly endorse the book as a mandatory resource for any person involved in seeing God's Kingdom established in every corner of the world.

Adriaan Adams, *MovingIntoAction, South Africa*

Research in missional movements has a long history but very few have ventured into closely looking at mobilisation for missions. This book unravels what goes on behind the scenes to mobilise people whom God has called to the frontlines. This research and reflection is a milestone in mission history and anyone keen to be involved or already involved in the ministry of mobilisation must study this book. The urgency to understand what we are doing in mission mobilisation takes centre stage as the mission context has changed.

John Amalraj, *Executive Secretary, Interserve India*

Too much mission research is either monocultural (North-American), or devoid of a theological context, and very often both. *Mission in Motion* falls into neither of these traps; it is a genuinely international piece of research into the factors that encourage people into involvement in mission with a solid theological base. This is an important book which will be a standard reference for practitioners, mobilisers, and academics for years to come.

Eddie Arthur, *Director of Strategic Initiatives, Global Connections, UK*

As part of the emerging missionary movement, the Korean Church experienced an explosive growth in the number of missionaries from 93 in 1979 to more than 20,000 in less than 40 years. However, recent years have seen the downturn of the Korean missionary movement. The number of new missionaries sent to the field in 2015 was just one percent of the number already fielded in the previous year—that is, about 200. This crisis situation is challenging us to reexamine the path that we have walked and the road that lies ahead. This fascinating book will help us do this right.

Dr. Felipe Jinsuk Byun, *Director of Global Missionary Training Center, South Korea*

Mission in Motion is a thoughtful book and a must-read for leaders who are shaping the mission movement from everywhere to everyone. Authors Gold and Matenga tackled a topic that can fall prey to some tiresome treatments; they succeeded by bringing historical perspective and tethering them to the emerging perspectives from around each distinct regions of the world. Thus, appetizers led to a feast! The question is—are we willing enough to critically reexamine mission in light of the emerging paradigm?

Rev. Samuel E. Chiang, *President and Chief Executive Officer, Seed Company, USA*

Jesus said the laborers are few, pray therefore. I believe we have to have a prayer support group praying for missions mobilization then we do as God directs and we will see fulfilment of multitudes going into missions. Secondly, I believe missionaries will come not just from the West but some of our most powerful missionaries will come from the nations below the equator. I believe every nation should send missionaries to every other nation on earth. May God bless you in your efforts to mobilize missionaries.

Loren Cunningham, *Founder, Youth With A Mission*

Drawing together voices from around the world, *Mission in Motion* thoughtfully explores the complex issue of mobilisation for global mission. In today's context, what does mobilisation actually mean? Who is called, and for what? How do different understandings of what mission is confuse it all? This book is not about agency or church empire-building, but about aligning with the Lord's heart to see his kingdom grow, and for God's people everywhere to be engaged in effective mission, locally and cross-culturally. Read it!

Rose Dowsett, *OMF International [retired]; former Vice-Chair, WEA Mission Commission, UK*

The research undertaken by the WEA Mission Commission Mission Mobilization Task Force is a unique worldwide project looking at the different ways people are recruited, trained, and sent into missionary work. The outstanding growth of mission movements in countries traditionally seen as mission fields changes the whole missionary enterprise around the globe. Innovative ways of mobilizing people into part or fulltime ministry are seen in the needed creativity of traditional sending countries and the inspiring freshness of the newer sending models. We can certainly learn from both. *Mission in Motion* enriches our understanding of how mobilization is done today and encourages us to a deeper reflection on how we best can facilitate people to engage in God's mission.

Dr. Bertil Ekström, *Executive Director, WEA Mission Commission, Brazil*

The Apostle Paul set a pattern of transcultural mission that accompanied his practice with a continuous reflection about it in light of God's word. Missiology has developed through the contribution of successive generations of that kind of reflective practitioners of Christian mission, in a great variety of contexts and moments. This book is a contemporary effort along this apostolic line that benefits from the incredible amount of information about missionary practices that we have now at our disposal. I hope that the missionary drive of the Holy Spirit moving in sending churches from the majority world nowadays will be helped by this book in the indispensable task of reflecting about their practice.

Dr. Samuel Escobar, *Facultad Protestante de Teología UEBE, Spain*

Mobilizers take note: *Mission in Motion* is a must read for any mobilizer wanting to better understand the complex and global phenomenon that we call mobilization. This influential book provides numerous case studies and examples that give practical insight and definition into the ministry of mobilization.

Ryan Emis, *Director of Global Partnerships for the Center for Mission Mobilization; Founding member of the Global Mobilization Network, South East Asia*

This is a global look at mobilization that will both embrace and challenge some commonly held beliefs. If you are a missions mobilizer this book is one which you should consider reading.

Dr. Ted Esler, *President, Missio Nexus, USA*

Occasionally a new book about some aspect of mission grabs my attention. *Mission in Motion* is one of them. This book delves into the "complex" topic of mobilization for mission. I say complex simply because thoroughly exploring this topic is not for the faint-hearted. The authors have given a thorough perspective on the global-glocal complexities of mobilization for God's mission. This is done with sensitivity and supported by qualitative research from practitioners. This resource needs to be in the hands of everyone who takes the calling and sending of God's people into God's mission seriously.

Dr. Kirk Franklin, *Executive Director, Wycliffe Global Alliance, Australia*

To open this book is to open yourself to a wisely-moderated conversation with scores of mission mobilizers from all over the world. You might well find yourself talking back, as I did. And therein lies the value of this book—it will provoke fruitful conversations about the important work of mission mobilizing. The helpful analysis of our present-day ambiguity about the nature of mission is set next to a robust diversity of approaches to the work of mobilization. It's for pastors and professors as much as it is for mission leaders.

Dr. Steven Hawthorne, *Editor,* Perspectives on the World Christian Movement, *USA*

Are you looking for encouragement and guidance about where to direct your efforts in working under God to mobilize people into mission? This comprehensive study of what facilitates and hinders people along their journey into mission will be a tremendous help. Excerpts from multiple conversations with missionaries and mission mobilizers in nine countries allow readers to access both a diverse range of perspectives and discern common themes. Particularly helpful is the emphasis that emerges on missionaries' sense of divine calling that grows in the context of a wide range of human factors.

Dr. Richard Hibbert, *Director of the School of Cross-Cultural Mission, Sydney Missionary and Bible College, Australia*

This book is a treasure store of practical wisdom for an under-researched area of mission practice. My seminary classes will be the richer for the insights and discoveries unearthed and presented by a first-class team of authors. Some missiological assumptions are challenged and will inevitably generate new practices for the formation and recruitment of future missionaries. The missiologists dilemma—whether to theologise or mobilise—is no longer as stark as it once was. With this book, the next generation of mission mobilisers will be blessed with an informed and missiologically rich resource that rests on more than mere opinions or possibilities. *Mission in Motion* deserves its place among the growing rank of excellent offerings from the WEA Mission Commission. In sum, this volume nails it!

Rev. Dr. Darrell Jackson, *Senior Missiologist, Morling College, Australia*

This carefully crafted research on mission mobilization comes at just the right time as evangelicals around the world grapple with mission in the new contexts of global Christianity and religious pluralism. One important highlight is the serious gender challenge where women continue to have an outsized role in mission without a corresponding place in leadership. This rich book offers both penetrating critique and encouragement for the way forward.

Dr. Todd M. Johnson, *Director, Center for the Study of Global Christianity, Gordon-Conwell Theological Seminary, USA*

I strongly recommend *Mission in Motion*. It will greatly help pastors of congregations learn how to work more fruitfully within the global church. It provides significant insights for leaders serving in diverse types of faith-based organizations. For mission scholars it provides an exemplary example of how to conduct global research and communicate findings in relevant and meaningful ways for busy pastors and practitioners. I am so impressed by this book!

Dr. Mary Lederleitner, *Author of* Cross-Cultural Partnerships*; Consultant for Learning Strategies, Leadership Team, Wycliffe Global Alliance; Researcher and Adjunct Professor, Trinity Evangelical Divinity School, USA*

The research presented in this book provides answers to questions that many of us have been asking about how, why, and to what this generation of mission workers are being called. *Mission in Motion* offers an important reflection into the factors that contribute to and inhibit global engagement, and raises many more questions as we wrestle with the implications. Written with a global perspective, this book will significantly benefit all those engaged in prayerfully and practically mobilising labourers for the harvest.

Dr. Joanna Lima, *Pioneers International Leadership Development, Thailand*

I am deeply appreciative of the efforts of the research team in producing this volume. It is a practical overview of the motivations and methods mobilizing for the mission of God. The team doesn't shy away from the complex reality of "missional anomie." The overview of regional characteristics followed by a deeper look at both accelerants and retardants provide the breadth necessary to gain a global picture. This type of work adds an important dimension to our understanding of missiology. The most significant contribution may well be the conversations generated in the boardrooms of denominations, mission societies, schools, and foundations.

Dr. Doug McConnell, *Professor, Leadership and Intercultural Studies, Fuller Theological Seminary, School of Intercultural Studies, USA*

A few years ago I contacted a number of mission networks to learn from previous surveys about mission mobilization. To my amazement, little could be found. I am so grateful we now have *Mission in Motion* as a resource for everyone involved in recruiting and launching missionaries. This book has both depth and breadth. The material is like a treasure trove of valuables with many pearls never discovered until now. I look forward to applying these insights and encouraging other mobilizers to do the same.

John McVay, *Missions mobilizer; Researcher, launchsurvey.wordpress.com*

This is a valuable mission resource that emanates directly from voices of the global church. With a kaleidoscope of church and mission leaders expressing observations and opinions as the basis behind the book's research, one is confident that this is a truly updated view of what is transpiring in the most key issues related to mission mobilization globally. Every conceivable angle is covered.

Marvin Newell, *Senior Vice President, Missio Nexus, USA*

Mission in Motion brings clarity, depth, and analysis to both theory and practice of the significance of mobilization in mission and missiology. The mission of God's people and the missionary movement has always been in motion. An African proverb affirms: "If the rhythm of the drum beat changes, the dance steps must adapt." The mission of God unfolds in constantly changing contexts, with a constant gospel. The authors of *Mission in Motion* provide unique and valuable contribution to the study, strategy, and deployment of mission workers globally. The evangelical missions community is well served by this thoroughly researched, clarified, and outlined piece of missiological reflection and practice.

Dr. Lazarus Phiri, *Vice Chancellor, Evangelical University, Zambia*

The flat globalized changing world and the changing demography of Christ-followers around the globe gives rise to issues like defining mission, the call to full-time mission work, the mode of sending missionaries across the world, the agendas for mission, and the decline of classical missionaries; all of which cause the traditional mission world to question the way forward! *Mission in Motion* will challenge you to think more creatively about such things, to become more proactive in communicating the Good News to the ends of the earth. I warmly recommend this book for transformed Christ-followers, thinkers, theologians, missiologists, pastors, and leaders who mean business for the Lord.

Dr. K. Rajendran, *Associate Director [Leadership Development, Strategic Thinking, Global Roundtables, and Mission Commission Creative Networks], World Evangelical Alliance Mission Commission, India*

Many of us have longed for a second reformation—a rediscovery of the missionhood of the believer. Nothing excites us more than to see God's people align more fully with their Great Commission calling. *Mission in Motion* paints a picture of what this looks like in today's fast changing global environment. It affirms something I've long believed—that there is no substitute for the hard work of life-on-life discipleship and influence when it comes to mobilizing laborers for the global harvest.

Steve Richardson, *President, Pioneers, USA*

The title suggests that mission is a moving target and the text does not disappoint. Competent, well trained researchers apply a qualitative approach to extensive research that reflects actual concerns and issues relevant to mission in the twenty-first century. The authors present the findings in an engaging style that will serve a global readership. I applaud the intercultural approach that integrates global issues in a multi-national yet complementary manner. I commend this book to all who are engaged in mission: practitioners, organizations, churches, and supporters—all are critical for mobilization!

Dr. R. Daniel Shaw, *Senior Professor of Anthropology and Translation, Fuller Graduate School of Intercultural Studies, USA*

The face and expression of the mission movement is shifting and we need to keep in step with the new ways the Holy Spirit is mobilizing his church to the fulfil the Great Commission. By showing us where we currently are in the realm of cross-cultural mission mobilization, this book enables us to see more clearly where we need to go. It is a key resource for anyone called as a mission mobilizer. May we together take up our high calling and call forth Christ's body to her purpose in the Great Commission in this critical hour of human history.

Ryan Shaw, *International Lead Facilitator, Student Volunteer Movement 2, Thailand*

Many of us share the desire to see God raise up workers for his harvest field. This rightfully drives us to prayer, but is there more we can do? *Mission in Motion* takes us into the world of global mission to help answer this question. By listening to the voices of God's people all over the world we gain an invaluable insight into the factors that accelerate and retard people's involvement in mission. May God use this book for his glory among the nations!

Tim Silberman, *Lecturer in Missions, Sydney Missionary & Bible College, Australia*

Many books contribute to mobilization in missions, but few analyze it. This book is in rarified air as a must read for those open to having their minds stretched and hearts inflamed about the missions mobilization of God in the world today. It is groundbreaking and deeply thought-provoking. I was freshly inspired and riveted by the masterful blend of current realities and compelling testimonies into a mobilization roadmap for our day!

Mark Stebbins, *US Collegiate Missions Director, The Navigators; Mission Mobilization Advisor, Missio Nexus, USA*

I am personally so excited that the final product of *Mission in Motion* is available. I believe it will be a gift to the global church as we respond to the challenge of the least reached. Local churches, mission organizations, and training institutions will benefit greatly by this well-researched and thought-out product. I simply love the global scope of the book and it has some significant insights in how we mobilise the church in some of the newer sending countries. Every organisation and church serious about the Great Commission should have a copy of this book!

Peter Tarantal, *Associate International Director, OM; Director, World Evangelisation Network of South Africa; Chairperson, WEA MC Global Leadership Council, South Africa*

This resource is unique and thoughtful. There is nothing like it in the history of mission leadership: a long-gestated, theologically-driven research project, carefully studied and analyzed; a truly global venture with strategic voices from East Asia, South India, East Africa, Eastern Europe, the United Kingdom, the United States, Latin America, and Oceania; a variegated project with women and men of passion and analysis, i.e., reflective practitioners. Such books challenge the established understanding of both mission and mission mobilization as "the first definitive exploration of the ministries and methods of mission mobilization." I cannot recommend this enough, especially to friends and colleagues who share vision and passion for authentic, long-lasting mobilization of the people of our God on mission who can also read the times and speak with authority.

Dr. William D. Taylor, *Global Mentor, WEA Mission Commission; President, TaylorGlobalConsult, USA*

This book provides a helpful focus on why and how people have been called to become involved in what we have called, until now, missionary work, world mission, global mission, or cross-cultural mission. Of those of us who were indeed "called" within such a paradigm, it provides insightful and helpful understanding and analysis. But the book also introduces the helpful expression "missional anomie" to explore the reality that mission is in flux, in practice and in concept, and that many of us in the West are still struggling to engage with the realities of mission in the context of post-Christendom.

Richard Tiplady, *Principal, Scottish School of Christian Mission, Scotland*

This is a project I have waited for a long time! The results of the research both inspire and deeply challenge me as a missions mobilizer. I am eager for our organization to devote time to read, learn, reflect on the issues and incorporate the lessons learned into our mobilization processes. It will be very useful for training, understanding past and current trends in missions mobilization, as well as open up opportunities for ongoing discussion among current and future mission mobilizers. This is an invaluable contribution to the discourse on missions and especially mission mobilization in our times.

Nosa Tukura, *Deputy International Director, Resource Development, Missions Supporters League (MSL), Nigeria*

Global mission mobilisation consumes energy, time, and resources of individuals and agencies. Findings in *Mission in Motion* illuminate the hidden dimensions of mobilisation engagement and will inspire improvement in delivery and practices. Three valuable contributions are the concept of missional anomie; the four ideal-types of mobilization approaches; and the motif of fire to analyse mobilisation dynamics. The book's non-prescriptive, non-reductionist, and non-formulaic outcomes will generate creativity and innovation under God's leadership and will fan flames of momentum for kingdom growth.

David Turnbull, *Senior Lecturer in Intercultural Studies, Tabor College of Higher Education, Australia*

Mission in Motion cannot come at any better time than this one for any seriously mission minded churches in the global South. In all our efforts to mobilize churches for missions in Africa, the book is a wonderful tool that deserves to be high on the list of must books.

Peter Vumisa, *Director of Research and Mission Mobilization, Institute for Strategic Services, South Africa*

In *Mission in Motion*, a team of international researchers provide a much-needed service to today's church and mission community by exploring and faithfully sharing what Christians in and from a wide variety of contexts have to say about the nature of the mission enterprise and mission mobilization, what motivated their own initial involvement, and what they see as accelerants and or retardants to the mission mobilization flame. This carefully crafted and far-reaching work is well-worth the read!

Marti Wade, *Editor, Missions Catalyst, USA*

Across the globe most involvement in mission doesn't begin by answering the complex question, "What is mission?" Instead, people are fired up by the Holy Spirit through a whole range of factors that push, pull, inspire, and motivate them to be "beautiful feet" sent into the world (Romans 10: 14–15). Intentionally building mission motivation and fearlessly addressing factors that demotivate is crucial work for church pastors, mission leaders, and mission trainers. *Mission in Motion* reports well-researched "accelerants" and "retardants" of mission motivation offering the global church a valuable, comprehensive resource to fan into flames motivation for mission once again.

Dr. Ruth Wall, *Adult Educator; Chair, International Mission Training Network (WEA Mission Commission), UK*

The WEA Mission Commission has an outstanding history of resourcing the missions community with evidence-based research that informs us about best practice. *Mission in Motion* is a welcomed and vitally important addition to the existing literature. For the first time, the voices of respondents speak directly to us as we hear from them the factors that encourage or deter people who might participate in God's mission. There is much here for the missions community to reflect and learn from. But we can also rejoice that in tumultuous times, God is still calling women and men to serve him in cross-cultural mission.

David Williams, *Director of Training, Church Missionary Society, Australia*

Join the mobilization conversation on the *Mission in Motion* Facebook page!
facebook.com/missionmotion/

MISSION
IN MOTION

MISSION IN MOTION

Speaking Frankly of Mobilization

JAY MATENGA
MALCOM GOLD

forewords by **Paul Borthwick** & **Patrick Fung**

WILLIAM CAREY
LIBRARY

www.missionbooks.org

Mission in Motion: Speaking Frankly of Mobilization
Copyright © 2016 by World Evangelical Alliance Mission Commission
All rights reserved.

Scripture quotations in text, unless otherwise indicated, are taken from the Holy Bible, New International Version®, NIV®. Copyright © 1973, 1978, 1984, 2011 by Biblica, Inc.™ Used by permission of Zondervan. All rights reserved worldwide. www.zondervan.com.

Scripture quotations marked NLT are taken from the Holy Bible, New Living Translation, copyright ©1996, 2004, 2007, 2013, 2015 by Tyndale House Foundation. Used by permission of Tyndale House Publishers, Inc., Carol Stream, Illinois 60188. All rights reserved.

Published by William Carey Library
1605 E. Elizabeth St.
Pasadena, CA 91104 | www.missionbooks.org

Koe Pahlka, editor
Jay Matenga and Koe Pahlka, interior design
Jay Matenga, cover design

William Carey Library is a ministry of
Frontier Ventures | www.frontierventures.org

Printed in the United States of America
20 19 18 17 16   5 4 3 2 1 Bang Printing 1500

Library of Congress Cataloging-in-Publication Data

Names: Matenga, Jay, author.
Title: Mission in motion : speaking frankly of mobilization / Jay Matenga,
    Malcolm Gold.
Description: Pasadena, CA : William Carey Library, 2016. | Series:
    Globalization of mission series | Includes bibliographical references.
Identifiers: LCCN 2016036912 (print) | LCCN 2016037900 (ebook) | ISBN
    9780878080557 (pbk.) | ISBN 0878080554 (pbk.) | ISBN 9780878086535 (eBook)
Subjects: LCSH: Missions.
Classification: LCC BV2061.3 .G65 2016 (print) | LCC BV2061.3 (ebook) | DDC
    266--dc23
LC record available at https://lccn.loc.gov/2016036912

Join the mobilization conversation on the *Mission in Motion* Facebook page!
facebook.com/missionmotion/

CONTENTS

FOREWORD

From Paul Borthwick

As a North American committed to the mobilization of others for global mission, my mobilization *career* peaked in 2000 when I was invited to give the call to commitment at Inter Varsity's Urbana 2000 Student Mission Conference.[1] Many participants come to the conference already primed to commit themselves to something great in missions, and I was in the position of giving the challenge. To me, it seemed like an opportunity to shake the fruit off of trees that the Holy Spirit and other *mobilizers* had made ripe.

To help me in my preparation, I asked the conference planners, "What exactly are you hoping I will call these students to?" In other words, I was asking questions like, "What aspect of mission is our focus?" or "Where in the world do we hope they will go?" or "How long of a commitment do we want them to make?" and "With what type of agency do we want to send them?"

Because of the broad range of answers to these and other mobilization questions, I was left with no definitive direction. I tried hard to listen to my advisors and to the Spirit, and I preached. After the entire conference concluded, the organizers reported that over 5,000 young people committed their lives to cross-cultural missions as their vocation and over 10,000 committed themselves to maturing as *World Christians*. Awesome, right? But to this day I don't know where, with whom, or how long these folks have gone. Nor do I know how they ended up defining *cross-cultural mission* as a vocation or *World Christian* as a lifestyle.

How I wish I had read *Mission in Motion* before I prepared that message!

For any person committed to mobilizing others for global mission—recruiters, mission pastors, or mission professors—*Mission in Motion* is a must-read. *Mission in Motion* is essential, not because it offers a dozen new *how to's* or clever innovative ways of getting people involved, but because it forces us to think through the basic questions I was asking my Urbana hosts: What do we mean by mission? Where are we focusing? How long is the commitment of a *mobilized* person? And what role do agencies play?

When you read this book, you will find that *Mission in Motion* is unprecedented. The scope of the research and the global thoroughness of the interviews yield a resource

---

1   For readers outside of North America, Urbana is regarded as the largest student mission mobilization conference in North America. Every three years, 16,000 to 20,000 university and graduate level students come together for five days simply to be challenged to get involved in the global work of God.

that is unparalleled in the field of global missiology. This is not a book by mobilizers for mobilizers; instead it is an exhaustive research summary of mobilizers listening to the feedback of the mobilized and then making observations and posing further questions.

Readers will also find that *Mission in Motion* is universal. In the global church where we hear the missiological mandate of "from everywhere to everywhere," the voices in this book will assist mobilizers in places like Nigeria, Brazil, and India (to name a few of the so-called "new" sending countries) as well as those more traditional "senders" from North America, Europe, and Australia/New Zealand.

Be aware, however, that *Mission in Motion* is also unsettling. We'd all like to think that our programs, our churches, or our agencies will all fall into the mobilization category that the authors call "accelerants" for global mission involvement. *Mission in Motion* may shock and humble us when we discover that our policies, structures, and undetected organizational cultures are actually "retardants" that serve to extinguish the fires for mission in potential recruits.

But do not despair; *Mission in Motion* is also uplifting because the authors' goal is not simply to disclose the challenges for mobilization, but also to help us identify ways forward so that we together can be accelerants that fuel the fires of mission involvement globally.

Finally, read this research carefully because *Mission in Motion* is urgent. If we are seriously committed to playing our parts in calling others to their roles in the Great Commission of Jesus Christ, the research, voices, summaries, and insights of *Mission in Motion* will serve as an accelerant for each of us.

Paul Borthwick
Missiologist, Author, Mobilizer, and Teacher

From Rev. Dr. Patrick Fung

I was once asked to speak at a theological seminary in Sydney, Australia on Global Mission. During the question and answer session, a student stood up and asked me a pertinent question: "Why are we still using the phrase *mission mobilization*? It is a military term that does not go down well in many cultural contexts and can be easily misunderstood."

In many ways, the student was right. Historically, the word *mobilization* was used to refer to the assembling of troops in preparation for war. In its original usage, mobilization was closely linked to the concept of military invasion and conquest. Thus it is no wonder that Bosch commented on the three-fold impure motives for mission endeavor: the imperialist motive of colonialism, the cultural motive of superiority, and the romantic motive of wanderlust.

What I particularly appreciate about this book is that it explores not so much *mission mobilization*, which unfortunately has been often used in a misconstrued way, but rather, *mission motivation* which has strong theological roots. There are at least three reasons why we should be motivated for mission. First, we are motivated by the glory of God and the vision of seeing all tribes, peoples, and nations worship our Lord. Second, we are motivated and inspired by the sacrificial lives of missionaries who have served God's purpose in their generation and so we are to follow in their footsteps today. Third, we are motivated by the brokenness of this world, and we pray desperately for the Lord's healing upon the nations and peoples. We want to be involved in God's mission to make a difference in the world that God loves.

This book does not attempt to give a single definition on mission. However, it highlights that mission relates to two common biblical denominators, namely Jesus' summary of the Law: "Love the Lord your God with all your heart and with all your soul and with all your mind. This is the first and greatest commandment. And the second is like it: Love your neighbor as yourself. All the Law and the Prophets hang on these two commandments" (Matthew 22:37–40).

This book embraces mission in the broadest sense—whether local or cross-cultural, whether evangelism that relates to personal salvation or social action—recognizing the spectrum of mission focus. However, it does focus on one main theme, namely, factors that accelerate or retard the mission flame.

This is not a book written by one person from a theoretical framework. Rather, it is the product of research based on extensive interviews with people involved at the grassroots of mission activities from different continents and cultural backgrounds.

Out of the many significant findings from the interviews regarding factors that may accelerate or retard mission motivation, two factors are particularly worth mentioning.

First, no resource is more powerful and accessible than persuasion. Though there is often an immediate impact from a missionary speaker, sustained contact and encouragement remains one of the best motivating factors into developing people in their understanding of and motivation towards mission. The new generation is looking for relevance and purpose. Thus mission motivation needs to be along the lines of discipling (mentoring and coaching) rather than lecturing; experience sharing rather than information transmission. Friendship is the key. The motto from Alison King, "From sage on the stage to guide on the side," challenges those who are involved in motivating the new generation for God's mission.

Second, the warning that mission mobilization is increasingly tempted to draw from "the industries of advertising, management, media, psychology, public relations, information technology, and even motivational/self-help gurus" for exciting, attractive, fresh new ideas to assist them to be better mission influencers. Yet it is clear from the research that people are weary of mission performance and instead are looking for mission motivation.

The reader may struggle with one issue in the approach of how this book is written. The research was done using a qualitative open-ended approach in the interviews. Some who are more statistically minded may have preferred a quantitative approach. However, the scope of the research covered respondents from a wide spectrum of backgrounds, including those from Africa, Eastern Europe, the Indian Subcontinent, East Asia, Oceania, South America and North America. Those interviewed spoke frankly of their experiences on the ground.

In 1865 a detailed research was conducted by James Hudson Taylor on the needs in China. It was published entitled, *China's Spiritual Need and Claims*. On the back cover of the book were the words, in both English and Chinese, "Come over, and Help us." This book motivated many in England in those days to become involved in mission. In the last chapter, Taylor issued a challenge:

> Beloved brothers and sisters, we cannot but believe that the contemplation of the solemn facts we have laid before you has awakened in each one the heart felt prayer—Lord, what wilt Thou have me to do, that Thy name may be hallowed, Thy kingdom come, and Thy will be done in China?

I ask the reader of this book to respond in a similar way, that each of us may ask the question, "*Lord, what wilt Thou have me to do, that Thy name may be hallowed, Thy kingdom come, and Thy will be done?*"

Rev. Dr. Patrick Fung
General Director, OMF International

PREFACE

This book represents an historic and unprecedented piece of research. The research project took nearly ten years to complete from start to finish. It is not a longitudinal study but rather a snapshot in time, which took far longer to process than it did to take. Nevertheless, the picture that developed was well worth the wait. Our hope is that this work will remain relevant for many years to come and promote much discussion and interest to foster more effective mission involvement.

As confirmation of the contemporary relevance of our project, while we were writing this book two localized studies were undertaken to investigate mission involvement in their contexts. *How Australian Missionaries Are Being Called and Choose Mission Agencies* (Hibbert, Hibbert, and Silberman, 2015) was researched in Sydney, Australia. *Mobilizing More Missionaries: Insights from Surveys of Long-termers and Prospective Missionaries* (McVay and Parrott, 2015) was the result of an online survey of 466 long-term missionaries from forty-six agencies undertaken in the United States.

Some variation is to be expected from different sample groups and methodologies, but the findings of both of these studies correlate very closely with our much larger project and there is significant overlap with the themes that emerged from our research. It took longer for us to publish our work because: 1) the wide scope of the project, 2) the enormous amount of data that was collected, transcribed, translated, collated, and analyzed, and 3) the researchers (including the authors) were carrying full-time responsibilities in their own spheres of service while investing in this project whatever spare time they could find.

As with most research projects, the research team commenced this one with an idea of what might be revealed in the data—an idea of the factors that help to motivate people to get involved with mission. In some ways individual interviews confirmed these ideas, but when taken as a whole, compared and contrasted with data from multiple cultures, we were taken aback by what we discovered, not just about how people are motivated into mission, but how our respondents understood the very concept of mission.

Unlike other books in the *Globalization of Mission Series*, this is not an anthology of edited works by multiple contributors. The research team felt that the analysis of the research data was best presented as one cohesive narrative presenting the outcomes of our analysis. While the whole team has contributed to its structure and content, reviewed, and approved of what you are reading, this book was cowritten by only two members of the team to aid cohesion and flow. Dr. Malcolm Gold was chosen for his sociological and analytical expertise, and Jay Matenga for his perspective of the global mission context and two decades of helping people into mission involvement.

ACKNOWLEDGMENTS

The research project represented by this book was made possible only through the collaboration of a committed research team. As revealed by their contributor biographies, every one of the researchers carried responsibilities in their own organizations while participating in this project. We all express gratitude to our respective organizations at the time for allowing us the space to pursue this project. Although from very diverse backgrounds, interacting on this project brought great joy to us all and during the process we built solid friendships. The team quickly developed an open, trusting dynamic, fostering a deep fellowship and appreciation of each other's contribution to the team. Times of "inefficient lingering" (attributed to Ajith Fernando) over meals and around discussion tables knitted our hearts together and we believe it ultimately led to increased fruitfulness. We want to acknowledge our heavenly Father in this regard for God's grace that blessed us with wisdom and creative insight as we dwelt together in unity.

Many other people have been involved at various times with this project, some brief, others longer, some catalytic, and others developmental. First and foremost, we would like to thank the respondents. They freely contributed a wealth of data without which this study would not be possible. We, and by extension the evangelical missions community, have been greatly enriched by what they have shared from their experience in mission. They represent voices rarely heard. In this work we aim to ensure their perspective is as a clarion to us all.

The team is also grateful to the WEA MC for commissioning this work. Aligned with the WEA MC are Executive Director Bertil Ekstrom and former Executive Director, Publications Coordinator, and Mission Commission Senior Mentor, Dr. William D. Taylor. Dr. Taylor deserves special mention as the one who called this project into being, identified those who would eventually join the research team, and helped ensure the project remained on track during the times it threatened to stall short of its destination. So *Uncle Bill* we thank you for your initiation, enthusiasm, and encouragement.

George Verwer was involved in a catalytic way at the beginning. The founder of Operation Mobilization led the WEA MC's Mobilization Track for a time and assisted with shaping the project in its genesis.

Tom Mullis was also involved in the early stages of the project's development and advocated for funding to help bring the project into being. We are grateful for Tom's involvement and particularly for the financial contribution from Perimeter Church in Atlanta, Georgia that helped launch the project.

Appropriate to the pan-cultural scope of the project, funding to complete it was generously donated by a Korean resourcing agency, Asian Mission. We are particularly thankful to Mr. Jae-Chul Chung for his assistance with the funding process, and research team member Min-Young Jung for connecting Asian Mission with this project.

Thanks also go to the team at Pioneers New Zealand who supplied resources, managed our funding, and maintained financial accountability for the project during the data gathering and analysis period, and to Missions Interlink New Zealand, which took over during the publication phase.

A more recent addition to the publication team was Koe Pahlka, editor extraordinaire, who has guided numerous *Globalization of Mission Series* books down the home straight to the finish line for the WEA Mission Commission. Our heartfelt thanks Koe for your professionalism, patience, and gentle prodding while the finish line seemed so close yet so far, and for your expert editing eye and design assistance. While on design, thanks are also extended to Paul Smith of Blue Sky Creative in New Zealand for his assistance with the cover art. The graphic combines a motif of audio and light pulses backed by fire and smoke to evoke the power of voices to ignite us, particularly God's voice. The *Mission in Motion* title carries double meaning as we recognize that the very notion of mission has become fluid, before discussing the way people are moved into mission.

Finally, we need to acknowledge two men who contributed a considerable amount of time and expertise to this project in its various stages but were unable to journey with us to the end. They are Carlos Scott and Trevor Gregory. Carlos is an Argentinian who undertook the South American aspect of the research project, but because of increased workload in his ministry could not continue to be involved beyond obtaining data from his context. Thank you Carlos for your contribution and your grace in persevering with our need to communicate in English! Trevor was the powerhouse behind the launch and interview phases of the project. He pulled our multicultural team together and held it together over the early years, guiding the process toward fulfillment from his base in Scotland until early 2011 when circumstances required him to entrust the project to the remaining team. Trev, we hope the final outcome is as you dreamed it would be!

*For our families who journey with us, encourage us, and
endure sacrifice with such gracious faith.*

CONTRIBUTORS

There was considerable debate within the research team as to whether or not we would include short biographies of the contributors who carried out this project. To a person, members of the team were reluctant to write about themselves; ultimately however we felt it would be doing the reader an injustice if we failed to provide some indication of our cultural and professional backgrounds. Contributions are presented in surname alphabetical order.

Alison Allen

Researcher, ROMANIA

I was born in Northern England into an evangelical church with a strong missionary emphasis: missionary prayer cards were a permanent feature in our home and sometimes the missionaries themselves would visit. I can clearly remember asking myself at a very young age, "If everything I hear at church is true, why aren't they all missionaries?" When I was eight my family moved to Scotland and I went through many of the experiences commonly associated with *third culture kids*.

At the age of twelve I made a personal decision to follow Jesus during a Scripture Union summer camp. Throughout my teenage years I attended many camps and training events organized by Scripture Union Scotland for high school students. In December 1989, I was gripped by the events in Central and Eastern Europe. This region, particularly Romania, fascinated me. By the time I finished high school it seemed a natural next step to study an East European language at university. I felt God leading me to study Romanian and German at the School of Slavonic and East European Studies in London.

In London I joined City Gates Church, which became and remained my sending church. My first (disastrous!) visit to Romania was in the summer of 1995. I then spent six months living in Bucharest whilst still a student in 1996–97, during which time I joined a church connected to the Timisoara Christian Centre network of churches. After graduating in 1998, I spent a year learning about ministry and mission in the network training program of Ichthus Christian Fellowship in London.

In March 2000 I moved to Bucharest to work with the church I had joined back in 1996. I also taught English to business people as a day job. After five years in Bucharest, I was asked to join Grace Churches International in setting up a ministry training school just outside Timisoara, where I stayed for eighteen months.

In 2006–07 I returned to London for a sabbatical year, during which I completed a master's degree at All Nations Christian College. For my thesis I researched the emerging Romanian missionary sending movement. Following my return to Romania in 2007 I worked to develop the area of member care for Romanian missionaries within the Partners in Mission consortium of mission organizations. I represented Romania on the Board of Member Care Europe in 2012–2014. I am also a member of the Central and East European Association for Mission Studies (CEEAMS).

In the summer of 2014 I married James Allen and returned to the UK and am now living in Ipswich. In 2015 I embarked on doctoral studies into the involvement in missions of the Millennial Generation.

Dr. Malcolm Gold

Lead Researcher, Research Analyst, and Research Team Co-Leader;
Researcher, UNITED STATES OF AMERICA

My conversion to Christianity was quite an unexpected event given the nonreligious persuasion of my family. Born and raised in Kingston-Upon-Hull in the northeast of England, my faith journey began at the age of fourteen (in 1979) and quickly set my life on a trajectory which would radically break with the cultural expectations mapped out for me. As a young person, with no prior church experience or knowledge, I joined a Pentecostal fellowship where my energies were spent on evangelistic programs and study. With its strong emphasis on outreach and ministry, I soon became involved in many of the church's activities. In 1984, with the support of my church (both financially and in prayer) I attended the Eurasia Teen Challenge ministry course in (what was then) Wiesbaden, West Germany. In retrospect my experience in Germany had three major effects on me and my future.

First, it revealed and nurtured my desire to pursue what some academics refer to as *the life of the mind*. Education had not been particularly stressed (or made easy) for me as a child. Family conflicts had diverted my energies away from excelling at school and the working class culture of which I was a part, as is often the norm, was quite bereft of the "cultural capital" (as Bourdieu would put it in Lane, 2000) required to equip me for any type of further or higher education.

Second, along with the experience of being in another country (my first time away from England) I experienced life with other attendees who were predominantly non-English. For the first time I was interacting with people from other cultures and being exposed to a diversity of views about God and life, which challenged (in a healthy way) my parochialism. The third major effect was that I met my wife Kathy while on the course. Much would transpire however before we were to marry. My first wife Desiree, whom I married in 1990, died in a tragic auto accident in 1991. In 1997, after renewing the acquaintance begun via Teen Challenge in 1984, I married Kathy.

The time between the end of the course and my first marriage was taken up with a mixture of ministry, secular employment, and preparation for university. I commenced study on my bachelor degree at Birmingham University in the United Kingdom in the autumn of 1991. In 1994, I graduated with a Bachelor of Social Science degree, joint honors in Economic and Social History and Sociology (BSocSc). By that time, I believe, my calling to ministry had shifted from the pulpit to the classroom and a vocation of higher education, research, and scholarship. That same year I began postgraduate study at Warwick University under the tutorship of sociologist Professor Margaret Archer and philosophy Professor Roger Trigg.

In 1996 I received my Master of Arts degree in Philosophy and Social Theory. Carrying straight through, I continued at Warwick, studying under the sociologist of religion, Professor James Beckford, to gain my PhD in sociology in 2002. The subject of my PhD thesis was an ethnographic study of the Pentecostal church I had first attended. The work was published in 2003 as *The Hybridization of an Assembly of God Church: Proselytism, Retention, and Re-affiliation* (Gold, 2003).

During the writing-up stage of my PhD thesis I had relocated to the USA. Kathy (who is US American) and I lived and worked in Canton, Ohio for sixteen years; she as a music teacher and I a professor of sociology at Malone University in the department of History, Philosophy, and Social Science. Malone is a Christian University for the arts, sciences, and professions and has its roots in the Evangelical Friends (Quaker) tradition. Although my faith journey started far removed from the sensitivities of the Friends heritage, I found a great resonance with the major distinctives of Quakerism, particularly their testimony to peace and commitment to social justice. In 2015/16 we moved from Ohio so that I could take a position as Chair of the Department of Sociology, Anthropology, and Criminal Justice at Messiah College in Pennsylvania. I regard my role in higher education as a vocation and ministry.

My involvement with the research team was initiated through an invitation to become involved by the original leader of the study, Trevor Gregory. Trevor and I had become acquainted in the 1980s while Trevor was working with Youth with a Mission in Hull. I feel blessed that our paths had occasion to cross again and that I could offer my services to this important work.

Jo Jowett
Researcher, UNITED KINGDOM

My journey into mission has had a number of unexpected turns, but the course it has taken has been exciting and fulfilling. I currently work as Mobilization Director for Global Connections, the United Kingdom network for world mission, a role that continues some twenty-four years after my first step to mission involvement.

Originally from Belfast, Northern Ireland, I grew up in a strong Christian home and mission often featured in our family prayers, not least because my aunt and uncle were missionaries in Brazil. I was always fascinated by their stories and as a child wondered what it was like to be a *real* missionary. After a few turbulent teenage years, God began to challenge me about my own part in his plan. My "please don't send me to Africa!" prayer wasn't answered in the way I expected.

A period of wrestling with God was followed by my first short-term mission trip to Kenya. I returned a year later and made my home in the south of the country where I worked among the Maasai at a rehabilitation center for disabled children. This was a time of intensive growth and personal transformation, which was to impact my life in the years to come.

On my return to the United Kingdom, after two and half years in rural Kenya, I went on to spend three years at Belfast Bible College studying Theology and Mission. This was to be preparation for longer-term service overseas but it seemed that God had very different plans for me. During the years at college I continued to be involved with Africa Inland Mission (AIM) encouraging young people to engage in mission. These were my first steps in what we understand to be "mission mobilization."

Following my graduation from Bible college, I worked a year with the African Children's Choir in a public relations role while I sought the Lord about my longer-term future in mission. An invitation to join AIM International as their Youth and Student worker based in London followed. Among the many and varied aspects of this role were planning, preparing, and leading teams of young people to serve in various parts of Africa. For me, the greatest joy of the job was seeing the focus of young people's lives being transformed by their mission engagement.

After six years with AIM, I took up the role of Associate Director with Christian Vocations, a UK-based organization focused on resourcing and mobilizing Christians for mission. Christian Vocations is now part of Global Connections, and my role includes production and editing the organization's publications, involvement in some of the major UK Christian events, and supporting joint mission agency initiatives. Other roles associated with my work include Chair of the Short-Term Mission Forum within Global Connections, Chair of European Christian Mission (Britain), and a Governor of Redcliffe College.

Birmingham, England is now my home and I am an active member of my local church. I have been happily married to Mark since September 2006 and have become a student of football and cricket as a result! Alongside my husband, I am closely involved with *Isubilo*, an HIV and AIDS ministry based in Zambia. On a more local level we also run a city center night project in Birmingham called *City Pastors*.

My journey in mission began almost thirty years ago; most of those years have been in active mission mobilization. It has been an honor to serve as the United Kingdom researcher on the team and throughout the various stages of the research I have been encouraged and have had my vision expanded by the stories of others who, like me, are still on that journey.

Min-Young Jung

Research Team Co-Leader; Researcher, KOREA

I was born into a Christian family in Korea. My maternal grandfather was one of the first Korean pastors trained by Western missionaries a century ago, and was sent to work in Jeju Island where my mother spent some of her teen years. Jeju Island was regarded as a mission field at that time, so I guess I inherited a missional gene from my mother and grandparents.

My own missional journey is connected to the corporate pilgrimage of the Korean church. The local church I attended in the 1970s, which later became my sending church, was one of the first in Korea that caught the vision of world evangelization and obeyed the mandate. The senior minister has been an ardent champion of world mission, and I have been influenced tremendously by the missional zeal of this church.

God led me to several important people who guided my next steps. Among them was an American Bible translator who visited Korea at a critical time in my life. My love of the Bible made it impossible for me to resist God's call to bring the gospel to numerous unreached people groups who are still without God's word in their native tongue. So, I joined Wycliffe Bible Translators, and after taking linguistic and theological training I was sent to Indonesia to translate the Bible into one of seven hundred plus tribal languages. Despite ups and downs, it was worth it to witness the people finally getting God's word in their *heart language*.

Since there are still some eighteen hundred language communities to go, I have been involved in mobilizing the church worldwide for the past twenty years. In the wake of Vision 2025, which has the goal of initiating by the year 2025 a Bible translation project for every language group that needs it, I was asked to lead the Asian Diaspora Initiative. This was a strategic initiative of Wycliffe to mobilize Asian Christian communities scattered all over the world. I am also an Associate of the WEA MC, and currently serving as an Associate Director of Wycliffe Global Alliance.

Following in the footsteps of numerous spiritual predecessors, I will continue my journey to the nations until all of them are given a fair chance to know the Lord, especially to have the written word of God in their own heart languages.

Jay Matenga

Project Leader, Research Team Co-Leader; Researcher, NEW ZEALAND

I was born and raised in a non-Christian environment in an impoverished part of New Zealand. My mother's ancestry is from the United Kingdom and my father is a fifty-fifty mix of indigenous Maori (his father) and various European ethnicities (his mother). I was led to faith in Jesus at the age of sixteen by the parents of a friend from high school. They took me under their wing as a seeking teenager and discipled me well, giving me a high regard for understanding the Scriptures and God's purposes.

Being from a working class background, academic pursuit wasn't encouraged beyond secondary school. Nevertheless, in my final years of high school certain teachers drew out some intellectual aptitude and encouraged me in a passion for learning. My first jobs were clerical but a yearning for understanding persisted, and when an opportunity arose to start training for ministry I jumped at it.

I turned twenty-one at Faith Bible College, a small discipleship school in Tauranga, New Zealand. There I met my wife, Pauline. We married in 1990 and immediately took the *Perspectives on the World Christian Movement* course at the recommendation of an elder of the church we were attending at the time. The course had a profound effect on my understanding of God's purpose in the world and led us to undertake three more undergraduate years of missiological and theological training at what is now the Worldview College for Intercultural Studies in Launceston, Tasmania (Australia). It was here that a calling crystallized to what Ralph Winter championed as the ministry of mission mobilization.

After graduating in 1995, Pauline and I worked in administration, public relations, and mission recruitment with a large international mission organization in New Zealand. During this time, I became increasingly concerned about the level of attrition among my peers in mission (GenX, born between c1965–c1980). A series of divine circumstances led me to All Nations Christian College (ANCC) in 1997 where I was privileged to complete MA research into the challenges facing GenX in mission. I analyzed the philosophical motivators of my generation (particularly postmodernism) and my thesis applied Michel Foucault's theories of power relationships to the missions context. This study led me to develop a set of principles for effective activation and empowerment of post-baby boom generations in cross-cultural mission from the West. I applied these principles in recruitment and retention strategies over a fifteen-year period as the New Zealand leader of one of the largest multinational missions to unreached peoples.

What has captured my missiological interest more recently has been the rise in mission personnel from new sending nations, and the struggles they experience trying to integrate into Western mission structures. This new challenge led me to commence a Doctorate of Intercultural Studies at Fuller School of Graduate Studies in 2014, seeking to identify ways to enhance intercultural relationships between missionaries from collectivist and individualist backgrounds.

Pauline and I fellowship at Eastgate Christian Centre in Auckland, New Zealand and I currently serve as the leader of Missions Interlink, the association of evangelical missions in New Zealand. I am also an Associate of the WEA MC. I joined the WEA MC Mobilization Task Force in 2007 and accepted leadership of the Task Force and Mission Mobilization Research Team early in 2011. It was a privilege to be invited to participate in this project and it has been an absolute joy serving with the research team.

Hikari Matsuzaki

Research Team Co-Leader; Researcher, JAPAN

I was born and raised in a Christian family in Japan. While studying in the US, I became a born-again believer and vowed to serve the Lord in cross-cultural missions. After majoring in Hispanic Studies at Monterey Institute of International Studies (California, US) and some years of working in various companies in Japan, I joined Operation Mobilization (OM) in 1991.

While serving with OM Ships for nearly seven years I was trained in cross-cultural ministries and coordinated programs in more than thirty-five countries in North, Central, and South America, the Caribbean, West Africa, and Europe.

Since leaving OM, my service to mission has included: Associate Coordinator of the Missions Mobilization Network (London, 2004–2006); Coordinator for Networking and Mobilization with Japan Antioch Mission (2007–present); a core member of the Diaspora Network Project (2008–2015), the Vice Chair (2009–2012), Chair (2013), and a committee member (2014–present) of the Japan Overseas Missions Association. I also encourage and coordinate intercessory prayer meetings for global missions at a grassroots level in Japan. Translating and introducing mission-related materials to the churches of Japan has been one of the burdens I carry.

I am an Associate of the WEA MC, a member of the Japan Evangelical Association Mission Commission, and currently live in Japan.

Duncan Olumbe

Researcher, KENYA

I was born and brought up in rural western Kenya, East Africa. Brought up as a nominal Catholic, I committed my life to Christ in my first year of high school through the witness of fellow students. Early influences in my life included growing up as a member of a local Pentecostal church where the pastor's family "adopted" and mentored me and involvement in student Christian groups at the two high schools and college I attended.

I trained as a Mechanical Engineer, my "dream" vocation, or so I thought at the time. Upon graduation I joined the staff of FOCUS Kenya (a national student ministry). What

I initially thought would be one year ended up being close to ten years, most of which involved mobilizing and mentoring Kenyan students into global mission. I am very grateful to the older staff at FOCUS Kenya who mentored me as I explored God's call on my life.

In 1994, while attending an Urbana-like student mission conference (Commission '94), I was made aware of the state of world mission and the need for more missionaries. During the commissioning service I made a public commitment to become a missionary. However, despite exploring various opportunities, especially in the 10–40 Window, lack of sending and support structures frustrated my efforts. Thankfully God finally led me to Careforce UK and in 1996–1997 I served in Oxford United Kingdom as a short-term missionary working with international students.

The Oxford experience was truly stretching and birthed the desire for more training. Miraculously God opened the doors to All Nations Christian College (1997–1999) where I, and eventually my fiancée Roseline, had excellent mission training. Soon after returning to Kenya Roseline and I got married and we have since been blessed with three very active boys—Roy, Ronnie, and Robert.

Back in Kenya I continued to serve with FOCUS Kenya as their Missions Director where I had the distinct joy of coordinating the Short-Term Experience in Ministry (STEM) program for fresh Christian graduate volunteers, hosting short-term mission teams from Intervarsity USA, Tearfund UK, and NKSS Norway, facilitating several Kenyan Christian Unions' short-term mission teams, and eventually serving as the Commission 2004 Director which brought together about 2,500 students and graduates from eastern and southern Africa.

In 2005 I cofounded Mission Together Africa (MTA) as a platform to address the many issues facing mission from Kenya and the rest of Eastern Africa. Through MTA I have been involved in mobilizing local churches, students, and professionals to take their rightful place in global mission. This involves facilitating contextualized training for our people being sent out and those coming to Africa, reflecting missiologically on mission matters as Africans, and strengthening global mission partnerships.

My other roles include being a member of the Global Leadership Council and cofacilitator of the Future of Mission Task Force of the World Evangelical Alliance Mission Commission, a member of Interserve's International Council, and the Chairman of KwaMataifa (Kenya To The Nations), a network of like-minded organizations that facilitates mission training for Kenyan missionaries. It has been a great privilege to part of this Mission Mobilization Research Team as the researcher from my base here in Kenya. I have learned so much from the team and the interviews.

Kannan Rajendran

Researcher, INDIA

I am trained in computer engineering from Tamil Nadu, South India, and became a first-generation follower of Christ in 2000 through the witness of some friends. In 2004 I joined the India Missions Association (IMA), which represents approximately two hundred missions in India and a large number of Christian workers. While with the IMA, I grew a great deal as a disciple of Christ.

Beginning in 2005 I have led the Research and Communications arm of the IMA. The main aim of the communications team was to provide information that will allow mission organizations, churches, theological institutions, and individuals to develop strategies in ministry that positively affect India and beyond with Christ's message and values.

I remain active in ministry and have had exposure to mission activity, research, and leadership. I have both assisted and led several think-tanks and research projects for missions and leaders in India and have connections with networks around the globe. My passion is to promote the relevance of the gospel to all peoples in this day and age.

Globally, I am part of the WEA MC Mission Mobilization Research Team and have been involved with the groups Ethne, Tentmakers International, and other global roundtables.

As you might imagine, the aforementioned networks, dialogues, and activities constantly challenge me as I mobilize appropriate people and resources to help societies and nations to consider, follow, and worship the Lord Jesus Christ.

INTRODUCTION

The mission endeavor is a complicated process commensurate with the era in which we live.[1] The context of Jesus' original commission to his disciples was one vastly different to the world we inhabit today. The clear and pristine call of Christ to his disciples to "make disciples of all nations" (Matthew 28:19) as they went into the world has undergone more than two thousand years of theological, ecclesiological, intellectual, and technological refinement as it has been interpreted afresh at various stages of Christian history. Guided by the Holy Spirit, it has been filtered, sometimes more, sometimes less, through the systems of the church, the philosophies of societies, the politics of nation states, and the mechanisms of economics. Through all this, one thing seems certain—that the process of mission for the people of God has become increasingly complex as it is redefined or at least reshaped for each new era and context. Far gone are the days in which the notion of *mission* was singularly apparent in the words of Jesus to his first century followers and then—by extension—all future generations of Christians.

Mission remains a hotly debated topic and it would be difficult to expect a clear consensus on a single definition across the global church today. Given the multitude of differing voices on the issue, should we try to impose an understanding of mission in a rigidly defined sense? While some would regard such divergent views as a hindrance to the overall design and work of God in the world, others may view the diversity more favorably and recognize that the one gospel has many incarnations, each valuable for its role in fulfilling the commission entrusted to Christ's followers.

The dialogue concerning mission continues to be an ongoing process with input from established orthodoxies of the church, denominations, streams, individual churches, sectarian religious groups, parachurch agencies, mission organizations, and theological institutions. In addition (and representative of numerous Christian traditions), individual theologians, missiologists, and reflective practitioners have contributed to the many different persuasions of mission interpretation and practice. Each of these contributors brings a unique perspective to bear. Rooted in their differing realities, they show us a side

---

1   Although our respondents use mission and missions interchangeably, we will mostly use mission in the singular for ease of flow. We understand mission (singular) to be the intention of God (the *missio Dei*), and for the purposes of this work we extend that to the outworking of God's intention through individuals. Where we use missions (plural) it is with reference to agencies, institutions, and other structured or otherwise clearly organized mission entities.

of the multifaceted purpose of God that is increasingly being understood as the *missio Dei*.[2]

This study sought to examine the lived experience and motivations of people involved at the grassroots of mission activity within the context of what David Bosch called "the crisis in mission" (Bosch, 1991, 7). Our intention was to investigate mission promotion and recruitment activities thought to be best practices by the evangelical missions community.[3] To help us achieve this, the research team created a project to gather data using qualitative open-ended interviews. That involved recording, with respondents' permission, conversations with people involved in mission, particularly those who encourage others into mission involvement. This data was then analyzed and this book presents the results of that analysis.

A quantitative approach, such as a standardized questionnaire, could have, in some ways, offered potential for greater statistical clarity. But our research team felt that a more nuanced approach was needed to obtain a deeper understanding of the different conceptual intricacies related to why people become involved in mission service according to their lived reality. Furthermore, an emphasis on cross-cultural *meaning* necessitated a multifaceted description of the interactive processes apparent in helping people become involved in mission. The scope of the research included respondents from North America, South America, East Africa, Eastern Europe, the Indian subcontinent, East Asia, and Oceania.

We have separated the book into six parts, some longer than others. Part one provides a necessary foundation to our project, establishing the rationale and contextual boundaries of this work. In chapter one we consider David Bosch's concept of *mission in crisis*.[4] For Bosch, the crisis was created by challenges resulting from sociological changes during the twentieth century. From this we developed our research premise. That is, if mission has been facing a crisis, then those activities or ministries integrally linked to mission must need to adapt to survive it. Of specific interest to us was the mobilization of resources necessary for mission to continue.

With reference to this crisis, in chapter two we briefly explore Bosch's thesis on paradigm shifts in Christian history and consider his suggestion that a new paradigm was emerging. At the time, Bosch believed we were at a point of transition between the former enlightenment and new ecumenical/postmodern paradigms. While continuing to explore the implications of being in a transitional period, in chapter three we introduce

---

2   A Barthian concept indicating the "intratrinitarian movement of God himself" which gradually became part of mission nomenclature following Georg Vicedom's introduction of the term at the 1952 world mission conference at Willengen. Christopher Wright further defines *missio Dei* as mission that "flows from the inner dynamic movement of God in personal relationship" (Wright, 2006, 62–63).

3   The "evangelical missions community" is the intended audience for this book. For us, the term broadly encompasses people who align themselves with an evangelical expression of faith and consider what they do as mission.

4   From 1972 until his death in a car accident in 1992, David Bosch was (among other things) a professor of mission, and served as chair of the department of missiology at the University of South Africa.

the concept of *missional anomie,* recognizing that multiple understandings of mission and mission practice are now apparent within our contemporary mission context, which remains in considerable flux.

Chapter four explains our chosen methodology for the study. In research-oriented books sometimes an author will casually suggest that if readers have no particular interest in how a study was carried out they may want to skip the obligatory chapter that discusses these methods—and more importantly, the philosophy of why one method of inquiry was chosen over another—and go straight to the meat of the study. We would rather encourage you to give some attention to the methodology of this study because we believe that doing so will help you better understand the conclusions we draw from the data.

The remaining bulk of our presentation draws on multicultural narratives from our respondents to illustrate themes revealed in the data. In doing this, we have obscured specific ministry locations by referencing only very broad regional boundaries to assist with respondent anonymity. This does not mean we have interviewed people throughout those entire regions; it just differentiates the voices from one another when other points of reference are stripped away. Also, to maintain anonymity we refer to the respondents' mission involvement in very loose terms. Respondents were involved in mission in different ways and we specifically sought to interview people with roles such as: mission leaders and missionaries, mission mobilizers (recruiters) and other mission organization staff, mission-interested church leaders, and mission-supporting church members.

We have sought to avoid being gender specific where possible for a number of reasons. This too preserves our respondents' anonymity and we believe it will keep our readers from defaulting to gender-specific assumptions (gender prejudices) when reading respondents' contributions. To achieve this, we use gender-neutral pronouns (they, them, their) in a non-traditional singular way. This is becoming much more acceptable in English language writing, and for our purposes we feel it is less unusual or awkward than other alternatives.

The anonymous stories we chose to publish represent just a very small sampling of our data and we reiterate this throughout our work. But we believe the global voices heard in this volume are sufficient to illustrate the complex diversity to be found today in the evangelical missions community. The voices represent a wide range of differing experiences, opinions, and understandings. Great care has been taken to not overstate certain voices and to avoid undermining others. It is also important to recognize that many themes emerging from our data sit within a broader context and are therefore better understood as subtext to even bigger concepts and issues, most of which we were not able to explore further within the bounds of our project.

Part two of our book explores what our respondents considered mission to actually be. Our data revealed diverse perceptions of mission, which required attention before we could move on to discussing what motivated or dissuaded people from engaging in mission. A wide variety of differences concerning the concept of mission were identified in our analysis but we will only look at the three largest categories of difference. As we do this we allow our global voices to speak to their preference or understanding of mission.

The variations we detected for each category best fit a continuum paradigm, with extreme preferences at either end and a great deal of overlap in between.

Chapter five explores the continuum of mission's focus, with concern for personal salvation at one end of the spectrum and an emphasis on social action at the other. For this chapter we split the subject matter in two and grouped sample global voices in the category that best fit their response. This does not mean they did not believe the other group's perspective, just that they had something significant to say about the category we place them in.

For chapter six we mix it up and deal with the issue of the locus of mission by grouping voices together according to their geography. This provides the reader with a view of the continuum within each region. In this case the continuum envelops differing opinions on where mission must take place in order to be considered authentically *mission*. The extreme ends of this continuum are local/same culture versus global/cross-cultural.

The hot potato of short-term mission is discussed in chapter seven. The continuum here is mission's length, from short to long-term. To present our data we chose to focus on short-term only, because the preferred model of mission in the evangelical missions community still seems to be long-term or career mission, however that is defined (we did not tackle the debate regarding what is considered *long term*).

In part three we finally arrive at our main subject matter, mission mobilization. We start the section with an introduction to mission mobilization, exploring how the concept emerged and became increasingly defined within the evangelical missions community. We then move to a more abstract investigation of mobilization in practice, identified in four different ways.

Chapter eight begins our discussion of the phenomenon of mission mobilization by tracing the history of the term within the evangelical missions community. The concept has been functionally in place for centuries, but to the best of our understanding the actual term, as we use it today, is a post-World War II development. We particularly identify the 1974 International Congress on World Evangelization in Lausanne, Switzerland as a major launch-point for our contemporary understanding of mobilization. This chapter takes a chronological approach to the emergence of mobilization as a mission-related ministry, exploring the concept's development, definition, and dispersal. We conclude with questions about the way the concept appears to be diversifying to promote more mission involvement.

The abstract application of our data starts to unfold from chapter nine where we identify certain broad aspects of mobilization as mobilization *ideal-types*. Our application of data in this regard is not evaluative, it does not indicate best practices; it is merely observational. We recognized different attributes of mobilization in our interview responses so we grouped them according to what they shared in common. At the end of the analysis we were able to identify four interconnected ideal-types and map them as interlocking quadrants. The means, models, methods, and mechanisms involved with mobilization fell into one or more of these mobilization ideal-types: educational, relational, formulaic, and pragmatic. Chapters ten to thirteen make up the rest of part three. Each chapter deals with and defines one mobilization ideal-type, with quotes from our global voices that best illustrate it.

Where part three discussed mobilization according to abstract concepts, parts four and five are more concerned with the lived reality of our respondents and what their experiences have to tell us about phenomena that helps or hinders mission involvement. Some of the territory explored under each mobilization ideal-type chapter emerges again in part four where we present the major accelerants to mission interest from our data analysis. Apart from prioritizing the major themes of relationships and education, the ordering of our subtheme data does not indicate any particular priority or rank.

Interactive relationships featured most significantly in our data as an accelerant of mission interest. There was so much data available we split relationships into two categories: familial and influential. We deal with family first in chapter fourteen, with our global voices speaking about the influence of their near and extended family members or spouse on their involvement in mission. In chapter fifteen, relationships of influence are widened and we explore five relationship-oriented categories identified in our data; influential individuals in general, missionaries, ministers, networks, and organizations.

In chapter sixteen, our focus turns to various forms of education and the process of learning as an important mission promoter. This chapter explores education in various contexts as mentioned by our respondents. We discuss them in a loose order from more formal to least formal types of learning, beginning with academic institutions, then church programs, courses and conferences, general literature, and finally, tough life experiences.

While significant relationships and learning opportunities helped accelerate and shape mission interest, we did not find much evidence of those things actually creating mission interest. Our respondents identified something quite *other* as the primary catalyst of their mission experience. We chose *Vocation* as the title for chapter seventeen because for many, vocation captures the idea that mission involvement is primarily rooted in a supernatural source, manifesting in what our respondents describe as a call. This is our most significant finding and it forces us to recalibrate our concept of mobilization away from something *we* do, to understand that it is something *God* does. We develop the concept of call that we detected within our responses by first considering whether a call to mission is a general expectation on all Christians or a particular revelation to some Christians. From there we listen to our voices as they explain different experiences of a calling from their lived reality. We note how a definite sense of call can assist with sustaining mission involvement and we highlight how a call can develop from an early age. A calling is not often an isolated, out of nowhere event. It is usually interconnected with other things, so we acknowledge that before moving on to identify specific references to the Holy Spirit at work in the mobilization process.

We believe the data indicates that a call is often received in a way that is relatively *nascent*, undeveloped. It often requires other things to strengthen and define it. That is where the other mobilization accelerants come to the fore, to fan the flame of a call if you will. The things we list next, in part five, as mobilization retardants, can therefore have a dampening effect on a person's call with the consequence of hindering involvement in mission.

You could say that it is all downhill from the end of part four. Part five has moments where the sun breaks through the clouds, but for the most part our presentation of elements that hinder involvement in mission gets rather gloomy. Nevertheless, part five contains very important perspectives and they deserve to be heard.

We open the section with the issue of funding in chapter eighteen. It will come as no surprise that there is a tense relationship between money and mission at the best of times. In the subsection on church giving we even see how having plenty of money available for mission can negatively affect mission involvement. Themes we touch on are some you would expect to find connected with money, which include teaching about giving, not having enough funding for mission, funding policies that restrict mission, and some wonderful testimonies of faith where God's providence is celebrated.

Chapter nineteen deals with some ways mission organizations retard mission involvement. Our global voices spoke of various mission organization policies and practices that hindered the advancement of mission and even times when an organization's staff had put people off. These represent unhelpful aspects of mission organization infrastructure, whereas the lack of infrastructure altogether was an issue for others, particularly from new sending nations.[5] The chapter ends with voices that expressed distaste in the way mission was being commercialized and marketed using competitive business approaches.

One of our more sensitive topics is presented in chapter twenty. Gender disparities could not go unmentioned because they are both a hindrance to mission involvement and a frustration in mission continuance. This is one chapter where the voice of women and men is made obvious as they spoke of experiences or attitudes that influence role distinctions, gender dynamics in general, and leadership issues that affect women specifically. Our global voices resonate with the opinion that mission is retarded when the potential for women to contribute fully is not realized.

The challenges to mission involvement widen considerably in chapter twenty-one where we look at various contextual issues that retard mission interest and involvement. Tragically the local church features first, with examples of Christian leaders and friends questioning missionary calls and discouraging mission involvement. We then briefly touch on wider societal issues. In case you are tempted to think that secularism, individualism, prosperity, and busyness are uniquely Western issues, our responses recorded in this section may challenge you to think again.

---

5   When we refer to "new sending nations" we are attempting to separate sending nations that once were mission fields from the traditional sending nations of the colonial era. Unless we are referencing a source that uses such terms, our aim is to avoid Westernized categorizations that reinforce ideas of otherness, like non-Western world, Third World, Two-Thirds World, Developing World, Majority World, and global South. Our term "new sending nations" describes a point in history or an empirical reality more than a location based on arbitrary geography, politics, economics, or some other colonial narrative.

As we did with our accelerants section, we conclude our section on retardants by turning our eyes from the material to the spiritual world and its effect on mission involvement. Whereas the Holy Spirit was the prominent focus ending part four, the powers of darkness are exposed at the end of part five. While this is a very short chapter, we feel the three representative voices we highlight help put our whole research project in perspective. They remind us that mission is a spiritual undertaking and we do not wrestle against flesh and blood. Therefore, the retardants revealed in part five are merely symptoms of a much deeper set of influences seeking to thwart God's mission.

We continue with that theme in part six as we conclude our presentation of global voices. With that perspective in mind, chapter twenty-three presents some ideas for accelerating mission involvement and minimizing the impact of retardants. We leave the evangelical missions community with a final challenge that we believe will encourage the flame of mission to spread, like wildfire.

PART ONE: CONTEXT

Who is wise? He will realize these things. Who is discerning? He will understand them. The ways of the Lord are right; the righteous walk in them, but the rebellious stumble in them.
(Hosea 14:9)

Missiologists and reflective practitioners of mission today are acutely aware of the importance of context. It is commonplace now to understand reality as something that is interpreted through the filters of language, culture, and a society's beliefs, values, behaviors, and by-products which in turn are influenced by all manner of environmental factors that nurture these attributes. To correctly understand anything we need to have contextual points of reference from which we can discern meaning.

In part one, we make clear the context for our project. It is rooted in a particular historical period of mission that we consider to be contemporary. It concerns the promotion of mission involvement, more specifically the concept of mission mobilization, which further defines what we mean by contemporary. With regard to the concept of mission mobilization, the 1974 International Consultation of World Evangelization features as a major landmark, so contemporary for us includes the past forty or so years. This period has seen considerable increase in mission research and we chose to anchor our contribution to that body of research to one particular missiologist/theologian, David Bosch.

Writing in the late 1980s, Bosch recognized that the concept of mission was facing significant change, influenced by contextual challenges that he saw as creating a single *crisis* in mission. This section of our book discusses Bosch's crisis and the factors contributing to it. By doing so we identify our project with his concerns and develop our rationale from there.

We note Bosch's preference for Thomas Kuhn's development of *paradigm shifts* (Kuhn, 1970) and see our project as contributing further insights into what Bosch saw as a major paradigm shift in mission, which we understand continues to this day. While mission historians define our contemporary era in different ways according to their agenda, we see the past forty years as an era of considerable fluidity in concepts of mission. Our data suggests this, and we introduce the concept of *missional anomie* to describe this condition.

Our convictions are not unfounded. They arise out of the findings of our research project, which are progressively presented throughout. The project, rooted in our contemporary mission context and anchored to the concerns of Bosch, was researched using a well-established social science qualitative methodology. The fruit of this methodology was data that not only helped us to better understand why people involve themselves in mission but also that mission itself remains a concept in flux.

CHAPTER 1

CRISIS

Let us first turn our discussion to the context of mission today and establish the backdrop to our study. What is this *crisis* of which Bosch and others speak? For some Western Christians the notion of there being a crisis at all may be quite unknown, thinking instead that the work of mission continues—"business as usual." Nevertheless, difficulties are still acknowledged; missionaries on furlough will talk to congregations about problems of finances, visa access, laborers being few, and other obstacles seen to hinder the activity of mission in various parts of the world. But these kinds of challenges are relatively familiar and have a long tradition in reports from the mission field over the past two hundred years of the modern (evangelical) missions movement. Congregations recognize these problems and earnestly pray for God's intervention. Many still give generously to the cause. If we were to take a little time to scratch beneath the surface, however, a less familiar set of issues and challenges would be revealed, ones which have been eroding evangelical understandings of mission for some time. To missiologists and reflective practitioners of mission it is far from "business as usual." As far back as 1961 Gerald Anderson wrote,

> The underlying principles and theological presuppositions for the Christian mission have been called into question and Christians are challenged to rethink the motives, message, methods, and goals of their mission ... The fundamental task, therefore, of the missionary enterprise today is to clarify the nature and meaning of its being. (Anderson, 1961, 3–4)

Times have changed since Anderson wrote and the clarification of the nature and meaning of mission's being has been fiercely debated since. Yet almost thirty years later, David Bosch (among many others then and since) still saw the question mark hanging over mission. Twenty-five years on from *Transforming Mission: Paradigm Shifts in Theology of Mission* (Bosch, 1991) we conclude the same. This suggests a range of issues far more foundational to the concept of mission than simple pragmatic difficulties like those mentioned above. Pragmatic considerations may be connected to the core issues but their nature is secondary or symptomatic rather than causal. To take a closer look at core issues, the research team decided to focus on Bosch's analysis of mission in crisis. We acknowledge that numerous scholars have attempted to articulate crises in mission and that Bosch's work is not exhaustive, but for us it provided a very useful entry point to a number of the major dynamics giving rise to the crisis.

Transforming Mission quickly became a standard text in missiological circles after it was first published and continues to be a primary source for students of mission. In it Bosch outlines, in quite concise terms, six factors that underlie the crisis to which we refer, not just within the realm of mission but for the "entire church, indeed the entire world" (Bosch, 1991, 3). We note that the context of mission has changed somewhat in the decades following the book's publication. Nevertheless, the succinct nature of his outline remains useful as it allows his readers considerable flexibility to add or subtract, elaborate, critique, or delve deeper into any one of the six points. We will briefly consider them to illustrate our context.

The Prominence of Scientific Rationale

> The advance of science and technology and, with them, the worldwide process of secularization seems to have made faith in God redundant; why turn to religion if we ourselves have ways and means of dealing with the exigencies of modern life? (Bosch, 1991, 3)

Here Bosch acknowledges classic features of the secularization debate. This remains an ongoing debate within disciplines like the sociology of religion and has spurned countless studies, papers, and books on the subject. The early figures within sociology, Durkheim, Marx, and Weber, all predicted the demise of religious life in the West. Durkheim and Weber especially wrote extensively on the subject of religion.[1] From their lead, subsequent study on the notion of secularization supported the claims of these three scholars throughout much of the twentieth century. More recently, however, the issue of the decline of religious adherence in the face of secularization has been significantly challenged. That is not to suggest that there is not valid empirical data that certainly infers a staggering decline in institutional religious practice and affiliation in various regions, nor is it to suggest that basic theorizing (attributing secularization to increased scientific rationale) is necessarily incorrect in some contexts. What is becoming apparent is a picture far more complex than the simple disappearance of religious belief, eclipsed by the reasoning and functions of modernity.

At this point we need to acknowledge (as Bosch does in his second point) that the secularization debate pertains to the Western world in which scientific thought, industrialization, efficiency, and capitalist production are significant defining features. China is another overtly secular context, but, with Bosch, we will locate our discussion at this point in the West. We need also to note that Western secularism does not present itself in a clear-cut way. While we can bemoan the apparent decline in religious belief in parts of Europe, how does one account for the vitality of the religious landscape in the United States, arguably the most capitalist nation in the world? Answers are not simple; while we can see evidence

An overwhelming majority of people on the planet believe in some form of transcendent reality.

---

1   Marx actually didn't write very much on the subject; this comes as a surprise for many people as, out of the three founders of sociology mentioned—Durkheim, Marx, and Weber, it is Marx's controversial understanding of religion which is most widely known. We can perhaps attribute this to the fact that Marx, by far, is the better known and certainly the most demonized. Few, if any, people of faith appreciate their sacred beliefs being reduced to an opiate!

of religious decline in some parts of the world, the very fact that an overwhelming majority of people on the planet believe in some form of transcendent reality must give us pause to recognize that secularization and sacralization are not as predictable as modern sociologists anticipated.

The Decline in Western Christianity

Linked to the former point is the reality that the West—traditionally not only the home of Catholic and Protestant Christianity but also the base of the entire modern missionary enterprise—is slowly but steadily being dechristianized. (Bosch, 1991, 3)

Bosch's second point adds some needed nuance to his first. In the text he goes on to make the same point as many secularization theorists concerning the decline in church membership in Europe and North America, which is a valid argument but not without its complications as we have acknowledged above. Here Bosch draws our attention to the dramatic shift in the *global* demographics of Christianity. A question arises from his second point—is the base disappearing or shifting? A decade later in his book *The Next Christendom: The Coming of Global Christianity*, Philip Jenkins caused quite a stir with his articulation of the shift in "the center of gravity in the Christian world" (Jenkins, 2002, 2). Although Jenkins' thesis is by no means original, he does a good job at putting the demographics of global Christianity into perspective.[2] He suggests that by the year 2025, out of a total Christian population of some 2.6 billion in the world, the numeric breakdown will be 633 million in Africa, and in Latin America and Asia, 640 million and 460 million respectively. "Europe, with 555 million, would have slipped to third place" (Jenkins, 2002, 3). In his own quirky style, Jenkins makes the comment, "Soon, the phrase 'a white Christian' may sound like a curious oxymoron, as mildly surprising as 'a Swedish Buddhist.' Such people can exist, but a slight eccentricity is implied" (Jenkins, 2002, 3). It is quite possible to take issue with Jenkins on a number of points and, in particular, to quibble with his statistics and calculations. However, that is best left to others in the field. The main point that Jenkins makes is sound; Christianity should no longer be understood as having its base in the West.

> Christianity should no longer be understood as having its base in the West.

A corollary to Jenkins' observation of a shift in Christianity's center is the fact that missionary recruitment is shifting with it. At the turn of last century Dr. Ralph Winter with Bruce Koch claimed, "More missionaries are now sent from non-Western churches than from the traditional mission-sending bases in the West." (Winter and Hawthorne, 2009, 509). Patrick Johnstone verified this with his *Operation World* research and more recently he has produced a visually appealing presentation of such statistics in his book, *The Future of the Global Church* (Johnstone, 2011). Johnstone maintains that "the globalization of the

---

2   Jenkins himself acknowledges the authors Andrew Walls, Edward Norman, and Walter Buhlmann as having written of the "shift" some thirty years earlier prior to the publication of his book in 2002.

mission force … is an unprecedented phenomenon" and notes that "from 1980 onwards the massive increase in missions was in Af(rica,) As(ia,) L(atin)A(merica), and especially Asia" (Johnstone, 2011, 228). He goes on to map out "explosive growth" in the global mission force between 2000 and 2010, particularly from China and India (Johnstone, 2011, 228).

Bosch saw the dechristianization of the West as a major challenge to continuing mission but hoped that a new paradigm would emerge as a result. Jenkins confirmed a shift in the geographical center of Christianity, and Johnstone proves Bosch's hope was not unfounded. Johnstone writes, "The whole paradigm of missions has now changed. The old, Western ways of forming relationships and strategies and working in the field will no longer do now that missionaries are being sent out from all over the world" (Johnstone, 2011, 228).

Increased Pluralism

Partly because of the above, the world can no longer be divided into "Christian" and "non-Christian" territories separated by oceans. Because of the dechristianization of the West and the multiple migrations of people of many faiths we now live in a religiously pluralist world … This proximity to others has forced Christians to reexamine their traditional stereotypical views about those faiths. (Bosch, 1991, 3)

Again, Bosch builds upon his previous point, creating another layer and reinforcing the challenges facing evangelical missions. He forces us to consider what mission should look like in a pluralist world and hints at the significance of dialogue with other faiths.

> We live in an age that increasingly understands and appreciates the importance of context.

Throughout much of the evangelical missions community Bosch's projection is coming to pass. Postcolonial pluralism is giving rise to greater degrees of cross-cultural and inter-religious sensitivity in mission praxis. We live in an age that increasingly understands and appreciates the importance of context; a globalized world where it is considered arrogant at best (xenophobic at worst) to think your worldview is the only valid view. While a triumphalist approach to mission activity is still detected, the desire to minister to those from another culture and religion with loving humility and respect increasingly underpins missionary intention.

Western Guilt

Because of its complicity in the subjugation and exploitation of peoples of color, the West—and also Western Christians—tends to suffer from an acute sense of guilt. This circumstance often leads to an inability or unwillingness among Western Christians to "give an account of the hope" they have (1 Peter 3:15 NAS) to people of other persuasions. (Bosch, 1991, 3)

Perhaps the sense of guilt to which Bosch refers can be linked to his discussion regarding some motivations for and aims of mission activity. Comparing Verkuyl and Durr, Bosch highlights various impure motives for the missionary endeavor. At the top of the list are "(a) the imperialist motive (turning 'natives' into docile subjects of colonial authorities)" and "(b) the cultural motive (mission as the transfer of the missionary's 'superior' culture')" (Bosch, 1991, 5). Additionally, he cites the "romantic motive" and the "motive of ecclesiastical colonialism" (Bosch, 1991, 5), the former referring to a form of wanderlust and the latter to the exporting of "one's own confession and church order to other territories" (Bosch, 1991, 5).

While we certainly should acknowledge the negative aspects of the Western missions movement throughout its history, elsewhere Bosch provides a significant balance to this issue. He states that, "I am convinced that the missionaries were, by and large, a breed fundamentally different from their colonizing compatriots" (Anderson, Phillips, and Coote, 1993, 176–177). Others have also written on this issue of postcolonial Western guilt and offer a more nuanced reflection. In his aptly titled article, "Christian Missions and the Western Guilt Complex" that appeared in *The Christian Century*, Lamin Sannah emphasizes the significance of Bible translation by missionaries and sees this as having, ultimately, a subversive effect on oppressive colonial rule. "Here was an acute paradox … Colonial rule was irreparably damaged by the consequences of vernacular translation—and often by other activities of missionaries" (Sanneh, 1987, 332). As the teachings of Scripture were made available in native languages and inculcated into the culture of indigenous groups, the subjugation and discrimination of colonial powers was often questioned and seen to be out of alignment with the teachings of Christ. In this way the missionary endeavor eventually had an emancipatory impact from Western rule.

> Postcolonial Western guilt is still a contributing factor in our understanding of the crisis in mission.

The Western missions movement also provided tangible benefit to the societies that emerged, as revealed through the statistical analysis of Robert Woodberry, who examined the activist attributes of what he calls "conversionary Protestants" and concludes,

> In cross-national statistical analysis Protestant missions are significantly and robustly associated with higher levels of printing, education, economic development, organizational civil society, protection of private property, and rule of law and with lower levels of corruption. (Woodberry, 2012, 268)

The influence of missionaries on indigenous groups was also not a one-way street; a level of reciprocity can be detected. In his book *An Unpredictable Gospel: American Evangelicals and World Christianity, 1812–1920*, Jay Case observes,

> When evangelical missionaries sought to influence the rest of the world, they inadvertently built conduits by which influences from new movements of world Christianity circulated back to affect American evangelicalism. (Case, 2012, 7)

It is reasonable to assume that this dynamic is applicable to other traditional missionary sending nations as well.

However, even in light of this more recent scholarship and its potential to help us view the history and development of missionary activity in fresh ways, postcolonial Western guilt is still a contributing factor in our understanding of the crisis in mission. William Thomas' theorem may well be applicable here. Thomas stated, "If (people) define situations as real, they are real in their consequences" (Thomas and Thomas, 1928, 571–572). Although the dynamics of mission and the involvement of the West in other regions of the world may be more complex than common perception may suggest, a common perception still remains.

The Increasing Divide Between the Rich and the Poor

More than ever before we are aware of the fact that the world is divided— apparently irreversibly—between the rich and the poor and that, by and large, the rich are those who consider themselves (or are considered by the poor) to be Christians. In addition, and according to most indicators, the rich are still getting richer and the poor poorer. This circumstance creates, on the one hand, anger and frustration among the poor and, on the other, a reluctance among affluent Christians to share their faith. (Bosch, 1991, 3–4)

From where does the "reluctance" stem? Assuming Bosch is still layering one point upon another, then this fifth component of crisis may be tied to the fourth—Western guilt. A truly Christian witness must surely include an element of sacrifice, but the enormous disparity between rich and poor only highlights a dismal record of selfless giving to those in need. Perhaps the thought of sharing one's faith assumes a sharing of other resources as well, and a more equitable distribution of global wealth? To come face to face with such need in the world would impinge upon the West's vast wealth; hence, a reluctance to participate. But that assumes a macro approach and mission activity in the modern era has typically been a micro endeavor—a more personal venture. More likely is the phenomenon where affluence induces apathy. As God said to the people of Israel, "Beware that in your plenty you do not forget the Lord your God and disobey his commands" (Deuteronomy 8:11 NLT). Following his lecture on prophetic imagination, Walter Brueggeman sardonically critiques the attitude of comfortable (rich) Christians and puts this quote in their mouths, "I don't mind dying for Christ, I can do that. But I do not want to be inconvenienced" (Suttle, 2015).

Affluence induces apathy.

But this is not just a Western malaise. A similar situation can arguably be seen developing in South Korea. Patrick Johnstone observes that mission "growth in S(outh) Korea continues but is likely to slow rapidly as a result of low birth rates and little church growth" (Johnstone, 2011, 228). Such indicators are often the by-products of affluence.

If impoverished North Korea suddenly opens up, will affluent South Korea be ready and willing to share?

Interestingly, the shift in the loci of Christianity will see a shift in the socioeconomic status of believers generally for, to quote Jenkins, "the typical Christian is not the White fat cat in the United States or Western Europe, but rather a poor person, often unimaginably poor by Western standards" (Jenkins, 2002, 216).

The Emergence of Majority World Theologies and Uncertainty of the Missionary Endeavor

> For centuries, Western theology and Western ecclesial ways and practices were normative and undisputed, also in the "mission fields." Today the situation is fundamentally different. The younger churches refuse to be dictated to and are putting a high premium on their "autonomy." In addition, Western theology is today suspect in many parts of the world … In many parts of the world it is being replaced by Third World theologies … This circumstance has also contributed to profound uncertainties in Western churches, even about the validity of the Christian mission as such. (Bosch, 1991, 4)

Bosch's sixth and final factor contributing to the crisis in mission is ecclesiastical and theological in nature. Bosch revisited these issues later in his book, making reference to the Commission for World Mission and Evangelism meeting in Bangkok. Commenting on one of the conference's statements that "culture shapes the human voice that answers the voice of Christ" (CWME, Bangkok, 1973), Bosch suggested that, "It should be clear that theologies designed and developed in Europe can claim no superiority over theologies emerging in other parts of the world" (Bosch, 1991, 189). This sort of postcolonial perspective on mission was a large part of the rationale behind the call for a moratorium on missionaries by John Gatu, General Secretary of the Presbyterian Church of East Africa, in 1971. The call was repeated elsewhere, most notably in 1974 at the All Africa Conference of Churches (Reese, 2014, 245), and in many ways Lausanne 1974 responded in defense of continuing missionary activity (Douglas, 1975). With reference to this call and its counter, later in his volume Bosch suggested that missionaries were in danger of reacting too defensively, thereby revealing self-interest and self-preservation. He went on to caution his readers not to make too much of the reaction against ongoing Western missionary involvement and discount mission altogether, reminding us that,

> Missionaries are in danger of reacting too defensively, thereby revealing self-interest and self-preservation.

> Mission is *missio Dei*, which seeks to subsume into itself the *missiones ecclesiae*, the missionary programs of the church. It is not the church which "undertakes" mission; it is the *missio Dei* which constitutes the church. The mission of the church needs constantly to be renewed and reconceived. (Bosch, 1991, 531)

Our research bears this out. The mission of the church is indeed being renewed and reconceived. As we will show, it is still far from certain what form mission in a postcolonial era will take. What our research shows is that it is taking many forms.

Another way of looking at the dominance of Western perspectives over the missions programs of the church is the concept of discursive power as understood within some postmodern schools of thought, which have informed postcolonialism. Discursive power theorists argue that those who dominate a discourse, or discussion on a subject, maintain power over those who may think differently. When recognized, this power is open to critique and pushback. Overlay this understanding on our Christian reality and we observe, with Bosch, that the dominance of Western thought in theological and missiological discussions is gradually being countered, as multiple perspectives force their way out of the margins and increasingly influence the conversation. In spite of Bosch's observations concerning the autonomy demanded of the younger churches from the 1960s, the power struggle remains in its infancy, especially within the evangelical missions community. Nevertheless, our data indicates that the status quo in mission will only face stronger challenges to adapt to new forms of mission as we move through and grow beyond our postcolonial era.

Paul Kollman adds an interesting perspective on the use of language in mission with his application of *metapraxis*, the underlying ideas behind action (Kollman, 2011). He argues that the narrative about an activity reinforces its practice in reality; while adaptive practices, in turn, reinforce the narrative. It takes time but the ebb and flow of narrative discourse is a critical influencer of paradigm shifts and this mechanism is important to understand when listening to what our global voices have to say about their experience of mission. We will return to this later; however, we note here that over the past half century this can be seen, for example, in the influence of liberation theology—a voice from the margins on behalf of the voiceless, emphasizing new aspects of mission activism for the sake of the poor and oppressed. Whether we agree with it or not, it is still studied in seminaries and mission courses today, albeit more as part of recent missions history than current mission practice. An indelible legacy has remained and many of the principles that liberation and similar theologies brought to the fore continue to influence mission practice, particularly in the realm of justice advocacy and holistic (or integrated) mission.

We need to leave further exploration of Bosch's crisis there for the moment, but we will return to it again. For now, we will move on with the overall trajectory of *Transforming Mission* and make a few more key observations that are pertinent to our study.

CHAPTER 2

PARADIGMS

Although quite abbreviated, the inclusion of the above factors indicating a crisis for mission is significant in that they introduce what Bosch saw as a new paradigm (or epoch) of Christian mission, an "emerging ecumenical paradigm" (Bosch, 1991, 182). He perceived dramatic changes occurring in the way mission is understood and carried out, a rupture from the former things. Although an unknown future may present itself as a source of great anxiety and intimidation, Bosch was keen to highlight the positive aspects of this transition while acknowledging areas of concern.

Drawing on Koyama (Koyama, 1980), Bosch used an East Asian sinograph to illustrate his hope for positive outcomes. The sinograph conveys the concept "crisis." Joining many optimistic interpreters of the symbol he broke it down into two elements—danger and opportunity—"Crisis is therefore not the end of opportunity but in reality only its beginning" (Bosch, 1991, 3). While it is acceptable to interpret the graphic script in this way, like most words its interpretation depends on the context in which it is used. The "opportunity" referred to could turn out to be either negative or positive. Nevertheless, we take Bosch's optimism at face value and agree that a period of change can present opportunity for positive outcomes.

Indeed, Bosch looked to the history of Christianity and suggested that in the past, "the church has responded imaginatively to paradigm changes; we are challenged to do the same for our time and context" (Bosch, 1991, 4). The concept of paradigm (and paradigm changes or shifts) was central to Bosch's *Transforming Mission*. After his short introduction to the crisis, the entire book explored, in considerable detail, the paradigmatic development of Christian history to the present, which he regarded as a period of transition to a new paradigm in the throes of which, we believe, we still find ourselves. To form a framework for his study, Bosch looked to Thomas Kuhn and his concept of paradigm change (Kuhn, 1970), and to Hans Küng (Küng, 1987) for his outline of epochs within Christian history.

We look at Kuhn's understanding of paradigm shifts below. First, let us consider them in an historical sense, as epochs of history. Küng postulated six paradigms of Christian history (which Bosch presented and analyzed):

1. The apocalyptic paradigm of primitive Christianity
2. The Hellenistic paradigm of the patristic period
3. The medieval Roman Catholic paradigm
4. The Protestant (Reformation) paradigm

5. The modern Enlightenment paradigm
6. The emerging Ecumenical paradigm (Küng, 1987, 157)

It is appropriate that we not limit our understanding of Christian history to Küng's historical sweep, however. The paradigmatic dividing up of Christian history after the Christ event has been done in various ways by different scholars; Kenneth Scott Latourette, Ralph Winter, and David Barrett among them. Although he acknowledged different ways of categorizing historic periods (Bosch, 1991, 342ff), Bosch preferred Küng's thesis possibly because his work was the most recent at the time Bosch was writing, plus Küng referred to periods of history specifically as paradigms. Regardless whether you view history as eras, epochs, pulses, or paradigms, shifts happen, and our data reveals that we remain positioned deeply in a new shift. With Bosch, our intention in referring to paradigm shifts in history is not merely academic; we reflect on the past for the insight it can yield to the future and specifically the future of Christian mission as it faces new crises.

> Regardless whether you view history as eras, epochs, pulses, or paradigms, shifts happen, and our data reveals that we remain positioned deeply in a new shift.

Bosch drew on Küng, who in turn was clearly influenced by Kuhn and his original formulation of the concept of a paradigm. Kuhn explained paradigms as "the entire constellation of beliefs, values, techniques, and so on shared by the members of a community" (Kuhn, 1970, 174). His understanding of the term specifically focused on shifts in thought within the realm of the natural sciences, but over time his thesis has been applied across disciplines, adopted by numerous scholars and adapted in myriad ways.[1] Bosch himself took some license in using Kuhn's ideas and regarded his views "only as a kind of working hypothesis" (Bosch, 1991, 184). In this way he was able to read Küng's paradigmatic epochs in a useful (and theological) sense.

Shifts occur in a contextual and cultural setting. Understandings and implications for mission are, therefore, commensurate with a person's "ecclesiastical tradition, personal context, … social position, … personality, and culture" (Bosch, 1991, 182). Obviously paradigm shifts do not occur overnight. Christians didn't wake up on Thursday January 01, 950 thinking, "Whew! I sure am glad those Dark Ages are over." Neither are paradigms without key protagonists on the side of both the former and the new. The stalwarts of the faith valiantly attempt to defend the old paradigm as the so-called revolutionaries of the new order effectively attack them (on increasingly multiple sides). Sometimes incrementally and almost imperceptibly, other times violently and suddenly, the world around us inevitably changes. Take a cyber look around you and you can see it happening right now.

In his discussion of the origins of missiology, Kollman added that paradigmatic shifts are reinforced by a *metapraxis* dynamic (Kollman, 2011). As we mentioned earlier, the theory

---

1   Two examples of Kuhn's scientific paradigmatic changes would be the eventual shift from Ptolemaic to Copernican cosmology, and Newtonian to Einsteinian physics.

of this dynamic is that new concepts or understandings are gradually embedded into a group's consciousness through incrementally accepted and reinforced philosophical (and theological) discourses or narratives. These eventually lead to a general acceptance of a new way as the standard—a new understanding of reality if you will. Kollman argues that shifts in mission practice have happened over time because the discussion about mission developed in a different direction, which is, in turn, increasingly adopted and reinforced (Kollman, 2011).

And so Bosch charted almost two millennia of Christianity within his chosen framework of epochs and paradigm shifts, arriving, finally, at his point in the transition from the enlightenment paradigm to what he preferred to call, with Küng, the ecumenical paradigm, after deciding to abandon the term "postmodern."[2] Optimism and hope are evident in Bosch's writing, yet his monumental study remains balanced in its tone and it left the evangelical missions community with considerable food for thought. Faced with competing and disruptive discourses, paradigm shifts are times of tremendous tension and contention, so to our current shift we now turn.

---

2   Bosch uses the descriptor postmodern at the start of his section on the newly emerging paradigm, but quickly relinquishes it in favor of ecumenical. In an endnote, he clarifies that his use of the term postmodern does not denote a kind of "antimodern" stance. Bosch's reason for dropping the postmodern term in this instance is curious. Even after a lengthy discussion on postmodernity earlier in *Transforming Mission*, in which he effectively critiques modern thinking along the same lines as many postmodern scholars, Bosch ultimately discards the term because, "It is, nevertheless, an awkward term, which I shall later replace with the notion 'ecumenical'" (Bosch, 1991, 531). Yet, in his later and last monograph, *Believing in the Future* (Bosch, 1995), he embraces post-isms more readily, dropping the ecumenical paradigm altogether and making only one reference to ecclesiastical ecumenism.

CHAPTER 3

MISSIONAL ANOMIE

Earlier, we highlighted uncertainty in one of the factors of crisis within Bosch's list, where he wrote,

> Western theology is today suspect in many parts of the world… In many parts of the world it is being replaced by Third World theologies… This circumstance has also contributed to *profound uncertainties* in Western churches, even about the validity of the Christian mission as such. (Bosch, 1991, 4, emphasis added)

We need not confine ourselves to just this one point of Bosch's thesis. All six of Bosch's crisis factors stir up degrees of apprehension. This crisis and a perceived uncertainty over the status of the missionary endeavor, its value, its place, and its future, form the backdrop to our work. To better synthesize the uncertainty Bosch was identifying and to help explain the diversity of definitions of mission revealed in our research data, we borrow a term from sociology known as *anomie*.

There are several different readings of the concept of anomie and some debate as to how the term should be used and what it actually means.[1] Interpretations range, not surprisingly, from the highly complex to the more digestible. For the current work, we shall be adding to the many interpretations already formulated. Similar to the way Bosch used Kuhn's paradigm concept, we will not attempt to claim a pure application of anomie and it is only right that we acknowledge this from the start. A certain liberty (and flexibility) will be taken in its application, but it is our conviction that anomie (even in our adapted sense) can help provide some cohesion to the context of this study, specifically when considering issues of uncertainty and crisis in mission.

Writing late in the nineteenth century, Émile Durkheim is generally credited as being the forerunner in the development and use of the term *anomie*, although the word itself predates him.[2] The root of anomie is also reflected in the theological understanding of

---

1   On writing about the many uses of the concept anomie over the years within the sociological community, Besnard states, "This word has been used with various and contradictory meanings, at times without any meaning at all, and eventually ended its career in the most complete confusion" (Besnard, 2003, 48). We're sorry that in Besnard's view our use of the concept may only add to that confusion, but we believe the term is far from meaningless.

2   In the original Greek, anomia means "lawlessness." The French philosopher and poet Jean-Marie Guyau (Guyau, 1885) developed a use for the term anomie almost ten years before Durkheim's *Division of Labor in Society* (Durkheim and Simpson, 1933).

antinomianism argued against by Martin Luther.[3] Antinomian was the label set upon those who took his doctrine of justification by faith alone to an unbiblical extreme, rejecting the keeping of any codified moral law. Antinomy (literally, "a conflict of laws") is derived from an ancient Greek understanding of contradiction or paradox (Honderich, 1995, 40). Kant used it in this way for his philosophy but we will keep with a more sociological application. For us, at its root, the word indicates a sense of normlessness and potential chaos without apparent restraint or adherence to a common guide to negotiate our condition.[4] In other words, we no longer have a reliable roadmap to help us navigate the shifting landscape, at least not one we all agree on.

> We no longer have a reliable roadmap to help us navigate the shifting landscape, at least not one we all agree on.

To help us better understand anomie from a sociological perspective we begin with a definition posited by the sociologist Robert Merton, "As initially developed by Durkheim, the concept of anomie referred to *a condition of relative normlessness* in a society or group" (Merton, 1968, 215, emphasis added). This is a fairly textbook definition and, although hugely underdeveloped, sums up the point we want to make regarding the concept's application to mission. The norms (expectations, understandings) of the mission endeavor appear to be in a state of disintegration within what Bosch refers to as the emerging ecumenical paradigm, leaving the evangelical missions community (particularly in the West) with no clear frame of reference for negotiating the various crisis factors that have arisen.

To flesh out the concept a little more, we should recognize that Durkheim's original formulation is concerned with two main developments. First, Durkheim discusses the transition (paradigm shift) from the premodern to modern condition in which the rapid growth of economic life is caught in a kind of liminal state, a period of ambiguity or disorientation, void of proper regulation (Durkheim and Simpson, 1933). In other words, a threshold period between what is now and what is not yet. On this, Besnard states, "Anomie is a situation characterized by indeterminate goals and unlimited aspirations, the disorientation or vertigo created by confrontation with an excessive widening of the horizons of the possible" (Besnard, 2003, 51). Second, Durkheim, in his famous study on suicide (Durkheim and Buss, 2006), suggests that an anomic state is characterized by an acute or abrupt change in socioeconomic status. People who, for example, may lose their income and savings due to some financial crash are unable to cope with a situation that is unknown to them; no norms exist to provide a model for how one should proceed.

While Durkheim's work is intended to give an account of wider societal structures and development, it is possible to apply his concept to issues present in today's missions community. The following is from Durkheim's *The Division of Labor in Society*, where he describes some characteristics of the anomic state. With only slight reconfiguring, we can

---

3   See Luther's Treatise against antinomians in Samuel Rutherford's work (Rutherford, 1648), a translation of which is available online here: http://www.truecovenanter.com/truelutheran/luther_against_the_antinomians.html.

4   Compare the situation at the time of the Judges, "In those days Israel had no king; all the people did whatever seemed right in their own eyes" (Judges 17:6 NLT).

identify aspects relevant to our current discussion; therefore, it is worth quoting Durkheim at length:

> Profound changes have been produced in the structure of our societies in a very short time; they have been freed from the segmental type with a rapidity and in proportions such as never before been seen in history. Accordingly, the morality which corresponds to this social type has regressed, but without another developing quickly enough to fill the ground that the first left vacant in our consciences. Our faith has been troubled; tradition has lost its sway; individual judgment has been freed from collective judgment. But on the other hand, the functions, which have been disrupted in the courses of the upheaval, have not had the time to adjust themselves to one another; the new life which has emerged so suddenly has not been able to be completely organized. (Durkheim and Simpson, 1933, 408)

In considering any particular focus of Émile Durkheim's work, it is appropriate to acknowledge the historical context in which he wrote. The latter half of the nineteenth century through to the start of World War I saw France under the political rule of the Third Republic. This was a period of a great many social tensions and one in which major political and social upheavals were only narrowly averted. Drawing on his context, Durkheim became an early pioneer in the discipline of sociology and produced a great body of literature covering such topics as social constraint and control, deviance, suicide, and religion. Throughout his work, themes of fragmentation and social solidarity are constant. For the former, his question basically was, "Why, in such a rapidly changing world, does society not fragment?" The latter point complements the first, "What is it that holds society together?"

While many take levels of social cohesion for granted, and thereby give little thought to Durkheim's questions, the concerns and concepts he articulated in the nineteenth and early twentieth centuries have a somber resonance with contemporary society. One could even argue *especially* for contemporary society, in which globalization has escalated and many live within plural societies characterized by diverse traditions, politics, socioeconomic status, and religious belief. The West is certainly far removed from an earlier premodern age of, what Durkheim called, mechanical solidarity; an age in which social cohesion existed through shared, fairly monolithic, beliefs (particularly shared religious beliefs).[5]

> We are in a state of *missional* (mission-related) *anomie* in which the forms and structures of the past are in a state of flux and a cohesive and accepted new way has yet to form.

---

5   For any reader with a particular interest in sociological theory, Durkheim postulates that modern industrialized societies no longer operate according to the model of mechanical solidarity but instead are, nonetheless, held together by organic solidarity. This is a form of social cohesion, which grows out of an increased division of labor. Members of society are effectively dependent upon one another to meet their economics needs, thus promoting a form of solidarity.

Within the context of issues facing the evangelical missions community, and therefore the context that forms the backdrop to this study, Durkheim's concept of anomie applies. We are in a state of *missional* (mission-related) *anomie* in which the forms and structures of the past are in a state of flux and a cohesive and accepted new way has yet to form. To link this discussion back to the factors of crisis put forward by Bosch, each point contributes to the anomic state being experienced by evangelical missions. To reiterate:

1. The prominence of scientific rationale
2. The decline in Western Christianity
3. Increased pluralism
4. Western guilt
5. The increasing divide between the rich and the poor
6. The emergence of majority world theologies and uncertainty of the missionary endeavor

Using these factors as a base, we identify three additional characteristics that contribute to missional anomie in our context twenty-five years later:

Hermeneutic Liberty

Closely related to Bosch's point 6, there now exists many differing interpretations of Scripture and doctrine within and between Christianity in the West and the rest of the world (even within the same denomination, the Anglican Communion for example). Philip Jenkins sums up the tension this way, "If Northerners worry that Southern churches have compromised with traditional paganism, then Southerners accuse Americans and Europeans of selling out Christianity to neopaganism, in the form of humanistic secular liberalism" (Jenkins, 2002, 201). While we cannot discount the many (positive) points of contact and relationship within global Christianity, we should also not discount the very real possibility of growing and seemingly irreconcilable schisms between Christians holding different doctrines due to their understanding of Scripture and theological formulations from within their, at once unique and global, context; even so among Christians of apparently similar traditions.

Plural Theologies

As a result of hermeneutic liberty there now exists multiple theologies from which people can draw; Bosch highlights this *within* the realm of alternate theologies outside of the West. But additionally we can include the various perspectives and modes of thought in the ecumenical (postmodern) paradigm of theology and mission within the West. Only relatively recently has it been possible to explore alternative theological ideas outside the *establishment* without mortal repercussions. As a result of this freedom many doctrines are being revisited, revised, and re-presented within the evangelical tradition. Proposed updates are not always readily accepted, but proponents of altered or new theologies in the

West are not being incarcerated or incinerated for their ideas—some may even be accepted for mission service! With theological and missiological ideas in the West increasingly many and varied, they are therefore less mechanical (monolithic) in the Durkheimian sense. This has the potential to tie in with another characteristic of the classic formulation of anomie, "The limits are unknown between the possible and the impossible, what is just and what is unjust, legitimate claims and hopes and those which are immoderate. Consequently, there is no restraint upon aspirations" (Durkheim and Simpson, 1933, 253). The question of validating orthodoxy immediately arises here, but that is beyond the purview of this study. Suffice it to say orthodoxy is in danger of becoming a fluid term.

Global Shifts in Christianity

Bosch observes the dechristianization of the West in his second crisis point; we add to this by noting the relocation of the center of global Christianity from the West to what Jenkins prefers to call the global South. Emphasis here is placed upon the fact that this is a development rarely witnessed in the history of the church.[6]

If we understand an aspect of the anomic state to be one of normlessness, without authoritative controls or a developed normative frame of reference, then our most recent shift in Christianity's center of gravity suggests a condition that is, for the West *and* the rest, incredibly destabilizing; but not without promise.[7]

> Proponents of altered or new theologies in the West are not being incarcerated or incinerated for their ideas— some may even be accepted for mission service!

Many of these characteristics will be recognizable as part of our so-called postmodern era and there are elements within *postmodern* perspectives that may help reflective practitioners of mission navigate their way through the current anomic crisis. Embracing the reality of an individual's experience without a compulsion to reconcile it (or force it to agree) with one's own perspective would be among those elements. However, an exploration of postmodern sociological and philosophical tenets is beyond the scope of this work.

---

6   An example of another time Christianity experienced a great global shift was when the center of power moved from the Middle East and North Africa to Europe. The emergence of Islam in the seventh century was a catalyst in that regard and the anomie apparent in our current major shift of the center of Christianity can also be perceived in what historians have traditionally called the "Dark Ages." Regarding this, Andrew Walls writes,

"In AD 600 the Christian heartlands, already justly claiming antiquity, lay predominantly among Greek-speaking people in the eastern Mediterranean; but the whole of that empire that had crushed the Jewish revolt now acknowledged the lordship of Christ. By AD 800 those eastern Greek-speaking heartlands were not only under Muslim rule; large sections of their populations were becoming Muslims. Latin-speaking African Christians were dying out altogether. How did Christianity survive the collapse? Because by the time those events took place Christian faith was taking hold among the northern and western barbarians whom civilised Christians had long feared and despised. New Christian lands emerged, replacing the old and shifting the Christian center of gravity as drastically as it had shifted after AD 70." (Walls, 1996, 256)

7   We are not comfortable with any classification of the world from the perspective of the West (e.g., global South, Third World, Two-Thirds World, Majority World, Developing World, etc.). Unfortunately, this duality dominates our era and it is difficult to avoid.

Instead, building on the elements just mentioned, we have chosen to let individual voices speak about their mission involvement as far as is possible without bias or judgment. It is our analysis of the conversations with these individuals from a variety of cultural backgrounds that revealed what we came to identify as missional anomie.

"Why, in such a rapidly changing world, does mission continue in spite of crises?" and more importantly, "What is it that motivates people to continue to be involved?"

Resonating with Durkheim's questions about society in flux, the backdrop to this study are the questions, "Why, in such a rapidly changing world, does mission continue in spite of crises?" and more importantly, "What is it that motivates people to continue to be involved?" These questions are constant companions in the analysis chapters that follow. By weaving diverse voices together with a consistent narrative around major themes evident in the data, our presentation highlights the anomic state of mission.

CHAPTER 4

RESEARCH METHODOLOGY

Researching a phenomenon is a perplexing enterprise because it attempts to elevate inquiry and the knowledge of a thing beyond that of mere speculation or opinion. Opinion has its place. It fills pages of newspaper editorials, the content of innumerable websites, and countless hours of radio and television broadcasts. Additionally within the evangelical world, opinion is the stuff of a great deal of popular Christian literature and specifically, literature which focuses on a principle task of the church—the dissemination of the gospel and extension of God's kingdom. We must be careful not to hinder the work of the Holy Spirit and deny the inspiration of God in the articulated hearts and minds of fellow believers, but it is important to recognize the distinction between claims grounded in opinion (including those based upon a particular form of scriptural interpretation) and those which are supported by sound scientific research. The distinction was significant for our research team and informed our decision to utilize tools of social science to aid our project. Social scientific research incorporates an internal sequence that shapes the parameters of an investigation and holds those who undertake it accountable to a set of guiding principles. If these guiding principles are maintained, the end result is the furtherance of knowledge built more firmly upon empirical data rather than conjecture.

In this chapter we will explore these distinctions further and explain the methods we employed to draw the conclusions we make in this book. We believe it is important for you to have confidence in the process to trust our results. Applying our method to a project with such a wide scope of investigation is rare in the evangelical missions community. It is much easier to collect and assess answers to simple questions or statistics than to obtain and analyze narrative data. Nevertheless, we were eager to get a deep, rich understanding of the current state of mission involvement across the globe; rooted in direct observation and experience rather than assumption.

Having said all that, we are not suggesting that all social scientific research is done well by default, while all opinion is poorly thought through and incomplete. Social research can often fail to maintain its foundational principles and the resulting slippage then becomes nothing more than opinion with a liberal dose of sociological jargon! To be done well there must be, first and foremost, a commitment to objectivity. While objectivity can exist in the world of opinion, it is not necessarily a prerequisite.

The difference (and discussion) between opinion and social scientific inquiry is common within sociology and the social sciences generally. To look more closely at the characteristics of investigation in the tradition of social research, consider the following definitions of sociology:

> Sociology is the *study of human social life, groups, and societies*. It is a dazzling and compelling enterprise, having as its subject matter our own behavior as social beings. The scope of sociology is extremely wide, ranging from the analysis of passing encounters between individuals in the street up to the investigation of worldwide social processes. (Giddens, 1989, 4, emphasis ours)

> Sociology is the *objective* study of human behavior in so far as it is affected by the fact that people live in groups. (Livesey, 2010, 1 quoting Barry Sugarman,1968, emphasis ours)

> Sociology is the study of individuals in groups in a *systematic way*, which grew out of the search for understanding associated with the industrial and scientific revolutions of the eighteenth and nineteenth centuries. (Livesey, 2010, 2 quoting Tony Lawson and Joan Garrod, 1996, emphasis ours)

There are obviously many more definitions of sociology, but these provide an indication of some characteristics of the discipline. Notice from the above definitions, the italicized points: sociology is the *study of human life, groups, and societies* in an *objective* and *systematic way*. First, and most basically, sociology focuses on human interaction and (aspects of) society. The second defining aspect of sociology and its practice is that of objectivity. To be objective is to look at a situation, event, or phenomenon in a non-biased way. Ideally, sociologists are committed to studying society, collecting data, and reporting findings as truthfully and accurately as possible. Some suggest that this sets sociology apart from other pursuits that involve human commentary. Bloggers, politicians, writers of newspaper editorials, newscasters, radio and talk show hosts, among many others, all report on societal issues but tend to do so with a particular agenda attached. While some of what they say may have some basis in fact, the end result is usually opinion shaped by an organization's bias or the commentator's particular worldview, informed by their own religious and/or political persuasion.

The thought has probably already occurred to you that sociologists are not omniscient in their work; they have potential for bias too. This is true. They are born into a culture and socialized in the values and traditions of that culture; they hold beliefs and political views and have agendas. They are not pure receptors and interpreters of social reality, as much as they would like to be. With that qualification made, however, there is a genuine striving in the sociological community for objectivity. It may be limited but the desire and attempt is there, as are the tools to assist.

The third point to notice from the above definitions is that of the *systematic* approach to the study of social phenomena. As the word suggests, to study something systematically is to proceed with a form of inquiry that adheres to a system or a set of clearly defined techniques. Within sociology, this system uses a scientific model in the process of collecting data. Sociologists have a variety of methods available to them to assist with conducting research. Their choice of method is somewhat dependent upon the social phenomena being studied and the desired outcomes. Methods can include the analysis of statistics, the use of questionnaires, various forms of observation, conducting interviews, and the collecting of life histories. Each data collection technique within sociology needs to adhere to a level of stringency, which has been honed and refined over many years of practice and discussion within the discipline to establish parameters of objectivity and authenticity. Population samples should be representative, observation should be unobtrusive, questionnaires should be clear, well-crafted, and unambiguous, interviews carefully designed, conducted, and respectfully recorded. The systematic quality of research extends not only to the collecting of data but to its analysis also. Statistics can too easily be manipulated or interviews conveniently edited to reflect the agenda of the researcher. No sociological method is without flaws, but a systematic implementation goes a long way to ensure as much accuracy as possible in the results they will yield.

Quantitative or Qualitative?

Research can be further complicated by the fact that there is no agreement on methodology (the underlying assumptions about how research should be conducted) nor which subsequent set of techniques will yield the most accurate results. This is so even within the framework of social science. As a discipline, sociology is not a singularly unified group. Instead, an active and continuing debate is present within the field. This debate highlights the distinction between what can be termed the *positivist* versus a *naturalist* approach to research. Other terms can be used which amount to the same thing: scientific sociology versus interpretist sociology and quantitative versus qualitative sociology. To understand better the complexities of these approaches and explain why we chose the method we used for the current study we feel it is necessary to provide a brief overview of the origin and philosophy and characteristics of these two approaches.

Early social theorists were influenced by the intellectual currents and (often tumultuous) changes of their day. The eighteenth, nineteenth, and early twentieth centuries witnessed significant shifts in both the economic and political landscape of Europe. Agricultural predominance gave way to the sweeping social and economic current of the industrial revolution. Rural life gave way to urbanization; religious belief, and the social order it reinforced, was challenged by a new modern and distinctly scientific rationale. It was from this emerging age of reason and science that early academic observers of society such as August Comte and Émile Durkheim sought to explain social phenomena using a scientific framework. Their aim was to develop a science of society that followed the cause and effect logic of experimentation found in natural sciences such as physics and chemistry. To use the term we are now familiar with, they applied a scientific *paradigm* to the study of society. This approach we refer to as positivism. Positivist research is conducted in such a way that a theory about causes is developed (or deduced) and then that theory is tested. It is then subsequently falsified or proven to be correct, thus creating a scientifically verified law or principle. In the study of social phenomena, the general methods employed in the positivist approach are *quantitative* in as much as the techniques employed to carry out the research enable the sociologist to easily convert the data into numbers and measure precisely the components of what is being researched.

The naturalist approach can be traced back to the work of Max Weber. Whereas in the positivist tradition the various institutions and forces of society effectively control individuals, Weber, by contrast, was concerned with understanding the *meanings* people attach to their everyday lives. The naturalist position is not so much concerned with a cause and effect analysis of social phenomena nor for the striving to formulate universal social laws. Its primary concern is to understand and describe social action. To translate this principle to a more pragmatic research methodology, this *qualitative* approach enables the researcher to gain a rich understanding of the social phenomenon or group under study. Instead of reducing data to quantifiable units, qualitative research draws heavily on description and often-lengthy interviews. To put it simply, quantitative (positivist) approaches utilize numbers; qualitative (naturalist) approaches utilize words.

The Current Study

After initial discussion among our research team in the early stages of the project, we chose to adopt a qualitative approach to analyze the lived experience of mission. A quantitative study had been considered and piloted which led the team to conclude that a major aim of any investigation into the issues surrounding mission involvement needed to be more open to the concept of collecting the articulated experiences of a decent and diverse sampling of people who had, either directly or indirectly, something of value to share about their involvement in the mission endeavor. The research methodology we subsequently chose was something of a departure from other *Globalization of Mission Series* projects, which have either been anthologies of edited commentary or the interpretations of statistics from quantitative data collection and analysis.

> We chose to adopt a qualitative approach to analyze the lived experience of mission.

We believe our deviation was necessary in order to produce fresh verified insight into our subject matter to share with the evangelical missions community. This should not be taken as a critique of opinion pieces or quantitative data collection, or as a refutation of the validity of earlier and ongoing projects. By adopting a qualitative approach, we aimed to develop a reservoir of descriptive knowledge, from a global missions perspective, and allow thematic patterns to emerge from the data itself. To achieve this, we placed our emphasis on very open-ended interviews and used appropriate analysis techniques to draw out meaning from the data collected.

Here are some logistics of our research project:
- The project was reviewed by the Human Research Committee of Malone University, Canton, Ohio and deemed to be in accordance with Title 45 Code of U.S. Federal Regulations, Part 46 (45 CFR 46).

- The members of the research team were given specific training in interviewing techniques and qualitative methodology during team consultations.[1]
- All the respondents interviewed signed consent forms (or verbally indicated consent if interviewed over the phone or by other means of telecommunication) prior to the start of the interview.
- Interviews were digitally recorded and then later transcribed in detail. Some were painstakingly translated from original languages into English.
- Nine researchers were trained and gathered data from their residences in nine different parts of the world: Korea, Japan, New Zealand, India, Kenya, Romania, UK, US, and Argentina.
- The principle researcher used qualitative analysis software to assist in coding and assessing the data.[2]

We used a semi-structured narrative interview method that introduced themes and concepts relating to issues of mission activity and experience and invited respondents to discuss the topic from their experience. In particular, the researchers guided discussion around how the respondents became involved in mission themselves. While the researchers introduced themes in their conversation, respondents were given the freedom and were often encouraged to expand upon areas of interest and concern that they considered relevant. According to Esterberg, in semi-structured interviews "the goal is to explore a topic more openly and to allow the interviewees to express their opinions and ideas in their own words" (Esterberg, 2002, 87).

In recognizing the apparent futility of attempting to establish a random sample of subjects to interview, our sampling was deliberate in that each team member conducted interviews with a selection of acquaintances and contacts as widely as possible within their network—people occupying different roles in mission who could provide input in relation to their involvement in mission. These included: missionaries, mobilizers, mission organization staff, church leaders, and church members. For economic and logistical reasons most team members limited their interviews to a geographic area that coincided with their normal ministry activity, but some interviewers engaged respondents from further afield, particularly if they were on home leave, or via digital communication tools (e.g., Skype).

While the ideal would have been to incorporate representation from many more countries, a number of factors made this impractical. Although a diversity of views from across the world is provided, the project does not claim to be representative of the entire region specified. Such a study would entail considerably more time and resources. Financial limitations are a constant issue with any research project, even more so within the missions context. Finding personnel willing and available to conduct research was also a challenge, particularly people prepared to commit to a lengthy process. Nevertheless, the cultural

---

1   Specifically, our Research Team Consultation, West Watch House, London, England, April 17–19, 2007. With supplementary training in Pattya, Thailand, October 30–November 4, 2008.

2   The software program used for this study was Atlas Ti. The name is an acronym for *Archiv fuer Technik, Lebenswelt und Alltagssprache* (technology, the life world, and everyday language). *Ti* simply refers to *text interpretation*.

spread of the team's interviews still provides a generous mix of global voices to present. We have no doubt that there is considerable opportunity for future research into our subject and it is hoped that this project will motivate others to continue the exploration.

The transcribed material was coded and analyzed. As stated above, with no hypothesis or theory to be tested the research process and analysis of the data from this qualitative approach is different in many respects from that of a quantitative model. In the absence of a clearly stated hypothesis, it is the intent of the qualitative approach to provide a rich descriptive account of the issue being studied. The American cultural anthropologist Clifford Geertz referred to this as a "thick description" (Geertz, 2000, 17).

Data analysis within this model usually employs a technique of highlighting, or coding, words, statements, or passages of the interview transcript in order to identify emergent patterns and themes. Coffey and Atkinson describe the process in this way: "a) noticing relevant phenomena, b) collecting examples of those phenomena, and c) analyzing those phenomena in order to find commonalities, differences, patterns, and structures" (Coffey and Atkinson, 1996, 29).

The following chapters set out the data. Describing the data is done in various ways. In some sections we allow individual voices to speak with narrative flow, either emphasizing the diversity of the respondents in a "mash-up" around a theme, or grouping regions together to highlight the variety in their respondents' perspectives. Overall, we make an effort to allow the diverse voices of a wide array of respondents from many nations to be heard as they describe their experience of mission, as they understand mission to be. To ensure the anonymity of the respondents, names have been changed, obscured, or simply not used; other precautions in the writing of respondents' accounts have been taken to further protect identities. Only once the data is presented and the voices heard do we attempt to comment on and draw tentative conclusions from the experiences they share.

PART ONE: SUMMARY

A well set context can differentiate an average picture from an excellent one. Once established, photographic artists blur the background context as they sharpen the focus on the primary object. One way of discussing the quality of context blur is called bokeh. The better the bokeh, the more pleasing on the eye is the picture. We are seeking to establish a good bokeh to help our primary object pop out of the picture. In our case, the primary object is what is commonly known as mission mobilization, but it is too early to discuss that further, we still have a few more contextual elements to put in place.

In many respects, the context for our research project was the history of the whole world and God's plans for the world unfolding in history. That is huge, too huge. To continue the photography analogy, it lay outside our depth of field. So we chose to view it via a shallower focus, through the lens of David Bosch. In his book *Transforming Mission* Bosch visualizes God's mission biblically and historically and identifies some critical issues that he saw contributing to a crisis. Although he wrote some decades before we started our research project, his perspective is still very relevant for mission today and therefore a salient backdrop to our study.

Bosch perceived broad philosophical and sociological shifts in the world that affected mission and challenged mission assumptions. He presented them as warnings but remained confident that God would help the church navigate around them to see the mission of God fulfilled. We incorporated the factors contributing to Bosch's crisis into our research agenda. They helped us shape the questions we developed, hoping to understand how and why people became involved in mission in light of these challenges. In the end we discovered a great deal of variation and observed additional potential threats to mission, expanding on those Bosch identified.

We believe the variety of responses to our exploration of mission was because the particular method of research we employed allowed them to emerge. While semi-structured narrative interviews have been in common use in many disciplines for a long while, this sort of qualitative method has not been popular with mission research until much more recently. The scope of our project was considerably wide, which provided data that was rich in its cultural representation, producing a wonderfully complex picture.

From our research we affirm that mission remains in a great deal of flux. Anyone who is experiencing frustration in the evangelical missions community will no doubt attest to this as patently obvious. Our study now confirms it and provides a systematic record of it in real terms, from the voices of real people, expressing how this anomic condition is experienced.

Questions for Reflection

1. What aspects of Bosch's crisis and/or our additional three factors do you encounter as part of your mission involvement? Assuming you are not simply trying to avoid them, how are you seeking to address those crises?
2. How can an awareness of the crisis of mission be used positively to strengthen your ministry?
3. How do the "profound uncertainties" that we believe manifest as *missional anomie* affect your attempts to encourage people into mission involvement?
4. Do you sense your understanding of mission shifting? If so, how?
5. How would you relate to someone with a different perspective of mission from you?

PART TWO: MISSION PERCEPTIONS

When Jesus had called the Twelve together, he gave them power and authority to drive out all demons and to cure diseases, and he sent them out to preach the kingdom of God and to heal the sick. He told them: "Take nothing for the journey—no staff, no bag, no bread, no money, no extra tunic. Whatever house you enter, stay there until you leave that town. If people do not welcome you, shake the dust off your feet when you leave their town, as a testimony against them." So they set out and went from village to village, preaching the gospel and healing people everywhere.
(Luke 9:1–6)

Interviews recorded during the course of our study allowed the respondents to discuss a wide range of issues connected with their perception of mission. In order to better understand the concept of mission mobilization, we felt it would be useful to know what the respondents considered mission itself to mean. The remit of the research project was not to provide a definition of mission and impose our own particular understanding of it upon our respondents, but to allow multiple viewpoints to emerge from the perspectives they provided.

This part of the book illustrates that our respondents' global voices reveal a wide variety of views regarding the concept of mission—particularly what it does, where it's located, and when it's done. While various understandings of mission have coexisted for a long time, the evangelical missions community has tended to hold reasonably tightly to a particular method of mission practiced over more than two hundred years of the *modern missionary movement*. From the late 1700s the standard experience of mission has followed the model of European colonial expansion. In very general terms the accepted mission narrative has been that of long-term, cross-cultural (if not specifically overseas), donation funded, gospel proclamation activity (or means to that end), with the intention of establishing and strengthening churches where few or none existed. Students of mission will be well aware of the other streams of mission understanding, which have been labeled in different ways at different times, but we will consider this understanding of mission a *traditional* one for the evangelical missions community.

We are firmly in an age where the traditional evangelical narrative of mission is no longer dominant. Missions have been struggling with this for decades and Bosch recognized it as a crisis. Our research confirms it. Adding weight to our perception of missional anomie is the diversity of voices advocating for the legitimizing of alternate understandings of mission, a broadening of the traditional parameters. As a result, the *what, where,* and *when* of mission now clearly struggle for common definition. The narratives are now plural and the traditional perspective wanes in ever increasing measure as the paradigm continues to shift.

In this section we highlight some of the ways mission is diverging from traditional evangelical norms. To anyone who has been reflecting on mission practice over the past couple of decades what our voices have to say will not be all that surprising. As we have emphasized, the evangelical understanding of mission has been in the midst of dynamic change for some time. Nevertheless, the voices articulating a different understanding of mission deserve to be heard. Mission can no longer be rigidly defined if the following perceptions are to be taken seriously. To illustrate the shifts, we look first at perceptions of mission activity along a continuum between personal salvation and social action. Second, we notice issues connected with the locus of mission along a continuum with local at one end and global at the other, with consideration of whether or not mission needs to be cross-cultural. Finally, we recognize that the length of mission engagement is varied along a continuum between short-term and longer-term or career involvement, with a particular emphasis on voices with a perspective on the effects of short-term mission.

> As a result, the *what, where,* and *when* of mission now clearly struggles for common definition. The narratives are now plural and the traditional perspective wanes in ever increasing measure as the paradigm continues to shift.

CHAPTER 5

THE WHAT: MISSION'S FOCUS

Personal Salvation ↔ Social Action

While there was significant overlap between broad perceptions of mission, distinctions in emphasis regarding the goals of missionary activity were clearly evident in our interview data. As we compare perspectives of mission that focus on salvation alone against what has sometimes been referred to as the *social gospel*, we thought it best to present the differing views as part of a continuum, with extremes at both ends of the scale, rather than polarized opposites set up to conflict. We will use this continuum model to explore the *where* and *when* of mission for similar reasons. Some qualification should be made though, especially when we use such loaded words as *extremes*, as neither extreme necessarily denies the possibility of containing elements of the other. For example in this first continuum, the data shows that often social action still plays a role in missionary activity, even with voices asserting the predominance of mission as first and foremost a means to salvation. The same can be said for those who appear to be strong advocates of more social applications of the gospel; the possibility of bringing others into an encounter and relationship with the Christian God is also present in the activities and agenda of the mission worker. With reference to the relevance of this exploration on mission mobilization, we believe the differing emphases of each continuum help inform our understanding of motivation when it comes to participating in the mission endeavor.

> We believe the differing emphases of each continuum help inform our understanding of motivation when it comes to participating in the mission endeavor.

Mission as Personal Salvation

I've always believed that the mission of individual Christians as well as the church was to save the lost souls and world by witnessing the gospel. (Minister in India)

Let us first hear from those who perceived mission as primarily the work of conversion and the salvation of the "lost." Consider the thoughts of an East European minister as he recounted a conversation with another minister.

And I shared the vision with him: I said, "Look, (pause) I'm thinking what God could do." And he looked at me at the beginning, curiously. Then when I'd finished, he said, "I'm not interested, that kind of thing is not my area." He was saying that he's more interested in social issues, not in missions.

This comment is significant because it highlights the conceptual gap between those who understand their work in missions as predominantly that of seeking salvation for the lost and those who emphasize social issues. Here, the respondent did not recognize social issues as being part of mission at all. Others we spoke with were more tempered in their responses but still provided clear examples of the perception of missionary activity with an emphasis firmly on evangelism, aiming for evidence of a salvific response, like this next mission worker in India.

> **Interviewer:** And so the (*name of church*) that you went to, they were a lot more evangelistic?
>
> **Respondent:** Very much so, they clearly presented the gospel, they pleaded with people to make a commitment, after that they lead them to baptism and then the Lord's table. They encourage you to share your faith very actively, they go from village to village, actually because of the (*name of assembly*), in our neighboring villages, they have gone from door to door and shared the gospel very actively. They have taken the clear gospel to every doorstep in our villages, yeah.
>
> **Interviewer:** So the (*name of church*), they have defined missions very clearly as evangelism—would it include anything else?
>
> **Respondent:** Yeah, basically, the main emphasis of the mission is to preach the gospel clearly and to lead people to make a personal commitment to the Lord Jesus Christ.

A church leader from the United Kingdom shared similar views.

> I think the first thing you have to have a love for is the gospel. I'd want to find out what part gospel preaching plays in their ministry. Because that is the heartbeat of mission—a love for souls and to see God saving souls and to see souls won for the Lord. That has to be the emphasis to all missionary work. And so I think we need to have a strong gospel preaching aspect and evangelistic aspect to our church, to outreach.

Even a mission motivator in East Asia, when asked, "What does global mission mean to you?" responded similarly:

> A task Jesus commissioned to his disciples and those who believe in him to make forgiveness of sins and the eternal life in him known to all the creation, both locally and globally.

The winning of souls or salvation of persons who do not have a personal relationship with God can also be seen to be the ultimate reason for mission activity for this student of mission in Eastern Europe and also as a direct motivating factor for their mission service.

And that makes me continue the choice and aims that I have, the dreams that I have, and the passion for people who don't yet know God. They have a general notion of God, but they don't know him personally, intimately. That makes me stay faithful, makes me persevere in my dream that I have for missions.

A number of respondents described the goal of mission as a ministry to the unreached; a reasonable indication that evangelism and conversion was the predominant goal of mission activity for them, like these two responses from South America:

> For me "the mission" is Matthew 28:19–20—the command and the privilege to declare to the world that Jesus came to the world to reconcile us with God. The evangelization of the world, from those around us to remote places and people. It implies to feel God's burden for the unreached, to pray, to give, and to work for them.

> Understanding that they (unreached peoples) do not deserve less than me the message of salvation. God loved them and sent his Son Jesus for them as he did for me. We have no right to keep it for us alone.

Evidence of a preference for a personal salvation outcome in mission is also implied by an overtly spiritual orientation to ministry. While social activity can be a valid spiritual activity, the emphasis on a manifest spiritual experience tends to sit easier at the salvation end of the continuum. A respondent in East Asia illustrated this with their telling of a dramatic encounter.

While social activity can be a valid spiritual activity, the emphasis on a manifest spiritual experience tends to sit easier at the salvation end of the continuum.

> A local pastor, his wife, and I went over some Bible verses with her to make sure she really understood salvation; we laid hands on her and prayed. Then, she was dramatically delivered from evil spirits and literally became a new person. With that extraordinary experience Romans 10:14–15 came to me. When I reflected on the verses and other experiences I had had since young, I was convinced that God had a purpose and led me to this unreached people group for them to hear the gospel. I headed back to (*location*) the next day and shared with my pastor what happened. He said "a door would be opened if God was leading you to that."

The above responses are examples from the data that advocate the purpose of mission as a means, primarily, to salvation and of evangelizing the unevangelized, but the team's interviews also revealed a broad sweep of perceptions regarding this. Consider the sentiment of one mission motivator from the United Kingdom,

> (*A certain Christian discipleship ministry*) does the same thing with missiology and does things like biblical basis of mission, examples of mission, and thinking about issues around serving God in other cultures. Its basic objective is driven by the needs of the unevangelized, the unreached. That's its major focus. It tends to be focused on evangelism amongst the unreached so it's not full-blown mission

as I would see it, not balanced mission as I would see it in the sense of it's not word and works and not so good on local and global either, although it does encompass both.

This respondent echoed much of the terminology present in the interview excerpts above (e.g., evangelism, unevangelized, unreached), but clearly indicated that the needs of the unreached (which in the context of the interview infer salvation and conversion activities) did not constitute the entirety of the respondent's perception of mission—"It's not full blown mission as I would see it, not balanced mission."

A similar call for a more holistic approach was evident in the voices from the United States, yet many of them still prioritized personal salvation. After calling for a pendulum swing back toward a "biblical gospel" from leaning toward a social gospel, one mission organization motivator balanced their comment with,

> We are definitely preaching that the gospel encompasses both word and deed— it's a holistic ministry.

A university chaplain in the United States held a similar view,

> I think the spiritual goal, the spiritual conversion, I think that's ultimately the end in mind.... When people come to Christ that includes the whole person, you know, and that affects their social life, everything. But what I mean is that sometimes to get people's attention, to get to their heart, you've got to love them, you know, instead of just preaching at them. You've got to love them; you've got to serve them.

Not everyone we interviewed seemed to appreciate the attempt to achieve a balanced integrated approach to the whole person, however. There were passionate advocates toward both ends of the continuum. We've heard from a sampling at the salvation end, from more extreme to moderate; let's now hear how those toward the social action end articulate their passion.

Mission as Social Action

> *And I stayed with them in (location) for one year and a half and I was able to take nursing training to be able to go back to the mission field and use my skills, because I realized it's so important to help people practically not just tell them, "Jesus loves you but, you know—bye bye."*
> *(Missionary from Eastern Europe)*

The opening account from an East European mission worker regarding mission as more social action oriented is an insightful example of the perception of mission work leaning toward that end of the spectrum. As such, it is worth expanding on. They went on to say,

> I really wanted to be able to use my nursing skills and not only that but to learn more. So I found a missionary, like a medical clinic that was working, there is a missionary doctor who's been in (*location*) for twenty years and he's very much dedicated to helping the by providing healthcare ... And it turned out to be a blessing. Not only an opportunity for me to serve the (*people group*), but also to improve my language skills and to learn more about treating and diagnosing patients. Learning more about the tropical diseases. Yeah, how to deal in situations like that.

The reference to a long-serving missionary doctor *dedicated* to providing healthcare was important for this respondent to mention. Their esteem for the missionary doctor is evident. That esteem, together with their focus on medicine and disease in the mission context, implies a deep passion for meeting certain human needs. Yet they still considered themselves and their colleagues to be missionaries.

In South America a pastor discussed their involvement in mission activity to Africa in medical terms also.

> The project to (*African country*) is the most recent, the missionary we are sending is a professional nurse and she will work in a health project with malnourished children.

For many in the evangelical missions community, this African country would be considered one of the most unreached and hardest to reach nations in the world, yet this South American church saw malnourished children as a primary need, worthy of them sending a professional nurse to help. From the context of the interview it was clear that they understood this to be legitimate mission work.

An Indian respondent referred to medical work as part of their mission sphere too. In addition, their part of the work was administrative, and the ministry included "philanthropic social work" but was still clearly on the "mission field."

> But in the year 1998, I'm sent out to mission field ... That is in (*location*), and majority are Hindu, next is Muslim. Christians are very few in number. So, I was posted there as an administrative secretary of the mission field. I have around 150 workers within that area, and we have four schools. Two are high school level and we do medical ministry and philanthropic social work, and I was there for three years term. So, that is my mission field experience.

This East African infers that "spiritual" work is separate from the practical work they describe. They do not indicate that practical activities may also have an inherent spiritual dimension.

This next East African voice takes care to emphasize that the gospel is "not only spiritual" but seeks to achieve many social objectives as well. An interesting observation here is that this East African infers that "spiritual" work is separate from the practical work they describe. They do not indicate that practical activities may also have an inherent spiritual dimension.

I think the third thing is that they are able to address a gospel that is not only spiritual but a gospel that is holistic; a gospel that addresses the other needs of the people and subsequently people open up for them because they would go with schools, hospitals, they sometimes dig boreholes for the communities. They would go with ways that would be able to open up people for them. We as evangelicals are sometimes a little nervous about what we have termed as social gospel and yet through this direction they are able to open us to the people. So I think we need to be open towards reaching out as missionaries, particularly when you go to a difficult terrain, the Muslims and other regions, that is not just preaching only but preaching and also good works that create openness, and the Catholic church has been very good at that.

Implied in this response is the need for a salvific outcome (people "open up" to the message) but the good works enable that to happen and therefore it could be argued that they take a kind of priority.

This excerpt from an interview in Oceania reveals that the respondent considered the local church context as mission (we will discuss the locus of mission later) and that social activities were legitimately mission, as each person's passion is encouraged.

> **Interviewer:** So would (mission) be encompassing working with the poor and the marginalized in your own city? Is there a link there between the global priorities and your somewhat local priorities in terms of mission?
>
> **Respondent:** Well yes in the sense that both of them sort of are related to, what would you say, getting out from your comfort zone of just looking inward and thinking about me and my comfort and my faith, all that sort of thing, to actually looking out to those who are disempowered, (those who) are struggling with all these different issues, like mental health, and problems with kids in high schools, and all that sort of thing. So in the end what has happened is that people, because we have had that sort of focus and vision, what has happened in the past is that usually individuals have stood up and said, "I've got a passion to do this." So we have someone start up a work that involves ministry to people who have got mental illness in the community, or initially it was with the hospital locally but that basically closed down, … and that has been a major focus of this church. Then somebody else got up and said, "I am committed to youth at risk," and so started a ministry, and large numbers of others all joined it and went that way. And someone else said, "I'm interested in vulnerable women," and all that sort of thing.

Others echoed the leaning toward community activism revealed in the last quote, indicating that there is an increasing desire for social justice to have a legitimate place in the understanding of mission. Also from the Oceania region, this respondent observed a growing passion for social justice/activism, particularly among the emerging generation. They referred to this perspective as "missional," a term we will revisit in the next section regarding the *where* of mission.[1]

> **Interviewer:** (with reference to young people in the church) Do you see a missional awareness growing in that particular generation?
>
> **Respondent:** I think that it is growing. I think that one of the key aspects of that generation, the under-thirties bracket and society as it is at the moment, is that there is a very strong social justice angle for that generation. I think that it's happening in society as a whole, but that age group is the one generation or age group picking up on this theme. And many of them are seeing that and working that in tandem and hand in hand with mission, however they want to define that. So for them social justice is mission.
>
> And it's maybe more that, that the older generations, the older age bracket thirty-plus even forty-plus perhaps, is more bent towards mission through word. I could be wrong there, and I think that there are always exceptions to the rule. Whereas the younger age bracket, we are seeing it more mission through deed. So for them mission is a practical outworking reaching out to people, insuring that justice is done. And this is exactly what we've seen in my church situation with at least two of these young people going of late, where justice is the key focus of what they have been going to do. So maybe it's just the flavor of the month, maybe that will change in time, but I think globally we are seeing the emphasis on poverty, we're talking food shortages, we're talking all sorts of things like that where people are being broken. And the young adults are picking up on it.

Again we see the dichotomizing of word and deed with reference to mission activity. The respondent recognized the influence of the public psyche ("globally we are seeing") on highlighting humanitarian concerns. This is an important factor in understanding the many sources of influence on the lives of current and prospective mission workers. We could ask how much the public forum is influencing our understanding of mission but that would be the task of another research project. Suffice it to say, our respondents are clearly aware of the needs of the world. We must refrain from speculating where they obtain information about those needs, the fact remains they believe the needs exist and are concerned about alleviating them as part of their mission activity, as this next voice from East Africa confirmed in the second point they made about mission engagement.

> Two, is the need to engage the contextual realities. I think with the hopelessness and desperation in this world, there are very pertinent crosscutting issues that are like issues of poverty, issues of justice, and governance in our region. There is a growing interest in social justice. I can see that increasingly in the last four

---

1   The use of the word missional by some of our respondents, from Oceania especially, is rooted in the missional church movement that started to emerge from the mid-1990s. Books particularly influential in this regard were, *The Missional Church* (Guder and Barrett, 1998) and *The Shaping of Things to Come* (Frost and Hirsch, 2003). For further learning about the concept *The Road to Missional* (Frost, 2011) is an accessible primer.

conferences that I have participated, that they are growing so that if we organize seminars with those issues people want to be involved. I think those two areas need to be engaged very clearly and appropriately.

Another manifestation of practical activity, as distinct from more overtly evangelistic activities, is the growing interest in conducting business overseas as mission, intersecting with justice issues, as this respondent from Oceania observed.

Following that there's been a whole wave of "business in mission" it seems to me—taking start-up businesses into countries and being a Christian within the context of a self-supporting business and the like. But it just seems like another whole wave with those coming out of high school, university students now—there's a real keen sense of justice. And so therefore it's not so much the teachers and the medical people that are going, now it's those who are training in law and those who can use some of those commercial skills to influence the world or their world for better.

Much more could be said concerning the place of business in mission, but not many of our respondents chose to focus on it. Rather, the issues of justice continued to reverberate toward the social action end of the continuum. Here, a respondent spoke of education as an activity related to social justice, which they describe as helping people "get a fair deal."

We've got (*name*) over in Thailand at the moment, she's working in education. We've got a good number of young people from our evening congregation who are going into various short-term mission projects—particularly (those) related to the issues of justice and wanting to see people get a fair deal out there.

This next respondent from the United Kingdom focused right in on social justice activities when asked where their passion lay with regard to global issues.

Interviewer: Are there any particular things in terms of global issues that really capture your heart and get you going more than others?

Respondent: Poverty, the awful AIDS crisis in Africa, and slavery as well—that really does challenge me to the core.

When one has a particular sense of concern for need in the world, whether that is perceived as spiritual or social or a combination of each, it can be difficult to hold all the possible ways of engaging with the world in some sort of balance.

The issues they listed align very closely to those mentioned by others as justice oriented. The importance of this response is the depth at which the respondent was affected by these issues. They felt very strongly about them.

Strength of passion can be detected at both ends of the personal salvation ↔ social action continuum with both perspectives well represented in our research, along with many who try to hold the two extremes at least in creative tension if not attempting full integration. When one has a particular sense of concern for need in the world, whether that is perceived as spiritual or social or a combination of each, it can be difficult to hold all the possible ways of engaging with the world in some sort of balance. A more likely outcome is what we have seen illustrated here, that an individual's passion emerges as a priority and dominates their activity; perhaps not to the exclusion of other aspects of mission but it can potentially eclipse them. As we stated at the beginning of this section, it is unfair to say that the respondents we quoted only held the views attributed them, they could well acknowledge the validity of other mission activities, but they chose to speak of that which was closest to their heart.

In light of many of our respondents' clear preference for one end of the continuum over the other we ask, "Is a view of mission that is integrated in thought as well as action an achievable or even a desirable aim?" If not, is that a cause or result of missional anomie? If so, could it be part of the roadmap out of missional anomie?

CHAPTER 6

THE WHERE: MISSION'S LOCUS

Local ↔ Global / Same Culture ↔ Cross Culture

If the *what* of mission creates in us a sense of tension, the same is likely to be the case when we consider what the research discovered about the respondents' understanding of the *where* of mission. This issue was a dominant one and revealed some fairly strong opinions. Some argued strongly for a mission is everywhere approach, others contended that the concept of mission should be reserved solely for cross-cultural ministry activity. While Bosch argued for a broader appreciation of the activities of mission, he was concerned that the term was being applied too widely. Quoting the mission historian Stephen Neill (from Neill's 1959 book, *Creative Tension*), Bosch states, "If everything is mission, nothing is mission" (Bosch, 1991, 511). But, as we also conclude from our research, he goes on to concede, "It remains extraordinarily difficult to determine what mission is" (Bosch, 1991, 511). Furthermore, Bosch felt it was dangerous to try to limit the scope of mission in order to lock down a definition on something that is essentially infinite. With academic flair he warned that this would tempt us to "incarcerate the missio Dei" (Bosch, 1991, 512).

Clearly not *everything* is mission. Participating in immoral acts can never be mission, but ministering where immoral acts are perpetrated can certainly be mission. Can it? Even if the location of those immoral acts is the neighborhood you grew up in?

But Neill need not fear. Clearly not *everything* is mission. Participating in immoral acts can never be mission, but ministering where immoral acts are perpetrated can certainly be mission. Can it? Even if the location of those immoral acts is the neighborhood you grew up in?

We now turn to such questions as our voices highlight how it has become quite difficult to delineate where mission is. For this section we think the most appropriate way of presenting our data is to group the responses according to where the interviews were undertaken. We will continue to group them into broad global sectors to avoid revealing too much information about specific respondents. Our aim is to reveal this particular continuum in tension within each respective region.

Eastern European Voices

Currently I am involved in mission with the Indians I have met. That's mission in the true sense of the term mission; evangelism is working with those the same as you. (Missionary in Eastern Europe)

We first tune in to the interviews conducted in Eastern Europe and allow those voices to illustrate the views along the local/global, same culture/cross culture continuum. The contrast is elegantly set up in the quote above, which we present more fully here.

> Currently I am involved in mission with the Indians I have met. That's mission in the true sense of the term mission; evangelism is working with those the same as you. I'm directly involved in this kind of mission at the moment. I know other missionaries and I support them however I can, but being involved through prayer or maybe through material support isn't direct face-to-face involvement.

This is fascinating for a few reasons. One, it distinguished between mission as a cross-cultural activity and evangelism as a same-culture activity. Two, this was a person who considered themselves a missionary even though they were living in their home country. And three, while they supported other missionaries (presumably also working cross-culturally somewhere) they felt the need to prioritize "face-to-face" engagement across a cultural divide in order to be involved in mission themselves.

The distinction between mission and evangelism was not at all apparent to the next respondent. Neither was the need to see mission as cross-cultural. We admit that "those the same as you" referred to above could mean the same age, socioeconomic status, soundness of mind and body, etc.; but in the context of the interview we understood it to simply mean those of the same ethnicity/culture. With that clarified, this respondent who worked for a mission organization had no difficulty in seeing mission as something more akin to what some might call community outreach.

> It's a small church, but there are already young people involved in missions. One works with handicapped people, another works with the elderly in (*location*), you know, with the marginalized.

The next respondent, a missionary to the area, would likely disagree with the previous respondent's view of mission. Exhibiting a tone of critique within the surrounding context of the interview, this missionary observed that their host culture had too localized an understanding of mission.

> Most, a lot of people when they think of mission, they think of the city churches sending people out into the village to do church in the village or start a church in the village and that's mission.

The missionary would no doubt be pleased to hear the testimony of this next respondent, a local minister whose perception of mission shifted after they became exposed to teaching that defined mission as "crossing cultural barriers."

> I didn't see mission as anything other than church planting, in the same culture, obviously, or in terms of encouraging smaller churches. That was my perception of mission. When I came to understand that missions means crossing cultural barriers, however, at first I was very reluctant to believe that (we) could do such a thing. God helped me to get to know closely the American and British models, and later also the (Latin American) model of cross-cultural mission, and that made me feel in my heart a desire to mobilize (my church) to do this ministry.

It is interesting to ponder how models of mission activity defined elsewhere in the world, and not just the West, were significantly influential for this minister who is now influencing others according to the same models.

South American Voices

> *I do not use the word mission, because many people think cross-culturally when we speak of missions, and when we speak of evangelism it is something local. In our teaching, we put everything together, the urban, the rural, and the cross-cultural. (Minister in South America)*

The South American pastor quoted above expressed a frustration you may well be tempted to express in utter desperation by the time you have finished this book—"I do not use the word mission!" What's the point? It has become so fuzzy. Here our friend was clearly erasing the dividing line between the "here" and "there," and the "us" and "them." Their church threw it all together, in every context. This portion of their interview did not reveal what they considered mission activity to be, but the scope of their mission-related activity, revealed throughout their interview, is intentionally broad.

A member of another South American church who has an interest in mission sought to raise mission awareness in their church as an influencer. Similar to the pastor above, they saw it as their responsibility to be aware of mission in both a local and global sense.

> Along with another couple, we basically work to raise awareness in the local church about the importance and responsibility we have as Christians to be an active part of God's mission in the city where we are, our country, and the rest of the world.

However, each person cannot be everywhere at once so we return to the tension regarding what a person focuses on? Or in this case, *where* does a person focus their mission attention? The same respondent answered quite pragmatically with, "Wherever we are," in this additional quote.

I understand missions from a thorough approach. To be able to take the message of Jesus Christ not only with words, but covering all different areas of a person: social, spiritual, etc., and most of all understanding that all of us can be transmission agents of God's love wherever we are.

Not all churches share these views though. As we heard from the respondents in Eastern Europe, South American churches could also have the tendency to limit their mission focus on the local as this church member explained,

In spite of having a missionary ministry, my church considers missions as the informal opening of extensions or churches in other parts of the city, provinces, and countries.

Not so for this next church. Our interpretation of this church member's response is that the church sees no boundaries on mission—mission is everything they do.

My church does not understand the existence of an area for the mission or missions. Its existence and all its activities as a church (liturgy, education, social action, fellowship, etc.) are part of the mission.

Integrating church and mission so closely does not have to negate the possibility of mission activity in a more traditional sense. The next mission-oriented church member saw no need for a gap between the two, but did seem to understand the need for mission activity as distinct from local church activity. However, the sphere of that activity is not necessarily cross-cultural, as one could understand "inhospitable places" to mean. With reference to Acts 2:8b they saw a combination of near and far places incorporated. Furthermore, they viewed it as a whole church ministry not just an individual's decision to be involved.

I understand that missions are the task our Lord Jesus Christ delegated to the church in Matthew 28. There is no gap between us (the church) and them (the missionaries). Missions are not carried out only in inhospitable places, but in our Jerusalem, Judea, Samaria, and to the ends of the earth ... Missions are developed jointly, as a church, not as individuals.

Not to be limited by space, our next South American voice boldly declared their understanding of mission was to share the love of God with *every* man and woman. Presumably they meant there was no restriction on who mission work ought to apply to, as opposed to a personal goal to share with seven billion earth inhabitants, but they did take care to emphasize the underprivileged as a particular concern to mission.

Missions is to share the love of the incarnated God with every man and woman, especially with the underprivileged—the poor and excluded.

We conclude our sample of South American respondents regarding the *where* of mission with the response from another pastor. This respondent was happy to embrace the idea of mission, and rather than provide a general broad sweep they carefully articulated where they have chosen to focus their mission activity.

Interviewer: In what kind of missions is your church involved at a local, national, and global or cross-cultural level?

Respondent: At the local level, evangelizing the neighborhood. At the national level, working in several (nearby) provinces … And at the global level, supporting missionaries in India, Africa, and Cuba.

This sampling represents the South American voices in our research quite well on this subject. The data revealed a sense of mission that included near, away, and far away ministries. There was not much of a reference to cultural distance in these responses but there was certainly a desire to minister to anybody who needed to hear the gospel and see it worked out, wherever they happened to be.

Oceania Voices

Most of us live in Western societies that have become increasingly cross-cultural in themselves, multicultural, needing to learn how do we cross cultures within our own societies. And so there's, you know, this concept of the missional church has sort of taken hold. (Mission Agency Leader in Oceania)

There was a distinct shift in mission terminology among the respondents from Oceania. As we noted earlier, a number of these respondents used the term "missional." The mission organization leader quoted above (technically a missionary to as well as a mission leader in their country of residence), observed that this term had "taken hold" in their host country. Let us listen to this leader a little longer.

> But I think that the church will begin to realize … that most of us live in Western societies that have become increasingly cross-cultural in themselves, multicultural, needing to learn how do we cross cultures within our own societies. And so there's, you know, this concept of the missional church has sort of taken hold, people now are realizing, well if we're a missional church and called to reach our community we actually need to reach, you know, different worlds within our community. And I think the step from there will be to say, well if there's different worlds within our community there's different worlds out there as well. And so I think that realization will start to come more.

A "missional" church seems "called" to "reach (their) community," a community that is seen to have "different worlds" existing within it.

There is a lot of hope for mission in a global sense from this respondent's commentary on mission in a local sense. They felt that an increasing awareness by local churches of multicultural realities in their context might ultimately lead to greater involvement further afield. In addition, this voice seemed to assume that mission was a cross-cultural activity, even when it is locally engaged in. What did it mean to be *missional* then? We get some clues from the record above. A "missional" church seems "called" to "reach (their) community," a community that is seen to have "different worlds" existing within it. The multicultural nature of the respondent's context clearly influenced their idea that mission, as a cross-cultural exercise, could legitimately be localized; yet they still carried a desire to see that translated into action further afield.

We get a little clearer picture of the term *missional* from this next respondent who was involved with mission sending and training for a variety of organizations over time.

> **Interviewer:** So what about the scope of mission, where would you see it in your understanding? When you say, "mission" would it invoke overseas, would it invoke cross-cultural, or would it invoke the whole spectrum of local to overseas?
>
> **Respondent:** It would invoke a whole spectrum I think. Mission to missional. I mean these are massive discussions at the moment. We see it all the time in the environment that I'm working in: theological education. (In) the church environment, I think, mission is very much a local and a global. I think it still has a lot of context around the global, the overseas, the leaving where you are at to go. But I don't believe it can be just that. It is very much a working within the environment that you are situated so mission can easily be within, you know, across your backyard fence to your neighbor, across town, across, or within, your country. And I think that's something that we see more and more.

"Mission to missional" was a telling observation concerning the concept of missional. Missional was not, strictly speaking, mission for this respondent. They were exposed to discussions on the distinctions while working at a theological education facility. So theological students who would graduate to become influencers in their own fields of service were exploring the term. From the context of this response it seems that the students would graduate understanding that ministry "across your backyard fence to your neighbor" right out to the edge of their nation's boundaries would be considered missional. Beyond that, we might assume, would be considered mission.

But missional is clearly in various stages of development and understanding in Oceania because this next voice would likely be a little uncomfortable with the over the back fence nature of the term. They wanted to see cross-cultural specifically included in a definition, but they conceded it was not a popular focus. In their recounting of an experience they illustrated that the term "missional" included other facets instead.

> And missional, that includes cross-cultural (laughs), not just "missional" … I'd love to harness all of that energy that's for the margins and the poor and fair trade. I was at (*a Bible college*) at their global mission day. It was a prayer day for global mission and they asked all the agencies who wanted to to come and set up stands and everything. What stole the day was a guy showing a short video on *coffee!* And they put out the fair trade coffee in the middle of the quadrant there and I spoke to, maybe one or two people that came across to see what we were doing, and all of the mission people that were there were lonely (laughs). And the fair trade place was just the hubbub of activity, you know. It's kind of like there's something about these justice issues, "One-life," all this kind of thing,

that's captured the imagination of Western youth and it's good and it's right ... but how do you harness that and bring it in? You know what I'm talking about? Least reached people groups. That's a justice issue as well.

You should be able to detect some frustration in this mission motivator's response. Their role was to raise up concern for "least reached people groups," but their promotion was eclipsed by a fair trade coffee promoter. From this response it seems evident that a concern for justice and the poor, and fair trade coffee, should be added to our understanding of the term missional.

> It seems evident that a concern for justice and the poor, and fair trade coffee, should be added to our understanding of the term missional.

The next respondent was at the end of a long career in mission service when interviewed. From their viewpoint they saw the emergence of something the others called missional and suggested that it could be considered mission, embracing many local as well as global activities.

> **Interviewer:** And so that's a fairly long involvement or period of involvement in mission—over that time and even before, what did mission come to mean to you in your experience?
>
> **Respondent:** Well when I was a young fellow whenever you used the term mission it seemed to automatically imply overseas mission in those days. Mission today embraces what we used to call home mission as well as overseas mission and so ... in terms of what mission is, I think it's really what Paul was saying, "All things to all men, and by some means we might win some," sort of style and it can involve ... well, I was flying aircraft for fifteen years and I felt I was fully involved in mission. Others might be doing all sorts of things. Once again they're used by God to lead others to himself.

Once upon a time, "in those days," mission automatically implied an overseas activity. Not so today. This experienced Oceanic voice reckoned the tide had shifted. The boundaries of mission appear blurred.

Without reading too much into these responses we can detect a common thread with an understanding of *missional* in this context as it relates to our continuum from local↔global or same culture ↔ cross culture. Missional clearly seems to be localized, whereas most of these respondents had a desire to see those involved missionally growing in their concern for mission globally as well. Through the use of this term these respondents kept local and global mission activity fairly neatly separated.

We detect an attempt to explain a shift in mission locus by applying new terms to the situation; such is a tendency in the context of anomie. The emergence of new ways of thinking about an issue require new terms to help articulate what those new realities are and mean. It is part of paradigm emergence; a gradually (mostly) acceptable shift in understanding. This younger Oceania respondent illustrated it in this way.

Respondent: Yeah, I guess that's been formulating. Originally I thought the word mission just meant overseas evangelism, but I guess more recently it means a lot more, it's a broader context. I don't know how to describe it. So, I guess (it means) sharing about Jesus, proclaiming the gospel, not only through word but also through deed. And just (pause) trying to live a life like Jesus in my day-to-day context. So it's both local and overseas.

Interviewer: So you feel a sense of being involved in mission locally here with what you are doing?

Respondent: Yeah. Absolutely. We'd love to get to know our neighbors more and sort of be more missional in our local community.

"Sharing Jesus," "neighbors," "local community," "missional." Here we saw it again, in the growing understanding of a church member who had active involvement with global mission overseas. Mission for them was now as much local as it was global.

Our next representative was a mission educator and motivator who tried to bring some clarity to what was considered mission in their local context. They believed that not all Christians are called to "go" somewhere else to do mission but they maintained that mission should be a cross-cultural activity.

Right. Well I think first of all one of the things in (the *Perspectives on the World Christian Movement* course) is that we talk about the fact that not everybody is called to actually go as a missionary in the normal traditional sense of geographically moving in a different way or going cross-geographically. But certainly we see mission as going cross-culturally, and for many people that means reaching out cross-culturally right where they are, in fact we encourage them to start doing that right where they are with the idea in mind that if they're not doing it very effectively here at home there's no guarantee they're going to be doing it any more effectively in another geographic location.

We conclude our exploration of the *where* of mission from our voices in Oceania at the "mission is cross-cultural" end of the continuum from this mission motivator,

So on the one hand it's dealing with the individuals and couples who have shown some kind of interest in those areas and on the other hand it's dealing with whole churches and leaderships and sometimes even denominations and trying to see how we can help mobilize them into mission and sometimes that is both local and global: cross-culturally amongst unreached people groups. Sometimes that is just local, sometimes it's just global. It could be short term it could be long term. It doesn't really bother us, but I suppose at the end of the day we have a real heart to see churches planted amongst these areas so it tends to be a long-term church planting focus amongst unreached people groups.

The scope of mission for this respondent was clear: "cross-culturally amongst unreached people groups." However, this was a minority view among the voices from Oceania. The sample we took from the region was clearly developing an understanding of mission that echoes voices from Eastern Europe and South America who perceived mission to be broader than the narrow confines of unreached people, cross-cultural, or even global. The activities of mission were being applied locally, and for many of Oceanic respondents this was considered missional.

This was our first sampling of voices from a predominantly Western perspective. How did the views here resonate with other Western voices? We turn next to the United Kingdom to get their perspective.

United Kingdom Voices

I think, correct me if I am wrong, the word comes from "missio" which is "sent" in Latin, and as I was saying a moment ago we are sent into the world. The world can be our next door neighbor, it is our community, it can be overseas and I see it in a holistic way. (Church Leader in the United Kingdom)

It is worth continuing the quote above because the respondent expanded on their understanding of the *where* of mission and the interviewer sought further clarification.

Respondent: I think it is a bit of false distinction between home and overseas work although I can see certain aspects you need to distinguish.

Interviewer: So, from that point of view, to have a group within the church that's handling overseas connections as a specialty ... does that reinforce a distinction, or do you think that's appropriate because of the nature of the church's involvement and the very nature of the kind of ministries that happen cross-culturally?

Respondent: Yes, but there are also various groups within the church that are set aside to work with the elderly and others to work with young people.

Interviewer: You feel that it's appropriate to handle world mission separately aside from local mission.

Respondent: Yes, of course I do because there are certain things that need to be discussed and decided upon in planning and having a policy for world mission.

Is it possible to do mission in a holistic way while dividing structures remain that plan and create policy for each distinctive ministry?

So while they argued the distinction between "here" and "there" is false, the interviewer teased out the fact that their ministries were still clearly set up to focus on local ministries as distinct from "mission" oriented ones (whether local or global) because of administrative need. This perhaps illustrates the tension that theological dissonance concerning mission creates within a context of missional anomie. There is a desire to remove the barriers and define mission in a more inclusive way (including local and neighborhood/near-culture ministries) but structures remain that can reinforce the distinctions. Is it possible to do mission in a holistic way while dividing structures remain that plan and create policy for each distinctive ministry?

While this respondent did not use the term "missional" as those from Oceania did, the same sense is apparent in their "holistic" and "local community" references. This was further evident when they continued to discuss their local ministry engagement and its relationship to their encouragement of overseas mission activity.

> Yes, that's right, you know in church life you don't get two people with the same gifts and we try to create ways to serve in the local church across the whole diversity of ministries, and some people will prefer to work with elderly, some with those who need counseling. And similarly, I think that it's important for overseas mission to give people a diversity of opportunities to involve themselves. For some, it may be to sponsor a child, that's the best way forward, for others it may be to go out and offer some practical help in the mission fields.

The only other voice from the United Kingdom to mention something about the location of mission activity felt that mission could be anywhere, but for this church leader it was among unreached people wherever they may be.

> I think there's a bit of both in it that we have to have a whole vision of mission. That mission is not just about going to the far-flung corners of the world, the unreached people—there are unreached people on our doorstep.

Although few responses are noted on this topic, the United Kingdom voices spoke of a broadly integrated view of mission as "holistic" or a "whole vision of mission." Certainly the possibility for mission to happen "on (their) doorstep" was apparent, while continuing to support mission beyond their national borders.

We now jump to our final set of Western voices before turning our attention to East Africa and East Asia. Did our friends from North America resonate with the "here" and "there" possibilities for locating mission activity, or was their understanding of mission's boundaries more defined?

North American Voices

> *We have a missionary at our church that's in Utah evangelizing the Mormons and so it doesn't have to be out of the country, but I think it does, I mean we're all evangelizing for Christ wherever we're at but an actual missionary I believe should be someone who has devoted his life, his or her life, to spreading the gospel full-time to someone who's not otherwise going to hear about it. (Church Member in North America)*

Immediately here, we are presented with a definition of "an actual missionary" from the North American perspective. We have used authors' privilege to introduce the North American perception of the *where* of mission in choosing the quote above, but we did so because we consider it a traditional understanding; the general perspective of most of the evangelical missions community for the last two centuries. Unlike our preceding voices, this one added longevity to their understanding of "an actual missionary." It was someone with a life devoted to spreading the gospel where it has not yet been heard. In one concise statement they conveyed mission as long term, cross-cultural ("someone not otherwise going to hear") and evangelistically oriented.

An historian based in North America, a former missionary to Africa, confessed that their understanding of mission had broadened since they were actively engaged in it. Whereas before it was,

> A two part model; missions as evangelism and then kind of helping those in need … the sort of thing you do outside the church and the work of the church."

It became part of a much broader scheme.

> It is the work of the church, and anything the church is called to do is part of this mission.

The shift from, "The sort of things you do outside the church," to, "It is the work of the church," resonates on a similar frequency as some of the South American respondents, but is somewhat unique among our Western voices. Their concluding comment on the *where* of mission in this regard became all encompassing.

> I see it as the great body of saints all called with different sorts of roles doing different things at different times but all part of this ever widening stream of blessing going on.

Our next voice shared this broader view of mission, but with a little more definition. This person saw mission as,

> More cultural, going into a culture that is different from your own. I considered myself a missionary in the military because it was an absolutely foreign culture to me.

However, there was not necessarily a geographic distance to the locus of mission here. In fact, they even considered the reevangelizing of "liberal churches" as mission at one point in their interview. Yet they too defined the activity of mission fairly traditionally as,

> Going into a place with the gospel and sharing the essence of the gospel in order to help people encounter Christ on a personal basis.

A traditional evangelical understanding of mission was reinforced by a self-confessed "essentialist" who resourced churches for mission. From the Scriptures, this person saw a model for mission's locus arising out of the activities of the first Apostles,

> So, like the apostle Paul … Paul, Silas, Barnabas, and the team; God calls them into a cross-cultural missional outreach that goes beyond Jerusalem into Judea, Samaria, and the other outmost parts. Like (author) Steve Hawthorne, I would say we're living in a day in the outermost parts. It is not to say there is a direct correlation to Acts; Jerusalem is where you are and Judea is the rest … But to me

that is still a pattern, we're living today and our concerns should be going to the outermost parts; that is, continuing to go to the people that have never heard.

Later in the interview this respondent clarified their perspective further,

> To me the hidden people, unreached people are the people that may be beyond the reach of God's tender mercy.

It was difficult to say from the context of the interview if this person would validate mission as some sort of activity in a person's "Jerusalem," but they took care to emphasize that a certain "missional" call of God should lead people to the "outmost parts" like it did the Apostles. Unlike the use of the word "missional" in Oceania, this respondent clearly preferred to limit it to prioritizing people beyond the current reach of the gospel.

Finally, for this region, the head of mobilization for an organization that specializes in helping to send people to "the unreached" reiterated the traditional evangelical view, leveraging unreferenced statistics to emphasize the need for missions to prioritize those without the gospel.

> You've heard the statistic before, less than 1% of evangelicals in the US are interested in missions and less than 1% of that 1% is interested in the unreached. We want to focus on those people who do not have a chance to hear the gospel. We believe other agencies and churches are doing a great job in reaching the reached and ministry to the reached. Our focus is unreached.

Of all the interview data we amassed, the North American perspective on the *where* of mission was the most consistent with a more traditional evangelical understanding of mission. From our data, the dominant narrative from this region involved presenting the gospel to those with least access to it, wherever they were, but it was more likely to be "out there" than "here" for those we interviewed. We will next explore how this compared with our respondents from newer sending countries.

East African Voices

> *It's them coming to us and we don't see how we are part of the mission of God and I think that is something that we need to reverse and engage. (Christian Leader in East Africa)*

Some of our respondents from East Africa concurred with the need for mission to start where they are. It is interesting to hear them wrestling with this in a postcolonial context where until recently, mission work was something they *received* not something in which they engaged. As Christians in East Africa participate in God's mission they are asking questions similar to those above, "Where should our priorities lie?"

Our first Christian leader from East Africa articulated this very thing. In their context, mission was essentially something "foreign—it's them coming to us." But in the interview they were considering it to be something more, and it was something more personal.

> Yes, especially when we think of our context. I think there has been a general belief which seems to be perpetuated over the years that mission is meant for, or is foreign. It's them coming to us and we don't see how we are part of the mission of God and I think that is something that we need to reverse and engage because I think good mission will bear in mind the context and I think we are better placed in carrying out God's mission in our context.

"We are better placed in carrying out God's mission in our context." Here, mission seems to be more personal when it is perceived to be local. This voice argued for control of mission in their context, for carrying it out. They suggested mission in their context is something they now need to take responsibility for, not expatriates. In this sense mission seems to be associated with set activities. Whatever mission looked like in their context, as done by foreign missionaries, is now something they need to do themselves—not in partnership according to this leader, but a full take-over—a full reversal.

> Whatever mission looked like in their context, as done by foreign missionaries, is now something they need to do themselves—not in partnership according to this leader, but a full take-over—a full reversal.

The next respondent took the personal to another level. Not only should mission be something done among "the people" (presumably their neighbors or whatever context one finds oneself in) but it is something that includes the particular set of gifts you are blessed with.

> **Interviewer:** Let's get a bit theological now. What do you understand by *mission*?
>
> **Respondent:** Theological...? The Lord said, "Go and become fishers of men." I don't know, what is in the theological bracket?
>
> **Interviewer:** What do you understand?
>
> **Respondent:** In my interpretation, if I can take you as far as the book of Revelation, the first part has the letters to the churches and I believe each church, not church as in the building, church as the people of Christ, has a duty to the people ... basically I believe every person has a talent. And I believe those people who have been called to preach must do it. They will not be able to find fulfillment in anything else until they pursue that. So if you discover what your spiritual gifting is and what your spiritual destiny is, you will get to understand what your ministry is, and I believe for those people who have been called to reach out, and (those) who have been called to be pastors, and (those) who have been called to become missionaries.

The letters to the churches in Revelation were referenced here as an encouragement to put the talent God has blessed us with into action as *fulfillment* of our "spiritual destiny." They considered this an integral part of a person's calling, a concept we will deal with in more depth later in the book. The inference here is that there is a particular calling to be involved in mission as distinct from "reaching out" and "pastors" ministries. As Western missions recruiters increasingly focus on placing people in roles best suited for them, it is not insignificant that this East African voice is expressing a similar principle: God has gifted us, therefore our "spiritual destiny" is to work according to our gifting—because, apparently, we won't be fully fulfilled until we do.

Presented with the two extremes of the continuum we are exploring here, the next respondent revealed they are finding young Christians reluctant to engage specifically in personal evangelism within their context of "student ministry as a mission component." This is a phenomenon that has become more noticeable in the West.[1] Apparently it was quite evident in East Africa, at least from this leader's perspective.

> **Interviewer:** How, in your experience with the students, how do you try keep the balance between those two extremes?
>
> **Respondent:** That has been the most difficult thing to do because our students tend to downplay outreach, reaching out to their fellow students, and exalt an outreach event or an evangelistic outreach to the remote parts of (*location*). It's a very difficult balance. Again, it is informed by the narrow discipleship programs or narrow training approaches. And so I think one of the things that we are trying to do is to engage with the students, particularly people who are in charge of missions, both evangelism and missions departments as they're called in other institutions, and to help them get a clear understanding that if we are able to consider student ministry as a mission component, we need to ask ourselves, what is it that we consider when it comes to missions out there?

While this response also contained the *what* aspect of mission ("reaching out to their fellow students"), here we are more interested in what it revealed about the *where*. This student leader wanted mission to include local "student ministry" as part of their understanding of mission, as a component. They did not dismiss mission "out there" but they did lament mission not being activated in the students' own context. Who did they blame? The disciplers. How were they seeking to bring mission into the local context? Through influencing the influencers in the "evangelism and mission departments" of "institutions," presumably these were the ones responsible for training in outreach "here" and "there" in Christian student ministries.

Rather than engage evangelistically with those around them, the students referred to in the last response chose to prefer big outreaches and distant missions. There is something impersonal about such things, but at the same time there is a sense of safety in the anonymity and camaraderie those contexts offer. It begs the question, as these young Africans emerge in awareness of their talents are they reluctant to apply them more personally and locally, or is it just the evangelistic aspect of ministry they are reluctant to engage in?

---

1   Rick Richardson recently observed, "The faith trajectory of emerging adults may be summarized as movement from the Moralistic Therapeutic Deism of their teens toward the bricolage (tinkering and picking and choosing) of their twenties. This trajectory presents challenges for evangelism and discipleship and for recruiting the next generation of committed cross-cultural missionaries" (Richardson, 2013, 83).

Unfortunately, definitive answers to such questions are beyond the scope of our research, but the questions emerge from our data and therefore remain valid. They add to the complexity of attempts to define mission. Furthermore, they are among important questions that arise out of a context of missional anomie. They are questions that arise not only from our East African, East European, South American, and Western region responses, but also ones that exist in the Asian regions remaining to be heard.

Indian Voices

(Missions is) something God has put in your heart with a purpose ... time bound or task bound—a specific task God has given you. (Christian Leader in India)

Mission is "a specific task God has given you." Could it be more personal? Furthermore, this Indian leader believed mission started at home.

Interviewer: How would you define missions? What do you say it is?

Respondent: It's something God has put in your heart with a purpose ... time bound or task bound—a specific task God has given you.

Interviewer: Would you say it is cross-cultural?

Respondent: In older days, missionaries used to go from one state to another, but now you can see that changing. Everywhere missionaries need to be raised from their own community. From their own people's group.

See how far we have come from "older days?" Our first respondent from India clearly saw that the times were changing. Archaic views of mission as something done out there "from one state to another" are no longer valid in this view. God is raising up people with a heart for their own people, and our respondent validates them as missionaries. Our next Indian voice would agree, the unreached "may be across your road."

Interviewer: How would you define mission?

Respondent: Go to the unreached and preach the gospel. It may be across your road or it may be across country. That is what I define as mission.

Interviewer: In regards to what you're saying about the attitude that people have to their own ministries and the collective body of Christ working for something greater, what is your idea of a missionary? The mission field—

Respondent: I am not a specialist on mission. But I will attempt to analyze some basic aspects of mission. *Missions* in the normal sense has been understood as sending people to Bible colleges straight after their academics and into the mission field. The "mission field" has been interpreted as reaching unreached people groups. Similarly, unreached people groups have also been misunderstood as people who are generally inaccessible in terms of geography. Our definitions and understanding of missions has to undergo a paradigm shift and needs to be redefined according to the present time.

> Personally, [I think] unreached people groups should be redefined as any and every form of inaccessibility, which can be subdivided into various categories. The list could be unending once we start. For instance, there could be inaccessibility due to class or caste difference, or status, education, whether a student or a worker.

This respondent was very generous with explaining their understanding of terms that are common in the evangelical missions community today. The terms are common, but this Indian leader's comments revealed that meanings were not necessarily the same. For example, in many mission circles "unreached people groups" refers to ethnolinguistic groups of people for whom the gospel message is not readily available in a contextually appropriate form so that it may be readily understood. This respondent observed that in their context it referred to groups of people who are geographically isolated from the gospel (presumably distant from a church or other Christians). It is not clear if they realized "unreached people groups" were originally more narrowly defined but here they were certainly advocating for a significantly broader use of the phrase.

According to the previous respondent mission needs to become an activity focused on "every form of inaccessibility." To that respondent the *where* of mission was everywhere the gospel, Christians, Christianity, the church, or the kingdom of God, is not accessible. In this sense mission would know no bounds. "The list could be unending." That would certainly resonate with our next respondent.

> I've gone to quite a (lot of) training … reaching out to students, and the view was wherever God has blessed you, you are supposed to be a missionary … (especially) if God calls you specifically to full-time ministry. Otherwise, you are already called as missionary in the area where God has put you to work.

You can be specifically called to ministry but if not, you are to be a missionary wherever "God has put you to work." The respondent reiterated this again later in the interview.

> The Lord taught me in the (*location*) that if the Lord has called you for full-time (ministry), fine; if not, still the Lord has called you to serve in your place of work. So everyone is a missionary.

"So everyone is a missionary" is a sentiment also implied in the response we received from an influential Indian teacher recorded next. Notably, this was the first voice in this whole section to refer to the kingdom of God as it relates to mission, where mission is seen to be "the overall plan of God … what God is doing in the world."

> **Respondent:** Mission in my opinion is, the overall plan of God. I refer it back to God's mission basically—to what God is doing in the world.
>
> **Interviewer:** And where would you see the believer's role in that?

Respondent: I think the believer's—our—role is very intricately connected into God's plan because I believe that God fulfills his plan through restored humanity. That's what I teach also. Unfortunately, the church's role in making people aware of mission is so limited, so triangulated. The question is bringing people to submission to the Lord and thereafter to salvation; and after that … there is nothing. And that has been my struggle in the church today. At (*ministry name*) seminars and at other programs where I speak at today, I'm always talking about how we need to be looking at what God is doing to establish his kingdom and that is huge. Personal salvation is an important starting point; in fact, it is a vital starting point … (but you need to be) restored into that relationship and then allow him to use you through the gifts and positions he has placed you in, the opportunities and positions he has placed you in and begin to serve him in his mission.

Once again this was a broad sweep definition of mission and one that was being promoted by a leader of influence. It is seen to be the task of every believer once they are secure in their relationship with God. For this influencer, mission was activating the "gifts and positions" God has arranged and serving in those positional contexts with those talents.

Our understanding of the next Indian response is that they would probably welcome the above teacher's understanding of mission influencing their church.

Interviewer: In your church, how would you define mission?

Respondent: In my church, in missions … I don't think, I mean in my church there was a lot of understanding, because in South India in that time when I first became a Christian there was some understanding of missions starting to dawn. Their understanding of missions in the church was always sending missionaries to some North Indian village or something like this, you know, among the tribal people and so on. So, that's how their understanding of mission was. There was also a lot of things that was done locally, but they never recognized it as mission because for them missions was always cross-cultural, even if you work amongst North Indian in South India, it's still not a mission because it's locally that the people are living; but if they come to North India, its cross-cultural and hence mission. That was the understanding, and I think that understanding is slowly disappearing at this point.

There was no hint of disappointment in this interview regarding the cross-cultural understanding of mission disappearing. Rather, there was a desire apparent for local activities to be considered mission, but their church seems to still favor the concept of mission being physically distant and perhaps socioeconomically distant ("the tribal people and so on").

A perspective similar to that attributed to the church in the previous interview was shared by the next respondent who used to think that mission was limited to "going out somewhere to a needy area" rather than working in their city of residence.

For me in my school and teenage years, missions was going out somewhere to a needy area and doing missionary work. I never thought that (*name of city*), the city that I lived in, that the city itself was a mission field. At that point of time going to a needy area, a tribal area, a place that there was no gospel, going there and doing mission work—that would be missionary work.

Our interviewer quickly picked up on this, suspecting a shift in perspective, and probed deeper.

Interviewer: Missions was perceived at that point as about going to tribal areas and to another country. What caused the change in your thinking?

Respondent: Definitely, my understanding of mission is that it doesn't have to be cross-cultural; there are needy people everywhere. The idea, that the *world* doesn't mean nations or people groups alone. I think understanding this dawned on me quite early on in my mid-twenties, a little before I went into ministry. That is when I realized that missions is not something you do cross-culturally alone, but you can do it within your city as well, although yes, that's the basic understanding.

The respondent's reference to "needy people" was revealing, as was their renewed understanding of the *world* as it relates to the scope of mission. Wherever there are needy people there lies the locus of mission. What constitutes the need is not explained but it definitely did not need to be cross-cultural in this person's growing understanding of mission. As we move further east a similar feeling was expressed.

East Asian Voices

(The local church) should teach there is no difference between local missions and overseas missions. (Church Leader in East Asia)

Our responses from East Asia on the subject of mission's locus are fewer than the rest, but it is appropriate we close our survey of this issue with these global voices. While few in number their opinion on the subject is very strong. Our first respondent distinguished between "global mission" from "overseas mission," something we had not come across elsewhere but the categorization is significant. The theme ran throughout the interview but here we have truncated three parts of their larger response into one section.

Interviewer: What does global mission mean to you?

Respondent: A task Jesus commissioned to his disciples and those who believe in him to make forgiveness of sins and the eternal life in him known to all the creation, both locally and globally … The thing is, the concept of global mission is different from overseas mission. The place where a church is a part of the world. In that sense, I think doing evangelism locally means taking part in global mission … (The local church) should take a local initiative in regular mission prayer meetings, training seminars, etc.; and should teach there is no difference between local missions and overseas missions.

In spite of making the distinction, for them there "is no difference between local missions and overseas missions" because together local and overseas form part of global mission—making "forgiveness of sins and eternal life in him known to all the creation." This is all encompassing. Clearly personal salvation is the valid mission activity here but mission is not limited to those with least access to the gospel or the geographically isolated. The *where* of mission, once again is deemed to be *everywhere*.

Our final voice on the subject serves to highlight the tension within regions regarding the locus of mission. This respondent wanted the term "missionary" redefined the other way, a little more restrictive. In their context they believed its meaning had become too "inflated," over applied.

> We should redefine the term *missionary* as it has been inflated too much. Yes, every believer should be a world Christian. But that doesn't mean that every Christian should be called a missionary just because he/she happened to be overseas or got involved in some type of missionary activity … There's a huge mess to be cleaned up.

Clearly personal salvation is the valid mission activity here but mission is not limited to those with least access to the gospel or the geographically isolated. The *where* of mission, once again is deemed to be *everywhere*.

The Asian leader's response here is unequivocal. They called for every believer to be involved in mission some way, to be a "world Christian" (a term popularized by the US Center for World Mission in its mission training material developed in the 1980s (Winter & Hawthorne, 1981)). But just because someone went overseas or was involved in missionary activity does not warrant the label "missionary." In the context of the interview, missionaries, who have earned the right to that label, are lauded and held in high esteem and this respondent feels we should seek to maintain that distinction. In their view, too loose an application has resulted in "a huge mess to be cleaned up."

To summarize this chapter, where shall we place the boundaries of mission activity? Enshrined at the first Lausanne Congress in 1974, the evangelical missions community has increasingly emphasized the need to prioritize getting the gospel to *unreached people* as defined in fairly narrow ethnolinguistic terms. Cameron Townsend and Donald McGavran pioneered this understanding by noticing stratification in societies and recognizing ethnolinguistic boundaries (Winter & Hawthorne, 2009). Particularly since Lausanne '74 it has been helpful in identifying where and why the gospel is not yet accessible to many people. While it may have had some strategic use, it clearly does not sit well with many of our respondents some forty years later. The world is no longer seen in such clear-cut terms. Cultures do not live in hermetically sealed bubbles unaffected by outside influences. The geographical areas where most people live are gloriously diverse and inter-acting. Furthermore, there are myriad sectors of every society that the gospel has yet to influence. Our sampling of global voices regarding this continuum is not definitive but the data does seem to be indicative of a desire to recognize a more general locus of mission. For the most part, our respondents believed that God prepares people for places that may not be considered mission in a traditional sense but still deserve to be acknowledged as mission.

So the *where* of mission seems to have become subservient to the *what*—obeying and serving God wherever he has put you for the sake of the world.

We close this section with an observation from missiologist Stanley Skreslet who published a survey of Christian mission concepts in 2012. We believe Skreslet's macro perspective, derived from missiological literature, summarizes what we have discovered in the voices of our respondents. Here Skreslet also encapsulates the dynamic of what we have identified as missional anomie.

> Christian mission as a subject has become a much more complex undertaking than at any time previously, with an expanding number of actors and types of organizations involved for many different purposes. The flow of mission no longer moves exclusively or even predominantly from North to South or from West to East, which means that it cannot be conceptualized as a North Atlantic project. A few large-scale organizations do not monopolize the conduct of this activity, as they seemed to do in centuries past. Mission now is truly "from everywhere to everywhere." It involves many lay persons and relatively few full-time professionals, who share faith and give witness *in their own neighborhoods* and around the world. The profound complexity of mission today also derives in part from the deep diversity that now marks a global Christian community. (Skreslet, 2012, 15, emphasis ours.)

CHAPTER 7

THE WHEN: MISSION'S LENGTH

Short Term ↔ Long Term

An actual missionary, I believe, should be someone who has devoted his life, his or her life, to spreading the gospel full time to someone who's not otherwise going to hear about it. (Church Member in North America)

We once again feature this portion of an interview with a North American church member because they articulated so concisely what the evangelical missions community has traditionally put forth as a prerequisite for "an actual missionary." From the outset of this section we again mention this affirmation of a life devoted to spreading the gospel as a point of contrast with the main focus of this section, which is positioned toward the other end of the continuum, the short-term end. Mission during the colonial era was, by necessity, a lifelong enterprise, regardless of the length of the life spent in mission. This colonial model of mission persists to this day but it is rapidly diminishing in the face of globalization. Since the rise of global travel post-World War II realities have exponentially changed. George Verwer and Loren Cunningham, among others, recognized this and began *mobilizing* young people for shorter engagements in mission from the 1960s. For many young Christians the *short-term mission trip* is now more of a rite of passage, particularly since global travel became more accessible.

For this section we decided that it was better to listen to what our voices had to say about mission duration, rather than revisit decades-old debates. In doing so we will not dwell long on the quotes but merely allow their viewpoints to speak for your reference. Much has been discussed about short term elsewhere.[1] We need to acknowledge too that our respondents were not of one mind concerning the shorter end of the mission's length continuum. We noticed references to tourism that we found worthy of attention so we attend to that, followed by issues of accessibility, a desire to clarify one's call, and perspectives on what is considered effective regarding a shorter-term perspective of mission. We will conclude by hearing from voices that highlighted some of the problems with shorter-term engagements to draw awareness of challenges further fueling missional anomie.

---

1   A good starting point for reading seriously about the complexities of short-term mission would be books like Dave Livermore's *Serving With Eyes Wide Open* (Livermore, 2013) and Brian Howell's *Short Term Mission: An Ethnography* (Howell, 2012).

Short-Term Mission: Mere Tourism?

In the evangelical churches in (local town) the thinking was that young people go on short trips to (foreign town) and pray on the streets and so on, but it's basically tourism. (Missionary in Eastern Europe)

What separates an authentic mission encounter from mere tourism? That can be a tough question because motives for engaging in mission are difficult to tease out. Nevertheless, our introductory voice refused to recognize a trip to a foreign town as mission just because they were ministering away from home, they also expressed that considering prayer on the streets "and so on" as mission was a stretch. This is how they went on to elaborate this point.

> Among evangelical Christians in (*location*) the line between a holiday and mission isn't very clear—(between) a tourist area and a mission area.... I've observed that in the tourist areas they are already well trained in discussions and are almost professional. They listen to you, but they are interested in selling something to you—in fact you don't reach them ... in their heart nothing is happening ... I think we are at a point where we need to think more deeply—to leave the tourist areas and to go deeper. And to find people in need.

What separates an authentic mission encounter from mere tourism?

In their interview our introductory respondent noted that short-term opportunities were promoted to attract young people. The struggle to avoid mission trips from just becoming rites of passage or Christian tourism is made all the more difficult by the way many organizations promote their short-term mission opportunities, particularly in the West. A mission recruiter from Oceania who was formerly a field worker observed this.

> I saw (*some short term promotional material*) recently that just made my stomach turn, but I can't remember the phraseology, but yeah I just thought it's all, it was all self-absorbed, all about the goer. And it obviously really connects with people and is in their language, but will it actually really change anything on the ground long term? From my experience no. Maybe in some places, yes... Yeah often it's complex, it's messy and needs to be highly kind of integrated. But we're trying to connect with people on a certain level so we water it down, we dilute it or we package it in a certain way that it gets them motivated and excited. Maybe it's ok if that's not the end of the story (laughs), you know if it gets them started.

Coupled together, these two voices, worlds apart, were identifying the similar potential for mission to be watered down to a youth-oriented experience rather than promoted as activities that make a difference along the lines of the *what* of mission. The potential effectiveness of these excursions are discussed further below, the point here is that motives are important when it comes to understanding how shorter-term mission involvement affects our perception of mission as such. Furthermore, if it is easier to become involved, does that mean everybody should get involved? To explore that further we next look at the issue of accessibility.

Short-Term Mission: Accessibility

I think that the world is becoming a smaller place and people are traveling much more freely and I think that's helped in terms of a growing readiness to be involved in short-term mission. (Church Leader in the United Kingdom)

Influenced by the Cuban Missile Crisis of 1962, Disney songwriters Robert and Richard Sherman penned "It's a small world after all." Since then the song has become a global phenomenon, the hopeful anthem of an emerging global reality that was becoming increasingly interconnected and accessible. As Christians for centuries followed European colonial expansion to advance what has become known as the *modern mission movement,* so the influence of politics and popular media continues to influence Christians' engagement with the world. Air travel, media, and the Internet have made the world increasingly small and immediately available—to those with the resources.

It is insightful that the United Kingdom church leader quoted above used the smallness of the world as rationale for their church's engagement in specific mission locations. They went on to say,

> One of the factors in thinking about our connection with (*overseas location*) was to say it is close enough to be able to get to in a day. To have the prospect of three days traveling when people are taking a fortnight's holiday from work or a week's holiday from work, then it's just nonsense. But you can get an awfully long distance now in a day compared with one hundred years ago.

That motivation might be appropriate for Christians within easy reach of what they would consider an overseas mission field. Would it hold for those further flung from such locations? New Zealand is at least a ten-hour flight from most non-Pacific Island mission locations. Nevertheless, the world still seemed small according to this Oceania mission recruiter living there.

> We had the ability to send people short term by themselves so we've probably, in the last four years, seen numbers slowly increase. So when I first started seven years ago (we were) sending out like ten short-term people a year and now this year I think we've got thirty-five.

The steady increase in shorter-term mission engagements over the past forty years is undeniable. Does this reflect an increased awareness of a mission mandate, a resurgence of passion for the Great Commission, or is it opportunistic? Whatever you conclude, the fact is, it is happening. As a mission agency leader from Eastern Europe succinctly stated, "It's much easier for them to become involved in short-term missionary projects."

Having noted that the mission field (wherever it is determined to be) is now much more accessible, we illustrate another recurring reason for it being an attractive option for many—some respondents felt it has become something of a *try before you buy* experience to assess whether or not longer-term engagement is something of interest to the individual.

Short-Term Mission: Taste and See

Short-term missions are a good medicine, or a good food by which they can taste what "missionary" means—what it means to be in another culture, what it means to live dependent on God, to see the challenges. (Minister in South America)

Accessibility has opened up a whole new range of options for Christians to engage in mission. As the South American pastor quoted above noted, it has provided the ability to experience mission, to assess it as an activity, without needing to fully commit to it in the first instance. The context of the opening quote was that short-term mission excursions can encourage those who choose to stay settled at home to be better informed about mission and therefore better supporters of mission.

Respondents in every region used similar rhetoric repeatedly to note that short-term mission can be an effective way to confirm whether or not one is suited to longer-term mission engagement, providing an opportunity to taste and see whether or not the Lord might be calling them to further commitment. A mission recruiter in Oceania explained,

> The idea of my role was to, like, be an impetus to try and get churches and youth groups to send out short-term missions as a way of connecting into the world of mission. And hopefully draw them into some sort of longer commitment towards the possibilities of it.

An East Asian church member's response would concur, "I also think short-term trips will eventually lead to (long-term) missions."

It would be wrong to think *the taste and see* aspect of short-term trips was just a manipulative tool to garner more recruits or support for mission though. Many of our respondents, now serving in longer-term mission contexts, felt their short-term experiences were critical in helping them assess their longer-term aims. As this missionary from the United Kingdom shared,

> I went to work in a hospital in India, in the north of India … I was there for a year and I felt, very much, my main purpose for doing this was just to test what I perceived to be God's calling on my life and how I would cope with working in that kind of situation, completely on my own in that I didn't know anybody at all. That was a really positive experience for me and that was more than enough confirmation for me.

And from East Asia, "I eventually got involved in short-term field trips, through which I felt called to become a missionary myself. So by now I have served for sixteen years as a missionary."

This outcome of short-term mission allows us to move into a broader category of which the one we have been exploring is technically a subset. It is worth highlighting separately however, because it is of particular significance to influencing peoples' motivation for mission and we will return to it again as the research unfolds. The broader category is that of the actual effectiveness of short-term mission so to that we now turn.

Short-Term Mission: Effectiveness

I think there is an area that needs to be developed and it is the commitment of a larger number of adults and young people in short-term missions and urban missions. I think many people's apathy is overcome once they are informed on the needs other people and cultures have and also through personal experiences of service. (Church Member in South America)

The effectiveness of short-term mission involvement can be measured in different ways. The most obvious is economic, is it worth the money spent? But what value can you put on the impact of experience? How do you assess costs against benefits? Short-term mission has received a lot of criticism over the past two decades for the amount of money spent in sending people (mostly young) all over the world, for the time invested in preparing and hosting them, and for the heartache experienced coping with the challenges associated with mismatched expectations and underestimations of difficulty.[2] Short-termers arriving with mixed motives and misapplied enthusiasm, ethnocentricity and immaturity, can create havoc for career missionaries and host churches, yet there is a life changing dynamic evident in our responses that is impossible to put a price tag on. Rather than dwell on the negatives we thought it more helpful to accentuate the positives as this better informs our understanding of motivations for mission involvement.

The quote above from our South American friend introduced us to a core rationale for short-term trips, "Apathy is overcome once they are informed on the needs other people and cultures have and also through personal experiences of service." That is effective. Short-term trips are disruptive.[3] They jolt people out of their Christian slumber into the stark realities of a world very different from their own. This response from a church

---

2   Steve Corbett and Brian Fikkert have an excellent chapter regarding the challenges of short-term teams in their landmark book *When Helping Hurts* (Corbett and Fikkert, 2009).

3   Intercultural educationalist Rosemary Dewerse provides incisive insight to this, encouraging her readers to "nurture epistemic ruptures" (Dewerse, 2013, 81ff) via regular mutually beneficial encounters with people from different cultures. From her own experience of short-term cross-cultural engagement, Dewerse concluded that the benefits of short-term cross-cultural exposures are often short lived.

"That sad thing, I have discovered, is that time can fade the impact of a rupture, lulling one into forgetfulness and a deceptive sense of security, which in fact is really the re-formation of the assumption—and the lie—that (cultural) ignorance is bliss." (Dewerse, 2013, 89)

leader's spouse in Oceania contained elements of this sort of awakening. Before they married, this respondent took a short-term trip to (*an African country*) and it significantly shaped their life.

> I think it was mostly an exposure trip for me, in that it exposed me to a different culture, it exposed me to poverty, it exposed me to how pastors work over in Africa, and just forming relationships with the local people was really significant for me. And also sharing about my faith and being put out of my comfort zone. I guess I look back and it was just a really exciting experience because it was just so out of the norm and so out of my comfort zone and I really grew from it, I learnt a lot from it.

A Christian leader in the United Kingdom shared that a short-term trip had similar significance for them. During their theological study they felt their training wouldn't be complete until they had experienced another culture. The trip that resulted had a deep impact on them personally.

> So I am really pleased that I went. I got a treasury of lots of stuff within and even though at the time it wasn't really quite what I thought it was going to be, I am really pleased that I went. I do not think that my training would be complete without that exposure.

Another interesting point to note with this quote is the value statement made, "I got a treasury of lots of stuff within." It leads us to wonder, is this a "treasury" that can only be obtained by those with enough discretionary income to expose themselves to the different and needy beyond their immediate context?

The answer weaves us back into the *where* and the *what* of mission and it is unclear whether the respondents who engaged in short-term mission, even from South America, East Africa, or East Asia only did so because of certain financial means. A mission leader in East Asia certainly thought that rapid economic growth in their nation helped facilitate short-term mission, but not without accompanying challenges.

> I think opening up of the (*East Asian*) door to the world in the wake of rapid economic growth for the past three decades contributed toward (*East Asian*) people's willingness to travel overseas. It triggered waves of short-term vision trips especially by many young Christians, which have caused both missions awakening and strategic problems.

An East African respondent spoke of the value of short-term trips from their context too. Financial means is noted as being a challenge, particularly for younger ones, but however they manage to do it, short-term excursions (beyond the boundaries of their nation) were deemed worth doing for the internal impact of such experiences.

> We started now talking of short-term trips for everybody within our discipleship programs. High school we have not been very successful because of realities, economic and school programs. On campus we are almost successful that

everybody ends up going for a short-term trip among the unreached people. We are not talking of going to preach in a high school, among the unreached people groups in Kenya. Several of them have made trips to Rwanda, Burundi, and Congo: this is an annual thing for our people we are discipling. And the whole idea is to cause them to encounter God in a personal level, yet in the fullness of his purposes for the nations, and after that we believe they will be in a position to make decisions that will influence their involvement in missions, whether as goers, senders … The rest are details.

"They will be in a position to make decisions that will influence their involvement in missions," loops back into an outcome of short-term experiences we highlighted as taste and see. From our data we detected that long-term mission respondents who had previously had some short-term mission involvement looked back on their shorter exposures as a worthwhile investment in the formation of their longer-term commitment. Beyond the personal impact on these respondents, the general consensus seemed to be that it also had a degree of value for the personal and spiritual development of others who undertook a short-term experience. Short-term trips were not thought to be effective if the experience was merely for experience sake, as a tourist trip would be.

We close this section with some food for thought from a respondent in the United States who coordinated field learning for university students. It is worth quoting them at length.

(The demand for short-term mission opportunities) seems to me to be coming out of churches and has become, in a sense, almost a rite of passage for the faithful Christian young person, because I have talked to more and more students who talk about, "Oh I had this missions trip to Costa Rica and my youth group went to Jamaica, and…" They are meaningful experiences but only on a certain level. I hear a lot of sympathy for the poor, a lot of response that we should be more grateful for what we have. But I don't know what long term kind of effect that has. This is a concern I have for our own experiences too; which is part of the reason for being careful with language because there's sometimes the assumption that when you say "mission trip," that how lucky for these Nicaraguans that we came down and built this house because they wouldn't have a house otherwise. Never mind that the tens of thousands dollars that was spent on your travel, and on your lack of skill, could have built half a dozen houses by local folks. And that's a tension I deal with everyday and routinely. I have people send me articles (regarding the cost of short-term mission) saying have you thought about this…? Well, yes.

> While short-term mission trips were seen to have some advantage in helping people shape their interest in mission, the phenomenon was not supported by enough data to warrant mentioning further as a mission accelerant, not even as a means of mission education.

Clearly short-term mission engagement is a complex issue. It has some value and can have a certain positive effect, especially for the participants, but challenges remain and the costs need to be seriously weighed against the benefits perceived, to assess whether or not a venture is worthwhile for all involved (visitors and hosts alike). Having said that, our study was not designed to assess short-term mission. All we can do is note that it is happening and it featured as part of the mission-oriented activities described by our respondents.

The discerning reader will notice that this chapter is the only time we touch on short-term mission. While short-term mission trips were seen to have some advantage in helping people shape their interest in mission, the phenomenon was not supported by enough data to warrant mentioning further as a mission accelerant, not even as a means of mission education. This correlates closely with other studies specifically designed investigate a causal link between short-term trips and long-term service.[4]

---

4   One such study was carried out in Hong Kong by Eleanor Chee for her Doctorate of Ministry degree (Chee, 2014, unpublished). In personal correspondence, Eleanor confirmed,
   "Although there was minimal movement after a short-term trip towards serving long term, it was not statistically significant." (Chee, February 2, 2016)
A similar conclusion was drawn by another study undertaken Australia, according to the journal article by Hibbert, Hibbert, and Silberman (Hibbert, et al., 2015).

PART TWO: SUMMARY

Global voices have spoken regarding current perceptions of mission. We listened and recorded representative perspectives in this section with a narrative flow constrained by the data available to us. We heard the traditional view of mission, which retains some dominance in the evangelical missions community, as well as voices that diverge somewhat from that stance. On balance, however, the divergent voices were considerably more present than traditional voices. Even those who might consider themselves somewhat traditional in their understanding of mission chose to discuss challenges to that understanding, so that the more divergent themes were even prevalent in their conversation even if it was overall a critical assessment of those themes.

We believe the variety of perspectives about the what, where, and when of mission leads us to confirm that the modern mission condition is in an anomic state where norms are no longer set in place. Each of our respondents would likely agree with Bosch, "If everything is mission, nothing is mission" (Bosch, 1991, 511). They were all invested to some degree in something they understood as mission. That is why we interviewed them. But they were invested in mission in very different ways. The scope of mission was remarkably broad.

What can we say then about mission involvement? How can we assess how people became involved in mission if we cannot clearly define what mission is from the data? While it will be impossible to weave the threads together to produce a meaningful definition, we can say something about a base common perception, but that only arises because of the sample we chose to interview. If we were to widen our interview sample it could reveal even more complexity and fragmentation regarding mission perceptions.

We chose to interview those connected with evangelical mission in some capacity so our sample, therefore, allows us to reduce mission down to some common denominators. When the differences are stripped away, mission within this research sample boiled down to two primary factors.

The first relates to belief in God. Because of the sphere of our research we can safely extrapolate an evangelical understanding of this belief (although trying to define that further would be a considerably more challenging research project!). So, our respondents' understanding of mission is rooted in their understanding of God.

The second factor is a matter of response to their understanding of God. Regardless of the shape their response took, they all felt it needed to make some sort of difference for good in the world. Whether it related to personal salvation or social action, locally or across some sort of sociocultural barrier, in a part-time capacity or as a professional career the respondents agreed that a Christian belief in God should promote action that makes a positive impact, which therefore could be considered mission.

These are very broad and loose parameters, but they are parameters nonetheless. Clearly there are things that are not mission, but our respondents would probably agree that the heart of mission, revealed in the two common denominators, is actually commanded by Jesus,

> "Love the Lord your God with all your heart and with all your soul and with all your mind." This is the first and greatest commandment. And the second is like it: "Love your neighbor as yourself." All the Law and the Prophets hang on these two commandments." (Matthew 22:35)

From now on our exploration of data will treat mission in whatever way the respondent perceived it to be.

We will not attempt to assume anything more about mission than this. From now on our exploration of data will treat mission in whatever way the respondent perceived it to be. Our primary concern for this project was, "How did you become involved in mission?" In assessing the responses, we now have to qualify that with, "as you understand mission to be?" In our opinion, anyone seeking to undertake serious research in the context of missional anomie will need a degree of comfort with this sort of creative-tension and ambiguity.

Questions for Reflection

1. How did you feel "listening" to voices that expressed a view of mission toward the other end of a continuum from you?
2. Why do you think those emotions emerged?
3. In what ways can voices from a different context or viewpoint enhance your own perspective of mission?
4. What will you need to adjust to adopt new ideas or perceptions of mission to help your ministry thrive in a context of missional anomie?
5. How does this information affect your view of mission mobilization and the ways you currently help others become involved in mission?

PART THREE: MOBILIZATION

The Lord had said to Abram, "Leave your country, your people and your father's household and go to the land I will show you."

(Genesis 12:1)

Before exploring the dominant reasons for our respondents' involvement in mission (as they understood it to be) it is appropriate to first discuss the phenomenon of mission mobilization (as we understand it to be). As we explain, the term is a relatively recent one, originating from the North American context. In some of the open meetings at mission conferences where our research team discussed our emergent findings, our reference to mobilization received some unexpected responses from those who were not previously exposed to the term. The reactions, usually from speakers of English as a second language, ranged from quizzical to quite concerned. Most soon joined us on the same page once we explained what we meant, but on one memorable occasion a participant refused to accept the term because for them it was too closely associated with military recruitment.

Indeed, the concept does arise from the military and we loosely track the popularity of the term as it applies to mission from World War II into the post-War era until it became embedded in the evangelical missions community's psyche at the 1974 International Congress on World Evangelization in Lausanne. From there, we see the concept become much more defined and dispersed to support the objective that, for a while, eclipsed all other objectives in the evangelical missions community—world evangelization.

Mobilization, used in a mission involvement sense, created quite the center of gravity in the 1990s as the turn of the century became a target in focus for world evangelization. This was because of a belief that if all the latent resource within the evangelical church was made available to the mission enterprise, the whole world could be evangelized in a decade. The turn of the century came and went, and—less of the world remains unevangelized. Resources *were* mobilized as a result of the concerted campaign to promote mission. But perhaps it was not enough, or perhaps the priority, while admirable, was not primary for many people.

In addition to encouraging the deployment of resources into mission, mobilization's center of gravity attracted many resources to itself, developing many motivational devices. These means, models, methods, and mechanisms of mobilization increased as enthusiastic promoters of mission sought to generate ever more interest in mission. Which brings us to where we are now, with mission in a crisis of fluidity and experiencing considerable anomie. How will the evangelical missions community continue to survive? How can we encourage more Christians to leave home and follow the Lord across boundaries? Is better mobilization the answer? If so, what *works*?

The primary reason for this project was to explore the phenomenon of mission mobilization and identify its key factors in the hope of discerning what influenced people to become involved in mission. Having established the mission context for mobilization, we now move on to look at the devices related to the concept of mobilization. From our data analysis we identified four mobilization ideal-types, categories of mobilization with common characteristics. There is a significant overlap between the ideal-types, but the distinctive attributes of each allow us to view aspects of mobilization from different angles. We explain each mobilization ideal-type in its own chapter as educational, relational, formulaic, and pragmatic. For each ideal-type we provide examples from our global voices. It is important to remember that we are not presenting these as accelerants of mission involvement, but rather just a representation of recurring activities and attitudes about mobilization that were evident in our data.

> How can we encourage more Christians to leave home and follow the Lord across boundaries? Is better mobilization the answer? If so, what *works*?

CHAPTER 8

CREATING MISSION MOMENTUM

Against the backdrop of phenomena influencing Bosch's crisis in mission and in the midst of apparent missional anomie, we wanted to know why people from "the whole church" continue to get involved in taking "the whole gospel" (as they understand it to be) into "the whole world" (terminology borrowed from the Lausanne Movement, 1974). Could it be that we are still riding a wave of mission impetus initiated over forty years ago? If so, is momentum slowing? Is the crisis Bosch identified creating friction as he expected or is the missional anomie that we experience actually lubricating momentum by allowing Christians to do in mission "whatever seem(s) right in their own eyes" (Judges 17:6)? Our research project was not designed to answer questions of volume flow (we'll leave that to the statisticians). We can, however, indicate what has contributed to people becoming involved in mission two decades after *Transforming Mission* (Bosch, 1991) hit the shelves.

Mission Mobilization Development

To provide some context to the concept of mobilization as it is used by the evangelical missions community we look back to the 1970s when a group of mostly middle-aged evangelical leaders gathered in Switzerland to "understand the times and discern the best course for the church to take" (cf. 1 Chronicles 12:32), creating the first International Congress of World Evangelization in Lausanne, 1974. Although mobilization was not the core rationale for this gathering, after the event evangelical missiologists, strategists, and mission practitioners began a concerted effort to accelerate the availability of resources for taking the gospel to the unevangelized world.

Via this statement at Lausanne Billy Graham drilled the concept of "whole church" mobilization into the bedrock of evangelical mission.

In his plenary address explaining why they were gathered in Lausanne, Billy Graham challenged leaders in attendance with, "The whole church must be *mobilized* to take the whole gospel to the whole world!" (Douglas, 1975, 31, emphasis ours). The use of the term mobilize with regard to mission was not new; George Verwer founded Operation Mobilization (OM) thirteen years prior and it is today considered one of the foundational pioneers of mobilization ministry. But via this statement at Lausanne Billy Graham drilled the concept of "whole church" mobilization into the bedrock of evangelical mission.

While George Verwer (OM) and Loren Cunningham (YWAM) and their staff continued to focus on training and sending ever more young people into mission service, Ralph Winter, also a keynote speaker at Lausanne, built on Billy Graham's idea of the church mobilized at Winter's US Center for World Mission (founded two years after Lausanne). Winter popularized the idea that all Christians can (and should) be involved in evangelizing the world, especially the parts with few or no churches and without ready access to the gospel. Using, among other things, the *Mission Frontiers* magazine and the course *Perspectives on the World Christian Movement* (Winter and Hawthorne, 1981), Winter (in partnership with Steven Hawthorne) expanded mission involvement beyond only those who go. He advocated for mission activity to also include those who send (via prayer and financial support among other things), welcome, and *mobilize*. In this way Winter validated new mission-oriented ministries.

It is beyond this study to undertake an exhaustive survey of key influencers toward mission service of the recent past. Nevertheless, in addition to those mentioned (Cunningham, Graham, Hawthorne, Verwer, and Winter), other pioneers of the advocacy and promotion of mission activity in the twentieth century will be quickly recognizable to the evangelical missions community: Brother Andrew, David Barrett, Bill Bright, Luis Bush, Willie Crew, Patrick Johnstone, Greg Livingston, Justin Long, Phil Parshall, Greg Parsons, Bob Sjogren, Bill and Amy Stearns, John Stott, and Thomas Wang to name but a few of the more prominent voices in mobilization of the mid-late twentieth century.

Mission Mobilization Definition

Like most Westerners growing up during or in the shadow of twentieth century wars, Cunningham, Graham, Verwer, and Winter understood something of military logistics. Their cooption of the military term *mobilization* was quite deliberate. Mobilization is the process of assembling and making both personnel and supplies ready for deployment, usually for a war. As the word suggests, it implies the making of something mobile, ready to be moved. In his article, "The Key To World Evangelization" on The Traveling Team's website, Steve Shadrach, Executive Director of the Center for Mission Mobilization in the US, quoted Wesley Tullis, former Director of Prayer Mobilization for Youth With A Mission, who defined mobilization as,

> Any process by which God's people are awakened and kept moving and growing until they find their place for strategic involvement in the task of completing world evangelization. (Shadrach, 2015)

Tullis' definition is helpful from the perspective of catalyzing movement and maintaining momentum against inertia, but in light of our research, we feel the objective is too narrow. We have simplified the concept in keeping with our identification of missional anomie and appreciation of the many factors, discussed later, which drew our respondents into their mission-oriented service. Therefore, we understand mission mobilization as the process of preparing Christians for deployment into some form of active mission involvement.

Notice our lack of specificity with regard to the outcome. The "task of completing world evangelization" is a consistent primary aim of the mobilization movement that was birthed from Lausanne, 1974, but as we explored in part two, it did not feature highly in our data as a singularly dominant mission objective.

Mission Mobilization Dispersed

Ralph Winter once stated that a vital purpose of the US Center for World Mission was to "rush out to all the churches with our arms full of good things" (Jennings, 1979). The objective behind this was to motivate evangelical churches and their members into mission-oriented action, preparing resources for deployment among people with least access to the gospel, which at the time were more popularly known as *unreached* or *unevangelized* peoples. From the early 1980s a plethora of posters and slides and brochures and books and videos and maps and statistics and studies appeared on the scene, all directed at encouraging Christians to see and respond to *the need* (unreached or unevangelized peoples). This was not a new mission awareness strategy. The fathers of the modern mission movement were motivated in similar ways. Awareness of difference and the need for the gospel in uncivilized *dark places* had long been a preoccupation of a globally aware section of Protestant Christianity during the era of European colonial expansion. However, during the late twentieth century technology was able to accelerate the whole church's exposure to the whole gospel needs of the whole world—to the point of information overload.

> Therefore, we understand mission mobilization as the process of preparing Christians for deployment into some form of active mission involvement.

Anyone involved in the mission mobilization industry over the past three decades, particularly from the West, will acknowledge the importance of print and presentation materials becoming ever more cost effective and accessible from the late 1980s. The industry of mission mobilization developed alongside easier and cheaper access to these technologies, coopting techniques and becoming more and more specialized. Larger mission organizations began creating specialist mobilization departments similar to the marketing departments of commercial entities.

By the mid-1990s the distribution of mission promotional material had reached a frenetic pace. Argentina-born Luis Bush and the AD 2000 (and Beyond) Movement added to the momentum with a focus on taking the gospel to the remaining unevangelized people groups by the year 2000.[1] In 1990 Bush popularized the term "10/40 Window" as a way to highlight attention on parts of the world most resistant to the gospel. Around this time the Internet became increasingly available and the Joshua Project became a valuable source of data in addition to print editions of *Operation World* (Johnstone, 1979, 1993; Johnstone, Mandryk, and Johnstone, 2001) and the *World Christian Encyclopedia.*[2]

---

1   http://www.ad2000.org/
2   http://www.joshuaproject.net/; http://www.worldchristiandatabase.org/wcd/

Global Mapping International further supported endeavors by presenting global statistics relevant for Christians in ever more graphic detail.[3]

By the end of the twentieth century, with every Western mission organization having access to desktop publishing technologies, the potential for mission promotion had reached unprecedented proportions, quite an expansion on William Carey's *Enquiry* (Carey, 1792).[4] By the time we transitioned into a new century the West was saturated with information. The need to help sort through oceans of data like this created vast wealth for the founders of Google!

Mission Mobilization Diversified

At Lausanne in 1974 Billy Graham lamented the many voices vying for the world's attention, saying what the earth really needed was to hear God's voice. Since then not only are the voices louder, they're more prevalent, personalized, and mobile. In accordance with increasing difficulty in being heard amidst the white noise of life, mission mobilization has grown more and more complex as practitioners seek new ways to grab the attention of congregations and point them, and their resources, to the white harvest fields. From our experience, mission mobilizers (those who lead, educate, and participate in mission promotional activities) are increasingly tempted to draw from the industries of advertising, management, media, psychology, public relations, information technology, and even motivational/self-help gurus for fresh ideas and new approaches to help them become better mission influencers.

In light of our identification of missional anomie, is all the promotional wizardry worth the effort or are mission mobilizers flogging a dead horse? Assuming technology is appropriate to the sending context, are more innovative ways to promote mission likely to make a difference in the amount of resource (e.g., prayer-time, people, money) being channeled to traditional forms of mission? In the recent past, what things have helped Christians become mobile and engaged in whatever mission means to them? Can they be formulated into more effective methods? During this extended period of apparent crisis in mission and patently obvious decline in traditional mission involvement (at least from the West), mission mobilizers are begging to know the answer to such questions.

This study identifies key factors that have influenced our respondents' mission involvement but we do not intend to present a method or advocate a solution to any perception of decline of traditional mission activity in the evangelical missions community.

As mentioned earlier, this study identifies key factors that have influenced our respondents' mission involvement but we do not intend to present a method or advocate a solution to any perception of decline of traditional mission activity in the evangelical missions community. Our data shows that people can be influenced to one degree or another by

---

3   http://www.gmi.org/

4   A copy of Carey's *Enquiry* can be downloaded here: http://www.wmcarey.edu/carey/enquiry/anenquiry.pdf.

all the techniques that mission mobilization specialists have developed throughout the modern missions movement to promote the cause of mission. In addition to noticing phenomena that aid mission involvement from our data we also identify things that frustrate it.

CHAPTER 9

MOBILIZATION IDEAL-TYPES

Our research project sought to discover what influenced our global voices to be involved in mission as they understood it to be rather than what they understood the functions of mission mobilization to be. Nevertheless, the data did reveal elements of mission mobilization that enabled us to group mobilization activities into *ideal-types*.

The Ideal-Type

The concept of the ideal-type is a sociological device used to categorize patterns or traits associated with a particular phenomenon. It is generally attributed to the German sociologist Max Weber who we introduced in the chapter discussing our methodology.[1] Weber wanted to develop a system of categorizing that would allow for comparison and interpretation of what is typical within a given phenomenon or set of experiences (in our case, reasons for mission involvement). It is important to note that Weber's concept of the *ideal-type* does not suggest that the given characteristics or properties classified are necessarily good or desired. So the use of the word *ideal* should not be understood to mean the best or most desirable or excellent (although they could be), but instead ideal as a concept in keeping with the Latin *idealis* as the *essence* of a thing.[2] According to Weber no ideal-type exists in the real world; however, the benefit of the ideal-type lies in its power to help with comparisons and provide a level of order and clarity to complex data (Weber, 1949).[3]

Weber's formulation and use of the ideal-type can appear to express nothing more than the subjective interpretation of data, but Weber would counter that no social inquiry is

---

1   For readers who may be interested, Weber wrote extensively on a number of themes regarding the emergence of the modern bureaucratic state as well as on methodological issues within the social sciences.

2   Regarding ideal-types, Weber wrote,

"An ideal-type is formed by the one-sided accentuation of one or more points of view and by the synthesis of a great many diffuse, discrete, more or less present and occasionally absent concrete individual phenomena, which are arranged according to those onesidedly emphasized viewpoints into a unified analytical construct." (Weber, 1949, 90)

3   What Weber is getting at is the essence of a thing. In the social world no ideal-type is empirically free standing; "In its conceptual purity," Weber writes, "This mental image cannot be found empirically anywhere in reality" (Weber, 1949, 90). Yet the utility of the ideal-type is evident in its power to aid comparison and provide a level of order and clarity to complex data. A common criticism of Weber's formulation and use of the ideal-type makes the very worthy point that the invention of such categories ultimately expresses nothing more than the subjective interpretation of data and yet Weber would hold that the process of positivist inquiry is no less subjective in that the framing of research is not something that can be scientifically established. On the contrary, what we study and how we frame the questions entails a level of abstraction from reality.

without elements of subjectivity. As we discuss what we have drawn out of our data it is fitting for us to acknowledge that whatever anyone chooses to study about human nature and how they frame their questions will always be influenced subjectively and is essentially an abstraction from reality. As we noted earlier in our methodology section, unlike the natural sciences, social science aims to seek knowledge from *meanings* and *motivations* attached to human experience and action.[4]

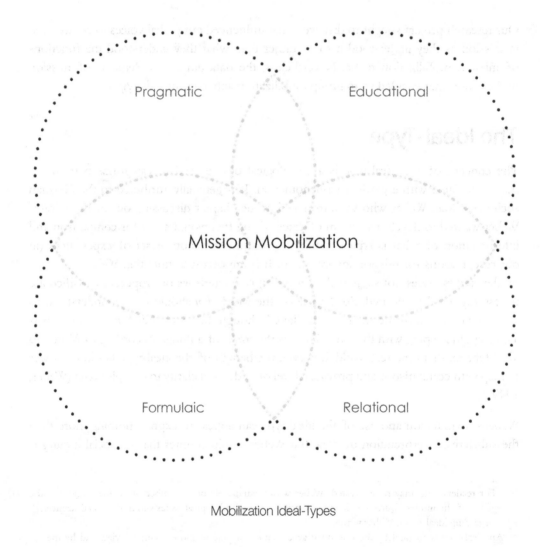

Mobilization Ideal-Types

Both interpretist and positivist approaches are in that sense subjective. Weber would further hold that social science is distinct from the natural sciences (and the methods it employs) in that it is possible, and should be an aim when studying human culture, to seek knowledge of the meanings and motivations attached to human experience and actions. A goal Weber considered more possible when utilizing interpretation than with the instrumental collection and analysis of hard data along the lines of positivist social science research.

4   Weber believed this was more feasible through an *interpretist* approach than an instrumental collection and analysis of hard data, and so do we.

Four Mobilization Ideal-Types

We now turn to the ideal-types we identified that group together activities related to mission mobilization approaches. Some of our questions were specifically designed to give respondents an opportunity to discuss their experience of encouraging people toward mission involvement. From their answers, activities were collected and grouped into common categories. Remember, we are still not dealing with reasons why people became involved in mission here. Rather, these are ministry approaches that emerged in the narratives which are used to inspire and assist mission service. They were not necessarily approaches that motivated the respondent, but ministry means, models, methods, and mechanisms that our respondents identified were or should be a part of general activity that encourages mission involvement. In other words, whether they actually work or not is not a consideration for this section of the book.

> Four mobilization ideal-types emerged from our data: educational, relational, formulaic, and pragmatic.

Four mobilization ideal-types emerged from our data: educational, relational, formulaic, and pragmatic. Each ideal-type represents a collection of mission mobilization activities mentioned by our global voices, and put together we believe they encompass the whole sphere of mission mobilization discussed. A graphic presentation of these ideal-types is charted on the previous page. Since there is significant overlap in the activities within each of the ideal-types, you will notice that our chart has a porous center.

We will now take a brief look at the elements of each of these mobilization ideal-types, illustrated with quotes from our respondents to help you better understand the sort of mobilization activities each one included. As we do throughout this book, the quotes we use are only indicative of a much larger set of quotes related to the point we are highlighting.

CHAPTER 10

MOBILIZATION IDEAL-TYPE 1: EDUCATIONAL

We use the term education broadly for this mobilization ideal-type in the sense that it encompasses multiple aspects of learning. It includes the transfer and development of understanding, knowledge, and proficiencies from a source to a recipient. It requires exposing learners to new information in ways that are relevant to them. When applied as an ideal-type to the ministry of mission mobilization, education seeks to develop an appreciation of the rationale, objectives, and opportunities for mission in the hearts and minds of would-be new mission adherents.

In New Testament terms, education is synonymous with discipleship. To be a disciple is to be a pupil or student of a particular teacher (Douglas, 1982, 285). As disciples of Jesus, we are therefore his students, learning from him. Those involved in mission mobilization ministries take this a step further, often taking one particular aspect of what we are to learn from Christ, interpreting it a certain way, and passing it on to whomever is open to listening.

Education need not be limited to an institutionalized transfer of knowledge or even a more casual course. It also doesn't require a single teacher to accomplish. Learning comes in many forms and means. Below we illustrate some of these with selected quotes. In part four we will revisit education with reference to specific forms that encouraged our respondents' involvement in mission.

Teaching

Although education is not limited to formalized methods, some of our respondents referred to it in such a way. This mobilizer from Oceania noted that courses could be effective mobilization tools. While admitting that they are not a complete solution, the respondent believed that courses were valuable for reorienting students to the importance of mission.

> There's, I suppose you could say, courses or workshops that we've found very helpful in mobilization, but they are only a part of the process. It's not an answer in itself, but it can be sometimes. A lot of people have the problem in their mind-set or in their thinking, in my opinion, of what they understand mission to be. And something that can bring about a fundamental change in their mind-set can really help in their mobilization. And sometimes things like *Perspectives,* or the shorter *Kairos,* or even shorter church-based workshops or things like that can

really help deal with some foundation stones and assumptions that may not be helping them being involved.

The respondent noted that having a wrong mind-set was a contributing factor in the lack of involvement in mission. The objective of mission education for them was to readjust foundational beliefs to right thinking about what mission should be. It seems once that is achieved, mission involvement would then be more probable.

Not content with individual students at a course, the same respondent also highlighted workshops they were in the process of developing that attempted to enhance the missions efficacy of entire congregations.

> Oh just on the workshops, a tool that we have found extremely helpful is we're trying to develop a number of different workshops for churches at different kinds of points where we can go to the church and sit with them and hear the vision that God has kind of put on their heart and where they kind of see themselves as their identity and involvement in mission, and then we kind of shape some of our workshops towards that to equip and train them to reach the vision God has put on their heart.

An East African church member sensed a similar need to educate congregations toward mission involvement in a more formal way than just hoping the congregation would respond to an invitation following the clergy's mission message.

> Just because you are clergy, you may not be the only person who is called to missions and just doing a simple invitation might not be enough. Sometimes I think you would need to teach people what missions is and how people can get involved in missions. I think they should have more sessions, or even a series where they teach and preach about mission work and that kind of a thing and what people have done, what changes have occurred and that kind of a thing.

Also in East Africa, a theological researcher added to this concept by giving voice to limitations of church leaders concerning their understanding of mission and called for more mission education resources for churches to access, presumably from outside of the church. The researcher's ideas echoed what the mobilizer from Oceania was developing.

> So if someone becomes a pastor, they can only give what they have and what they know. So I could say churches need to be educated for mission. We cannot blame them for lack of involvement as expected. Ignorance would play a crucial role. Educate the church for mission because, you know, the church is supposed to be the one catalyzing all these things, not (another organization). And for me, the church, our church has not been educated for mission. Think about a church that has been educated for mission; it will not just target the high school students, even in children's ministry, Sunday school, youth, whatever, so that's something that I would really love to see done.

It is important also to note that this respondent felt that the lack of involvement in mission was because of ignorance, which they claimed could be resolved through education. The desired result would be an engagement in mission beyond the targets of children and youth.

Anyone involved in the education process knows that effective learning needs to be reinforced, it does not happen at one time. Our next voice, speaking from a mission organization perspective in India, believed that mobilization requires education and replication over a lifetime.

> Mobilization is a lifelong process. Keep on challenging in all meetings and consciously challenge in all messages, at every seminar to rededicate. Even I rededicated, that's no harm, it's good (pause) renewing (laughs). Renewal is needed for everybody at every age for any leader. That is one thing, and on another side, keep on training the leadership traits, leadership skills, and leadership qualities. Hand it over. People keep with themselves. They don't want to hand the responsibility. So mission mobilization is an ongoing process.

A fellow Indian believes the minister has a special role to play in developing a mission mind-set through education, again within the context of whole-church discipling. Note particularly their use of the words "equip," "train," and "program" when it comes to motivating congregations to outreach.

> And sure the church plays a key role in discipling, in equipping, helping people to grow. But unless we're able to train people to go out and serve God through the different ministries available, evangelism is one of them, teaching is another, justice, health, and so many other ministries springing forth today. I was just reading about the guy who started (*name of organization*), there are so many opportunities if only pastors can help people identify, equip, and train them. We are beginning to see this happen. I have some wonderful stories about pastors who have allowed us to come in and do a program and finding out the church members have become outreach oriented where it was not there earlier.

Of course, education is not just for catalyzing mission involvement, it is also part of the ongoing lifelong development of the missionary. As this East African mission student told us, it is particularly important prior to serving in mission.

> **Interviewer:** Any parting shot, any final reflection, especially to do with mobilization? How can we have more people or what are some of the issues to consider?
>
> **Respondent:** I would say that it's not easy to send a missionary out when they are not trained. I would say that training for missions, especially when going for missions is really key.

We know teaching is not just for the classroom but our respondents tended to associate teaching and training with more programed methods. This is not surprising since a

Western model of classroom education, passionately promoted outside the West by past missionaries, remains a dominant philosophy of education. But it is not the only form nor is it necessarily the most effective way to transmit learning. As noted above, the New Testament model is more that of the master/apprentice relationship we call discipleship. When it comes to transmitting vision and passion for something such as mission involvement, the passing on of abstract concepts and information can be found wanting.

Discipling

We realize the subject of education is much more complex than we are discussing here. Furthermore, separating the mobilization ideal-type of education into two subsections is oversimplifying the reality. Nevertheless, we detected the distinctions in our data so it is necessary to reflect these in our results. For our purposes it may help to consider teaching as the transmission of knowledge and discipleship as the transmission (or sharing) of experience. Both involve the element of training, and both are aspects of education.

When it comes to transmitting vision and passion for something such as mission involvement, the passing on of abstract concepts and information can be found wanting.

When presented as part of a programed education process, teaching generally follows a set trajectory within a set timetable for desired objectives. Discipling is more about life-on-life learning and is much more dynamic, rooted in relationships of trust that seek multifaceted development in a trainee. The length of time is often more protracted than that of a classroom environment. Our first sample response from a mission organization worker in India expressed this reality.

> You will find that there is a great part of discipleship, and even I have discipled some people for seven years, eight years, with whom I could say they are still in the ministry, who are still in various other missions supporting, personally involved in ministry. So, the second part, when the people come in contact with you, you need to spend enough in discipling them and mentoring which is very costly and sometimes we feel that it might take a lot of our time and privacy and things like that. But still that is how it has to be done. It's very fruitful and encouraging when I look back after ten, fifteen years. Even now some people are there still in contact with me whom I mentored for years. Sometimes you have to go the extra mile and some of the people I know have fell apart and met with tragic ends.

In this quote, which is just a small part of a larger conversation, our Indian friend spoke of discipleship as a prolonged investment of time, energy, and privacy in others where a positive outcome is not guaranteed. Yet they saw it as a necessary component of leading people into and helping them persist in ministry and mission service. It was a tough ask but they reckoned it was worth it. After all, "that is how it has to be done."

While not specifically mentioning discipleship, the following references allude to the life-on-life educational experience we identify as part of a discipling process. They describe opportunities to model learning for others outside the classroom or church setting. A mobilizer from the United Kingdom explained,

> A lot of what we do when we're away is practical stuff but I would say almost fifty percent of their time is taken up with teaching them to listen to God in the place where he's sent them. Teaching them to look at things around them and tune into God and what he's thinking about, what they're looking at, and learning to pray into that. I guess that was the journey that God took me on. He spoke and my prayers followed accordingly. Then things became reality. Yes, I very much believe in that model.

This mobilizer used their experience of God as a model to lead others to encounter God when they were all away together. This type of modeling experience can be infectious and therefore a valuable method of inspiring and teaching others. A similar dynamic was identified by our next voice, a missionary in Europe, who observed that local pastors could catch a mission vision from missionaries. That is, supposing missionaries took the time to model that vision.

> We were talking about mobilization, and one thing that jogged my memory there is that often there has been a contact between a foreign missionary who has a mission vision with the local pastors, and the local pastors then catch it from the foreign missionary. And the foreign missionary can disciple the pastors a little bit and influence them that way. And some other people who have done studies in (*a research location*) saw that as a key spark there.

We will spend a great deal more time exploring the role of education as a motivational device in the lives of our respondents in part four. The samples above are sufficient to establish something of what we mean by education when applied as a mobilization ideal-type. We conclude our discussion with the following quote, again from an East African voice, because it incorporated a number of relevant educational elements. In a couple of sentences they referenced the church as the context for mission education and the need for a context-sensitive biblical and evangelical model of re-education. According to their view, education of this kind, identified as a mobilization method, would include making prophetic declarations and forming solid biblical doctrine concerning mission.

> (I'm) wondering, how do we engage the church in (*location*), (*location*) in particular, towards missions through a model that is both biblical, evangelical, but also taking care of contextual realities. And in my understanding, mobilization then becomes re-education ... So, for me, mobilization moves from the part of raising the prophetic banner to say that this is what the Lord is saying, which takes in our context, is a form of re-education to develop a biblical doctrine of mission, because that's what we miss in our churches.

CHAPTER 11

MOBILIZATION IDEAL-TYPE 2: RELATIONAL

The way we are listing our ideal-types does not denote any sort of priority or rank. We do not view any one ideal-type necessarily more important or effective than any other. We are careful to reiterate that, as mobilization ideal-types, these categories merely envelop what was mentioned in our data, not how often it was mentioned or how efficacious the means, model, method, or mechanism was. The next two parts of the book will deal with accelerating and retarding factors a little more in order of significance but even then it only reflects the experience of our particular respondents. Your experience may differ and you are free to prioritize differently.

Interpersonal interaction covers a great deal of territory and that is a large reason why the middle part of our mobilization ideal-type graphic remains porous. All of the ideal-types involve some sort of interpersonal interaction. None of us are immune to the influence of those around us, but we are most readily influenced by those we trust, those with whom we have a relationship.

> None of us are immune to the influence of those around us, but we are most readily influenced by those we trust, those with whom we have a relationship.

This relational mobilization ideal-type stresses the importance of relationship building in the work of mobilization. A mobilizer needs a particular set of talents to be able to build new relationships with the intent to spur people on to more mission involvement. Like most people-helping ministry, it is more art than a science. The influencer needs to be able to identify a person's unique calling and spot potential for development as a future participant in mission. This takes time and sensitivity and is often closely aligned with the discipling aspects of the educational ideal-type.

Given the propensity for certain characteristics to be present in multiple mobilization ideal-types, a strength of the ideal-type methodology is that it also clearly identifies contrast between them. This was most apparent when we categorized the relational aspects of mobilization. A response from a minister in the United Kingdom illustrated this.

> **Interviewer:** A lot of mission agencies, in their attempts to relate to churches, seek to come and do meetings that promote their organization. It's one model for communicating how mission is done. Is that something that you encourage here?
>
> **Respondent:** (Yawns)
>
> **Interviewer:** I'll take that yawn as a "no" then!

Respondent: That's how I react and how just about everybody I know reacts.

Interviewer: Is it because of the way some of the people who come to speak deliver their message or is it a bigger issue? What is it that puts you off?

Respondent: It's very hard to get excited about an organization. People want to get behind people—if they know somebody.

So, "People want to get behind people." In other words, do not bring your clever marketing material or presentations, do not try and present your organization's latest course or strategy, take the time to get to know us and then we might bother to listen. We can almost hear those who favor other mobilization ideal-types asking, "Who has that kind of time?!"

The minister we just heard from may well concur with this next mission mobilizer's response. From Oceania, this person did not see the point of speaking in churches about mission.

> For myself, and it might just be a personal bias, for myself I don't find speaking at churches a useful, a particularly useful, mobilizing sort of thing. Often because you only just have a short time and you just see the people once and you're in and out and on your way again sort of thing. So I don't do a great deal, if any, of that at all these days, and I certainly prefer to even take people on one-on-one.

Clearly this person favored the relational approach. As did our next voice speaking from Oceania about their experience mobilizing in North America. They were involved with organizing a large missions conference. From the context of the interview they gave an example of some out of the box thinking regarding missions' promotional presence at the conference. It was not well received by the organizations (and eventually the conference organizer capitulated) but the sentiment reflected both of our prior voices on the subject.

> Like for example, telling mission reps that that they could come to the conference, in fact that they ought to come to the conference because they are the resource, it is relational, but they could leave their booths at home thank you very much because we didn't want their booths we just wanted the people.

Perhaps it is a context thing, but on the subject of relational mobilization, the Oceania voices were more vocal as a group and quite pointed and skeptical of other mobilization practices. This experienced mobilizer for a mission organization saw the limitations of devices like workshops and courses. Instead they emphasized relational aspects such as practical coaching and mentoring.

> Like I was saying, you know, to just do a workshop or a course doesn't actually mobilize anyone, it can bring about some change and identify some next steps, but then you need a whole process to facilitate those next steps and follow up those people and stay in relationship with them and coach them and mentor them and suggest tangible practical next steps for them and maybe even actual mission opportunities that they should be seriously considering, which you know they would be good a fit into, because of that relationship.

Our Oceanic friend was not suggesting that workshops or courses had no value, but that they had limited value for mobilization. This fellow mobilizer in South America would agree.

> Conferences, congresses, seminars, forums, and preaching play an important part in the mobilization process, but the discipleship and the personal orientation confirm it.

Another experienced mobilizer in South America saw it similarly.

> After working six years in the north of (*South American country*), I think that personal visits and making friends is the most appropriate way for pastors and churches to start mobilizing in missions.

A missionary from India conceded that there is a place for pragmatic ways to raise the awareness of mission, but emphasized the need to put the effort in to nurturing people into mission service.

> Awareness is definitely a must. To build up awareness we need to use technology, teaching, writings, the visual media. (But) it's hard-core spending of time with people for nurturing into direct mission work … that's what we need to do for people who are willing to give their lives to missions.

This next mission mobilizer from the United Kingdom agreed that taking the time to walk with people in their journey toward mission is a necessary part of the mobilization process. It's not about asking, "What can they do for us, but what can we do for them."

> Relationship is the best way to mobilize people … we can depersonalize things in our eagerness too because we are busy. People take time, but I think the best way to mobilize and to nurture people into mission is through relationships—to spend time with people. It's about walking with people on that part of their journey, so when someone expresses an interest, you first invest in those people. It might be that they haven't got mission on their radar initially, but it often slowly comes to some degree of completion. So, we are not so much looking for what can they do for us, but what can we do for them and helping them discover what God's will is.

A very experienced mission leader and mobilizer in South America associated a relational approach to mobilization with the longevity of a missionary's service. They were also a rare voice connecting prayer (groups) with mobilization outcomes.

> There is nothing like personal contact and time to see the permanent results in mobilization. We talk from our experience. We will have been twenty-five years in missions next April. We have challenged many people but how many have stayed and why were they faithful to their calling? That is why we talk about permanent fruit. It is very important to mobilize through personal relationships and knowledge. In our culture, confidence is gained through relationships. Prayer

groups for missions in different cities of the country brought about a lot of fruit, and we visited them regularly. The missionary discipleship courses, for small groups, allowed us to have a more personal and direct contact.

Confidence is not only gained through relationships in South American cultures, it is a fundamental part of our human experience. It is too easy for relationships to get eclipsed by strategies, tasks, and objectives. As our friend above suggested, we can too easily depersonalize the mobilization process for the sake of efficiency. Sometimes we need to just slow down and see people, as this mission leader from Oceania encouraged.

Most people really just need someone put their arm around them and walk with them. Tell them they're OK, tell that yes, yes God did say that to you, yes you can make a difference, yes it's going to be hard to (be) there, but isn't it worth it?

This East Asian mission mobilizer thinks similarly. Their aim was to take the time to personally mentor others toward mission service, particularly younger people. Note their observation that people of the generation "of age" for mission now have different needs than those of a generation ago.

But I want to do what I can do, such as spending more time in personal mentoring for the next generation. I think every mission leader should be committed to personal mentoring if they want to upgrade the quality of future (*East Asian*) missions … The young people in this generation want mentors, so if mission leaders are committed to it I think there is hope. Most of the adult generation is self-made. But it is not helpful for them to demand the younger generation to do the same. They are different, and their circumstances are different. Thus it will not work. They desperately need mentors.

Since returning to the mission scene almost two decades ago this North American mission organization leader noticed a lack of people available to achieve the ideals of relational mobilization. Their comments remind us of how resource-heavy "high-touch" types of ministry can be. This is even more so if the relationship is expected to last as long as suggested here.

When I first came back into the ministry in 1997 I was told that for an average person it takes them about seven to ten years to get to the field from the moment they sense God's calling in their lives for missions work. A lot of that reasoning was because (of) the fact that there are very few people who walk alongside those people to help them get to the field. The difficulty in that is that many of the mobilizers find themselves going into the field themselves.

The good news in the North American's observation was that mobilizers get mobilized while mobilizing! This too is likely because they are in a place where they get relationally connected with mission opportunities and those relationships draw them in to active participation on the field. Such is the influencing power of a relationship. As you get to know people and trust is built up, then you become much more open to invitations to be involved. That is ably expressed by our final voice to speak as an example of the relational mobilization ideal-type. This United Kingdom minister closes our section in a somewhat more helpful way than it began.

It's interesting—I was talking to someone the other day, talking about always struggling for volunteers from church life and there was one particular area we were talking about and they were saying that they just can't get people for it. But when they had met with someone face to face and asked, "Would you be interested in doing this?" the response was, "Maybe I would be." Personal contact was the key—"I know you and you are asking me." If someone from some research organization had called me up and said, "I want to do an interview with you about ... I would have said, "I'm sorry, I'm too busy," but if it is you, and I know you, then I am happy to respond. There's something in that—how we engage with world mission—rather than it just being another big corporate thing. It's about that person who I know and care about, about what they are going through. I can get my head round that one person's living conditions and whatever. I think there is something in that.

> Such is the influencing power of a relationship. As you get to know people and trust is built up, then you become much more open to invitations to be involved.

CHAPTER 12

MOBILIZATION IDEAL-TYPE 3: FORMULAIC

Strategists usually *know* that relationships are an important part of the mobilization process, they can get their head around that, but they tend to view relationships much more as a means to an end, an abstract piece of the puzzle. Strategists would be much more comfortable in the formulaic quadrant of our mobilization ideal-type framework. They default to plans that help navigate through a given context and around identified obstacles to achieve desired results. Once again, it will be apparent that this ideal-type enjoys a great deal of overlap with the others. The act of influencing *people* requires a you to exert effort to move them from where they currently are to where you want them to be. To be successful that involves a degree of relationship, it includes some education and it is assisted by pragmatic tools.

A common understanding of leadership is to see it in terms of influence over others. After surveying the development of leadership theory covering more than a century, Peter Northouse settles on the following definition, "Leadership is a process whereby an individual influences a group of individuals to achieve a common goal." (Northouse, 2013, 5). This aspect of leadership will be immediately apparent to people whose aim is to motivate others toward greater involvement in mission service.

> "Leadership is a process whereby an individual influences a group of individuals to achieve a common goal."

The formulaic mobilization ideal-type sits well within a leadership framework as it relates to mission. It refers to the constructing of systems and the development of strategies to coach others into greater levels of mission involvement. Mission mobilizers who lean toward this aspect of mobilization are usually concerned with finding *keys* or replicable principles to motivate people so that the recruiter can achieve certain organizational goals. It is quite likely that this book will attract just this sort of reader, which is why we are careful to reiterate that we are not aiming to fulfill that particular expectation. One-size-fits-all magic bullets, panacea, or snake-oil solutions simply do not emerge from our data. We do however, identify phenomena that help and hinder mobilization. The onus will be on the mobilizer to relate those aspects to their context.

Those who lean toward the formulaic mobilization ideal-type will tend to have a macro approach to the *problem* of lack of involvement in mission. They seek *solutions* and work to develop a formula for resolving the problem (hence the name of this mobilization ideal-type). While not explicitly stated, when they were mentioned in our data we detected an underlying expectation that the given formula or process would have a certain universal quality to it, applicable to any situation. Scratch the surface of many mobilization techniques and they are likely to be underpinned by some sort of formulaic presumption.

It came as no surprise to us that the most ardent formulaic voices spoke out of the North American context. For a good while, North America, particularly the United States, has set the pace for mission thinking and practice for the rest of the world. The very idea of mobilization arose out of and was popularized by US Americans, and mass movements toward mission involvement are still being attempted there, in honor of, or in the hope of, replicating past mission booms like the Student Volunteer Movement.[1]

To illustrate the formulaic mobilization ideal-type we have selected two extended responses to use as case studies exemplifying the ideal-type. The excerpts come from staff members at two different North American mission organizations. Remember, our role is not to pass judgment or critique, merely to present the data as honestly as possible, making sure the context accurately represents the intentions of the speaker. We have also worked hard to maintain anonymity. That is difficult for lengthy responses such as these. Those closest to the situations may recognize elements and be able to put a face to the voice, but we would like to take that risk because we feel these contributions are valuable as case studies for our readers around the world. Our aim is to always honor the respondents for their insights and experience.

Systems orientation

Our first voice speaks in "systemic" terms concerning the way their organization works to meet its objectives in keeping with their vision and values.

> OK. Our mission organization is called (*mission organization name*). Basically we focus on leader-development in about twenty-five countries. We have two or three tasks:
>
> One, we can come alongside pastors at existing churches and help them experience renewal and then sort of have a systemical preaching model to then help them bring a renewal to their church. Secondly, we do some assessing, interviewing, and training of church planters. Then a systemic coaching pattern for coaching church planters in their first three to seven years. And then we have a younger leader training, a community-based training program primarily to try to raise up missional leaders. That's harder than we thought it would be …
>
> And then we have a business international group, all trying really hard to come alongside leaders and encourage and empower them to be more effective.

---

1   The latest iteration of the Student Volunteer Movement (SVM2) is championed by our friend and fellow mobilizer Ryan Shaw, author of *Waking The Giant* (Shaw, 2006), *Spiritual Equipping for Mission* (Shaw, 2014) and the new *Handbook for Great Commission Ministries* (Shaw, 2016), among others. US American by passport country, Ryan has located his family and the SVM2 team in South East Asia. The SVM2 website is here: http://www.svm2.net.

We're doing some pioneer work, primarily more with the churches than planting. My work has been in missionary training, both for our own staff and others. My focus now is really leader development with other agencies and then strategic life coaching with other leaders. ...

I am now spending the major part of my missionary career doing leader-development and strategic life coaching with mission agencies around the world, Majority World and Western. Based on the hypothesis that I believe, fifty percent of most missionaries and mission leaders who are in the world are in the wrong role. That is, they're not in a role where they are utilizing their spiritual gifts, which means they are in a role where they are not operating spiritual power most of the time. Again, it's not (a) mystery to me why we haven't reached the world, we're putting people in the wrong place. It is horrible, lousy stewardship and misappointment of people into the wrong roles. It's like we're trying to win the World Rugby championships and we have thirty-two scrumhalves and we wonder why we're not winning the game. You have to have a whole team. ...

To us, sodalic structures, mission agencies, need to be deployed missionary bands. That we flag the biblical DNA of giftedness in teams, just like you have Paul, Barnabas, and Silas and all that. I think they had sufficient array of the spiritual gifts but when they planted little church houses wherever. In Serbia and Ephesus, the people there saw the power of body life in the team, and it was not just an abstract concept. "There are only two of us but (we) want to tell you about body-life." It is not really a team thing. And everybody has a gift. I am more and more convinced, you could not have started churches in some places in two weeks and moved on unless the team modeled body-life to the people and they caught it by observation. Therefore, they could replicate it almost instantly. That's why to me one of the things we have to (do) differently than the majority of the world movements is we have to instill that part of the DNA of the team that we're deploying is also body-life. The team has to model body-life and operate by gifted power. You can't just have a bunch of wild Americans or a bunch of aggressive, monocultural (teams), and wonder why they are not affective. Because they are not a body.

I think the mobile missionary band in Acts were at least three to five. I don't think it was ever just Paul and Barnabas. We have Luke, and probably some supply people, and young John Mark. I think three to five is probably your essential core of body-life where each person has three to four gifts and their team functions as a full body. That does not mean they may be weak on hospitality, or they only have two guys with the gift of evangelism. For example, what does it mean that in the team you have no one with a gift of evangelism? I think it is the height of stupidity. I don't think everyone needs the gift, but you have to have one!

When I look back, my parents arrived in (*host country*) in '52 and by 1955 (*mission organization name*) had three hundred missionaries (there). That is a lot of missionaries in one country. Now very few of them had any missionary training. A lot of them came out of Bob Jones, Moody, Wheaton, etc., but the most training they had was as anthropology majors. The point is, what they did was send these people off one by one, maybe two by two, single women, into rural cities all over (*host country*). Most of them had the language at the fifty or sixty percent level, no more. I would say that ten percent of the people in the body had the gift of evangelism. So I am guessing that probably ten percent of those three hundred people had gifts of evangelism. So that means that two hundred and seventy of those people were mobilized into areas without the gift that was needed in a team to really win people to Jesus with power.

For example, my mother had the gift of evangelism and dad was quintessential apostolic leader and could lead people to the Lord, but mother won the people that flocked to the churches. Dad started the foundation, established leaders, and kept that moving, and mother won a lot of people to the Lord. Together they were a wonderful husband, wife team. A number of couples in (*host country*) had the gift of evangelism in the mix but I mean out of three hundred, probably thirty had the gift. So I am thinking, we should have structured thirty teams of about three to five to ten people, and deploy them into thirty key cities. We had about three hundred people scattered all over (*host country*), no teams, and then after thirty years we wondered why we only led about two hundred people to the Lord. I am saying, bad theology.

So more and more I am convinced that even today it is interesting that most mission agencies do not deploy in teams based on spiritual gifting and spiritual power. And I am thinking, whoa, we haven't learned a lot have we?

That was a long monologue to digest but we will leave it to you, our readers, to detect the formulaic aspects of this person's approach to the problem and consider their proposed solution. We admire the conviction expressed in this excerpt. As we tease out at the end of our *Accelerants* section, this is the sort of conviction that can help sustain people in their mission involvement.

Planner orientation

Where our previous respondent was more systems-oriented, this next respondent is a planner. Systems tend to be integrated and interconnected, with elements strengthened to support the whole strategy to achieve desired outcomes. Plans tend to be step-by-step processes within a more defined strategy that seeks to achieve an objective. Needless to say, these expressions of strategy are not mutually exclusive. They are just two variations on a theme and in our case the theme is the formulaic mobilization ideal-type. Here is how that played out in a different way with different objectives, but no less a strong conviction in the *solution* being proposed for the *problem* perceived.

Respondent: I can just give you a broad overview of what I think in terms of the best practice. I think people need three things. Broad and yet I try to keep it simple. And the three things are: a zealous heart, they need a workable plan, and they need a group for accountability.

I think what I have seen is, for instance, when people go to a big missions conference, they can get sort of whipped into a tizzy and will even willingly sign a commitment saying, "I want to go overseas." The real problem arises when they sit down and have to think about, "OK what does that really look like if I want to go to the 10-40 window to a Muslim people group? What do I really need to do between now and then?" So I think people really lack a workable plan, and then third, is that they really lose touch of any sense of accountability. ...

Systems tend to be integrated and interconnected, with elements strengthened to support the whole strategy to achieve desired outcomes. Plans tend to be step-by-step processes within a more defined strategy that seeks to achieve an objective.

People's passion would not be deceived—bad company corrupts good character, but even good character corrupts great character. So if you really have this heart and passion for overseas but no one else around you then it is just a matter of time before that sort of dies out. ...

If I call (*mission organization name*) they have a plan. You do an interview, you fill out some paperwork, but in terms of two to four-year kind of plan in what areas to really be moving toward, there was never such a thing. As far as I could tell, the closest thing I ever found to a missions training manual, was one called (*name of manuel*), are you familiar with that?

Interviewer: I've heard of it. I am not overly familiar.

Respondent: The authors are (*name of author*) and (*name of author*).

Interviewer: Oh yes! I spoke to (*name of author*) just the other day. He made reference to that.

Respondent: So that was the best I could find and that was just ten steps. But I kind of launched on my own research; Scriptures and asking a lot of mobilizers and goers a lot of questions. And boiled it down into ... something I call the Cairn Illustration. It's the process of seven areas to help people move through one step at a time, on their way to make their contribution cross-culturally ...

So this is in that second area—if your heart is stirred up. That happens a lot of times through conferences, connection with a missionary, the *Perspectives* class. We could talk some more about that. I took the *Perspectives* class and with the permission of the *Perspectives'* folks and (*mission organization name*) I boiled it down to eight lessons designed for people in the US military ... The second part of really helping people develop a plan is what this Cairn Illustration is all about. Do you know what a cairn is by any chance?

Interviewer: No, not in this context.

Respondent: Yeah, if you ever are climbing a mountain, and as soon as you get up above the tree line the way that the path is marked is by a pile of stones that men will pile up.

Interviewer: Yes, we have them. I always wondered.

Respondent: Yeah, those are called cairns. They're really marking your path. People that want to go and make cross-cultural apostolic contributions are talking about going above the tree line in the hard places. We want to help them develop their own personal cairn, their own pathway to the nations. The bottom rock is what I call Talmud training. Talmud is the Hebrew word for disciple. I like to define what discipleship is, that we have to grow in knowledge, skill, and character—all three of those. This is sort of (*mission organization name*)'s bread and butter.

Interviewer: I was going to ask specifically what you meant exactly by "Talmud."

Respondent: Yeah, it is just the Hebrew word for disciple and the reason I don't use the word disciple is because it is kind of a cliché, and for a lot of people discipleship just means, I go to a discipleship class for six weeks after I got baptized. That is really the extent of discipleship. We've developed a workbook that actually walks through each of the seven steps that we worked with an expert for each of these stages to develop. This is kind of (*mission organization name*)'s area especially the bottom one. I don't know if you saw the Willow Creek research, the big church in Chicago?

Interviewer: Some. Relating specifically to what?

Respondent: It's called Reveal. It was their studies on are we producing fully devoted disciples of Jesus? That was their vision statement and they wanted to know if they were doing it. They found out first of all that people's growth to becoming a fully devoted follower happens in four pretty distinct stages. (*Mission organization name*) for years had been using an alliteration, but it's Evangelism, Establish, Engage, Equip, and Empower. Those are the five. Willow Creek didn't realize that those stages even existed, so they obviously didn't know how to intentionally move people through the stages if they did not know they existed. They found out that they were doing a very poor job of producing the kinds of fully devoted disciples that they had hoped. They came out in a very humble, courageous way to say we're totally going to have to rethink what we are doing after thirty years and being the ones that coined the phrase "seeker-friendly churches."

That bottom rock, Talmud Training, is basically four stages. Within each of those four stages there are certain knowledge things you need to learn, skill things they need to learn to do, and certain character things that need to be developed in their lives. Those three things are going to change depending (on) which of those stages they are in. That's kind of the overview of the bottom rock.

The next one is Talmud Freeing. What I found in my research, thanks to (WEA Mission Commission books) *Worth Keeping* (Hay, et al., 2007) and *Too Valuable to Lose* (Taylor, 1997) is that there are several areas that bind people and keep them from really being able to live in a free way and to go overseas and then to stay in a cross-cultural context. We just listed five of them. ...

One of the things we developed in the workbook walks them through these four stages of maturity. 1 John 2:12–14 talks about little children, young men, and fathers. We walk through the knowledge, skills, and character issues and very concretely ask "How are you doing in this area?" sort of evaluate that and then begin to develop a plan to grow to the next level.

This excerpt reveals an organization that approaches their perception of the problem in a very logical way. They have carefully developed building blocks that lead people step-by-step to a desired outcome. They draw on established research and seem to be learning from the experience of others.

Note how both respondents presented the elements of their proposed solution in universal terms, as suitable for any context. They firmly believed that the world will be a much better place and mission would be far more effective if only others would realize and activate the keys they have discovered concerning church development or discipleship. This is not unusual. Myriad mission organizations exist because they feel they have a distinctive contribution to offer global Christianity. They may not express it in such well-defined terms as our two friends here but mission organizations' proposed solutions (usually described as vision and values) are unique enough to keep them from amalgamating with other groups seeking to achieve similar aims.

We can legitimately praise God for those drawn to the formulaic mobilization ideal-type. They are the type of people and organizations that love to *get things done*. However, our findings encourage us to encourage our readers to remember that there is more than one way to do things and rarely, if ever, are *formulaic principles* purely transcultural.

CHAPTER 13

MOBILIZATION IDEAL-TYPE 4: PRAGMATIC

The final mobilization ideal-type to emerge from our data carries with it the largest body of evidence when compared with the other three ideal-types. A sizeable cohort of those we interviewed seemed relatively unencumbered by the more theological, philosophical, and sociological considerations that underlie the other mobilization ideal-types. Even so, this mobilization ideal-type still overlaps with each of the other ones in many ways, drawing on the practical aspects of education, relationship, and formula and applying *that which works* in their context.

Pragmatic mobilization activity finds practical ways to carry out mission promotion, using devices to help influence people toward greater involvement in mission. Where an educationalist wants to influence through the learning process, the relationship builder through interpersonal interaction to build trust, and those of the formulaic type through developing strategies and systems to solve problems, the pragmatist just wants to apply that which will help achieve their goal. Over the past era in the evangelical missions community, that has most often manifested as "we must finish the task." For mobilizers, these means, models,

> The pragmatist just wants to apply that which will help achieve their goal. Over the past era in the evangelical missions community, that has most often manifested as "we must finish the task."

methods, and mechanisms are usually very tangible *tools* that promote needs and present opportunities for meeting those needs. From our interviews here are some examples of the types of pragmatic devices mentioned by our respondents. We will let them speak for themselves.

Church appeals

In this first phase we are focusing on bigger churches because there is more potential there. And in the churches (we work) through a message specifically linked to missions, challenging the church for missions and encouraging those interested to get in touch with us at the end. As a team we are available to go to a church when we are invited and to present everything about missions, to recommend a missionary to them. *Mission Mobilizer from Eastern Europe.*

Emotive presentations

Then when I went to (*location*) we were exposed to these mission people coming on a Friday afternoon to give a mission talk. It was showing that people need the Lord and it really spoke to me. You hear the mission talk, play the song, and there are pictures of people up there and it has such an impact. *Mission Mobilizer in the United Kingdom.*

Display exhibits

There was a whole mission emphasis there, you know, when it came to the aspect of serving, there were displays in the church of mission organizations invited to come in and the like. *Church Mission Supporter in Oceania.*

Distributed material

Interviewer: How do you—I don't want to use the term *marketing*—how do you tell people that (*mission organization*) exists, in (*location*)?

Respondent: Basically of course by our presence as much as possible, during conferences, or by talking in churches, by sending out email. We've got like a prayer bulletin that we send out weekly. We've got a website, we've got some promotional materials that, we're actually still developing some more, but we have some books, some leaflets. *Mission Mobilizer in Eastern Europe.*

Field video documentaries

The best thing now is the documentary videos from the field, more than the promotional ones. You can see a documentary of fifteen years ago, in spite of the lack of technology, the content is still good as long as it is narrated, and shows the field and has information. The tendency should be that. Documentary videos of seven to fifteen minutes, the National Geographic type, with good cameramen, and photographers and communicators, in inhospitable and remote places where there are unreached peoples, so they can film the places and testimonies of missionaries, the unreached people, and the community, well edited and with good ethnic music. This is going to be the strategic resource of the future. People do not want to see PowerPoint presentations anymore, they want to go to YouTube and see videos and download them. This is going to be the tendency—good filming equipment and cameramen—who can capture the reality at the field. Video clips that can even be downloaded to cell phones. *Mission Mobilizer in South America.*

Focus groups

We, this year, have also run an event for (*student ministry*) conference, which is a Christian student university group, and we ran a focus group for professionals in training. So we ran an experience that was very different, that had a group discussion at the end of it, to say, "What did you like, what did you not like, what impressions did you get?" etc.,—helping people to explore their view on mission. *Mission Mobilizer from Oceania.*

House groups

The monthly letters of missionaries have to be shared with the congregation so they know how to respond to them. Not only the missionaries who are far away do the task, we also have the workers who work in the extension projects inside the country. Many churches have Bible studies, Bible schools or seminaries of their own and I think that they should include the issue of missions where people learn about mobilization to missions during the year. If they have house groups they can include subjects about missions. *Minister from South America.*

Interactive role plays

We've developed a program called CSI Mission, which, you know, all around the CSI program, have you heard about this? So CSI starts with a dead body on the floor and then the rest of the program, you know, all of these crime programs is so how did it die, you know, how did this happen? So we start with a drama of a dead body on the floor, but the dead body is representative of a least reached people group and so then they are in teams and they have to go through an interactive cross-cultural challenge basically. Going to different areas of a room and breaking the code of a language, making certain cultural dishes, getting dressed up in cultural clothes, speaking a foreign language, finding clues that are adapted into photographs and jigsaws that have little adapted things, so they have magnifying glasses and little agent kits and all this kind of stuff. It's for youth groups and each team is looking at a different people group and at the end of the night they've built up a profile of which they actually get in their hand in a nice little brochure type thing. And then we kind of unpack for them "so what?," so you know what a people group is and give them a state of the world kind of situation, next steps and that kind of jazz. But it's geared at, you know, like we need ideas of how to capture the imagination of young people, but help them understand some of the realities of this almost one-third of the world that are yet to hear. Um, so yeah, I think there's people starting to develop some of these tools but they're not particularly widespread, they're not used a lot. We probably need to share them a lot more. So, you know, some of the workshops that we're doing that are working well I need to be training other people to do the same things if they're keen, and some people have expressed interest, so that it can go wider. *Mission Mobilizer in Oceania.*

Mission conferences

(*Name of conference*) is a mission mobilization conference that is organized by (*organization name*) every three years. So it's a triennial missions conference that seeks to present an opportunity for students and graduates to see their place and role in God's mission. And so it's organized with the intention of presenting a mission challenge to the students and graduates, through talks, through seminars, through plenary sessions, through Bible expositions, small Bible studies, and of course exhibitions. *Mission Mobilizer in East Africa.*

Mission focus Sundays

We tend to have particular Sundays where we focus on something specific. One of the great things about having the (ministry teams) in training is that they are here over weekends so, for instance, for part of their training schedule they come to us for two weekends in September and the second of those, I will expect them to lead the morning service to let them do that however they want to. Whatever they do, we are immediately given a focus on world mission because they are a team of usually four young people who are going, say, to India. They'll tell us, "This is what we are going to be doing, this is where we are going, this is who we are," so there is instinctively that focus. And then when they come back, usually in April, they lead another service when they talk about what they have done and how God has worked through them. We, as a church, have a practice of supporting different organizations such as (*organization name*). We will have a (mission focus) Sunday, not necessarily when the rest of the world is having a (mission focus) Sunday but we will have a focus. *Church Leader in the United Kingdom.*

Missionary reports

So there is that "breath" that comes through reports, that "breath" that comes from results. I'd say there is a very strong connection between the church which supports spiritually and materially and the people on the mission field who communicate things to the local church, concrete things, precise things, moments when they saw that the hand of God saved them, let's say, from the intention of being kidnapped, or other plans against them, very precisely at the moment the church was interceding. *Pastor in Eastern Europe.*

Special exposure events

The best way to mobilize is to organize events addressed to male and female pastors, women, and children. During these events, people who are interested in cross-cultural evangelization approach us. The contact with pastors and leaders starts there. Then we visit them and show them the tools we have available to motivate and train the church. *Mission Mobilizer in South America.*

These are examples of very practical ways to promote mission and mission opportunities. Other forms of pragmatic mission promotion mentioned by our respondents included:

- Book distribution
- Building relationships with Christian students on campus
- Frequenting specific venues
- Mission video (in addition to the documentary type which was mentioned above)
- PowerPoint or other slide-show presentations
- Securing speaking opportunities at Christian events
- Websites: promotional, educational, and informational
- Youth camp participation

We did not specifically ask what tools or mechanisms our respondents favored when it came to them promoting mission but many of them volunteered this information as part of their narrative. We're confident you will be able to add considerably to our list, further reinforcing the significance of pragmatism as a mobilization ideal-type.

PART THREE: SUMMARY

Our aim in grouping aspects of mission mobilization into four ideal-types was to provide a helpful framework for further discussion and research within the evangelical missions community. Again, we were careful not to make judgment calls with regard to these ideal-types or the means, models, methods, and mechanisms that were highlighted. Rather, we simply presented what was apparent in our data. Much more could be developed in each of these ideal-types by way of best practices for mobilization in any given context.

Proponents of the relational mobilization ideal-type preferred to emphasize activities that promoted interpersonal interaction. They were particularly interested in spending time with people and coaching them toward mission involvement. They are likely to encourage others to do the same.

Practitioners of the educational mobilization ideal-type were more likely to run courses or teach mission subjects in formal or non-formal settings. By default, they would prefer to point people to resources about mission and encourage learning by multiple means.

Formulaic mobilization ideal-type thinkers had a plan to promote mission involvement and a clear-cut strategy for bringing that plan to pass. Their interest was more in analyzing the scene and replicating their plan than engaging at ground level with people one-on-one. Their gift tends to lean toward guiding others to fulfill the plan rather than actually implementing it themselves.

Advocates of the pragmatic mobilization ideal-type used whatever worked to influence people to get from point a to point b. They probably carry around a resource bag or promotional kit full of material, ready for a variety of opportunities to encourage people toward mission.

These mobilization ideal-type snapshots are grossly simplified but they serve to accentuate some of the distinctive attributes of each. The scope of each type is much broader and in reality there is a great deal of interaction between each of them. Mobilizers are usually more well-rounded than each of these ideal-type descriptions suggest. However, our data suggests they will more than likely prefer one particular mobilization ideal-type more than the others.

Questions for Reflection

1. What ideal-type do you naturally gravitate toward?
2. How do you supplement your promotion of mission with attributes of the other ideal-types?
3. Did you find anything problematic about the attributes of any of the ideal-types? Why do you think that might be?
4. In which ways can this framework of ideal-types for mobilization help you to develop your own strategies or resources to foster greater involvement in mission?
5. Imagine that aspects of your ideal-type preference can hinder your attempts to encourage mission. What might those aspects be, why could they hinder, and what can you do to ensure they do not? You might have to ask someone with a different preference to help you detect your own biases.

PART FOUR: ACCELERANTS

I thank God, whom I serve, as my forefathers did, with a clear conscience, as night and day I constantly remember you in my prayers. Recalling your tears, I long to see you, so that I may be filled with joy. I have been reminded of your sincere faith, which first lived in your grandmother Lois and in your mother Eunice, and I am persuaded, now lives in you also. For this reason I remind you to fan into flame the gift of God, which is in you through the laying on of my hands. For God did not give us a spirit of timidity, but a spirit of power, of love, and of self-discipline.
(1 Timothy 1:3–7)

In this short passage we have a powerful example of encouraging mission interest in another. Timothy was not just a church leader; he was a missionary every bit as much as his teacher Paul. These five verses demonstrate some of the mission motivators that emerged as we analyzed our research. Paul's forefathers and Timothy's grandmother and mother exemplify the significant influence of family. Timothy's relationship with the missionary Paul speaks of the power of a missionary's experience as well as individual discipling (and therefore educating) toward mission. For this chapter we are coopting Paul's encouragement to Timothy to "fan into flame" his unspecified gift. Here we will explore what helps "fan into flame," encourage, promote, or accelerate mission involvement.

From our data we identified four accelerant categories worth expanding and one dominant influence.

Over the past two decades there have been a growing number of specialists contracted by mission organizations to promote their mission opportunities and attract new recruits. As we presented in the previous chapter, the variety of means, models, methods, and mechanisms has been growing too. The growth curves are interrelated as the evangelical missions community strives to promote mission involvement in an era that Bosch identified as one of mission crisis, and we have identified as wrestling with issues related to missional anomie.

For all the resource being poured into more complex mission promotion, we wanted to know what factors appeared to be effective in helping or accelerating mission involvement and what seems to retard or hinder mission-interested people from engaging in mission. The next two chapters will spend some time looking at those questions. This represents the heart of our research project.

Over the next five chapters, our demonstration of accelerants highlights factors from our research that helped to spur people on toward involvement in mission and sustain them in it. From our data we identified four accelerant categories worth expanding and one dominant influence. Each of these major themes is far more complex and nuanced than the activities described in each of our mobilization ideal-types. These themes represent what the majority of our global voices said was influential in their mission involvement and *their* experience of helping others become more involved in mission. Similar to how we presented our data in previous chapters, each of the four themes will begin with a theme overview and then introduce each related subsection before creating space for a sampling of our global voices to speak for themselves.

It should be noted that accelerants also have the potential to retard mission passion depending on how aspects of the theme are applied. Rather than split discussion about the inverse effect of a potential accelerant or retardant over both of the next two sections, we have chosen to deal with the negative and positive aspects of themes within the chapter where the theme is strongest. In this way we will treat the flipside of a theme as a caution, an aberration on the dominant potential of the theme.

CHAPTER 14

FAMILIAL RELATIONSHIPS

Somewhat surprisingly to us, the influence of family relationships featured consistently throughout much of the interview material data. By "family" we mean parents (mother, father), siblings, grandparents, spouses, and other extended relatives. We split the theme into two subthemes. We will cover extended family first and then look at the influence of spouses where the marriage relationship played some significant role in a respondent's journey into greater mission involvement.

We have listed the familial relationships theme first because it is a dimension of mission motivation that could too easily be understated or completely ignored by the evangelical missions community seeking to promote more mission involvement. As you will see, our data shows that encouragement of mission involvement by family members had a significant impact on many of our respondents. But it cut both ways. Some respondents spoke of family as a point of hindrance, where various forms of parental pressure and family responsibility were presented as potential obstacles. Rather than split the data between our accelerant and retardant sections, we will keep this theme grouped together and deal with both sides of the coin here because the weight of evidence is largely positive, and where family is seen to be a hindrance it serves to magnify the importance of this theme for promoting mission involvement.

Many of our respondents mentioned that they had Christian parents and that their upbringing was steeped in the Christian tradition. Typical of accounts is that of a Bible college lecturer in Oceania who stated, "I grew up in a Christian family; mum and dad and two of us boys, and was involved in church life at a Baptist setting virtually from birth." And an Indian minister concurred, "Yes, I have attended church all my life; I was born in a Christian home and made a personal commitment to the Lord at the age of fifteen while in my high school." This is echoed by a church member in East Asia who acknowledged the significant Christian input of their parents in their life, "My parents were the ones most influential. Since my early age I think I naturally learned from my parent's exemplary life. My father did not even finish primary education, but taught himself to read and write and has dedicated his life to evangelism. He was famous for evangelizing the whole block."

> As the primary socializing agent our findings confirm that not only are families influential in the internalizing of values and beliefs into their children, but also in the development of convictions and tendency toward Christian service and mission.

Family Helping

As the primary socializing agent our findings confirm that not only are families influential in the internalizing of values and beliefs into their children but also in the development of convictions and tendency toward Christian service and mission.[1] Significantly, a number of our respondents indicated that either their parents or family members had themselves been involved in mission. A missionary from South America recalled,

> I am the son of missionaries, and the subject of missions was always around at our home. My parents worked very hard so that the Argentinian church would have a missionary vision, and I helped in that task for a long time. Accordingly, my vacations always included evangelistic campaigns and missionary conferences when we were not living in the field itself.

Also from South America another missionary stated,

> I got involved because I had the calling to missions since I was little, through a specific word of God to me and through the example of my parents, who served as national missionaries in (*country name*) in the 80s.

A church leader in the United Kingdom shared with us that, "The influences of my grandmother who was a very godly lady and my aunt who was a missionary in Argentina were quite strong on me as a person," and that, "because my brother-in-law was a missionary in Peru and we now have a mission partner here who works there I'm very interested in what's going on in Peru." Even great aunts can have an influence, as we discovered in the following interview excerpt from a mission influencer in India.

> So then there was also a little bit of family history. One of my grand-aunts on my mother's side, she had become a single missionary to the Lutheran church and she served in North India for more than thirty years, and whenever she used to come back to South India she used to come and stay in our home during her holidays for two or three months. ... And when she stayed in our home when we were small, she used to tell us stories of how she used to go and share the gospel in remote areas in (North India); in walking through jungles, meeting wild animals, bandits, and all kinds of adventurous stories. As a little child along with my brother and sister we used to sit and listen to all those stories. She actually made our home as her home so for holidays she always came to our home so that connection was there, so I think that also played a part in the seed that has been sown in my heart for missions.

---

1   The family is the place where members of any given society learn how to interact and thrive in that society. In her book *Family and Social Change* Angelique Janssens suggests that the nuclear family has been left with only two main functions, the first of which is "the family is the main socializing agent of new members of society" (Janssens, 1993, 4). The second is to regulate the emotional stability of a family's adult members by offering safe harbor from a hostile world.

Even without the direct socialization from extended missionary family members or missionary parents on those who would become *missionary kids,* a general positive influence of parents is still prevalent. From a missionary in South America we heard,

> What made me sure of my decision at my eighteen years of age, to leave my city for the first time, and set out into something new, was the unconditional support of my tutor, my grandmother. In this new life of obedience, I learned that if she agreed to allow me to do what I wanted to do (missionary training), then I was taking the right path with God.

And a missionary in the United Kingdom told us,

> What happened was I remember a discussion in our kitchen with myself and my parents. I was sitting at the sink explaining how I felt. I had left school and was working in a bank and was keen to have a career in the bank, but I felt that there was something more and that maybe I should stop and do some Bible training. So they were very sympathetic and asked me pointed questions about finance, about where, what, and when.

Family influence is shown to be particularly significant when compared alongside other types of influence. In this next quote, note the emphasis placed upon a parent by this South American missionary.

> Since my early adolescence, I have been influenced by the biographies of missionaries, missionary films, worker's testimonies, short-term experiences, participation in missionary conferences, etc., and also by pastors who have collaborated in my congregation. But especially, I have been influenced by my father's involvement.

Family Hindering

As the former examples show, family can be quite a motivating force in both a general and specific sense, directly or indirectly, and especially from family members who themselves were involved in mission. Seeds are planted and a particular mission ethos instilled. Not all our interviewees responded, however, with the positive attribution of family as being a source of inspiration or motivation. Rather, some of those with whom we spoke indicated various forms of tension between their personal sense of call and desire to participate in mission service, and their family members' priorities. With regard to studying for mission, a student in Eastern Europe exhibited frustration with their Christian parents.

> One of the obstacles was my parents. They didn't agree. What? Me go to school? Far away? I didn't have their support; I could see they weren't … And I saw in Scripture that when you set out on a path it's important to start with your parents' blessing. And I could see that was failing. Even if they don't want to recognize it, God will work on their hearts and in time they will think differently, not just to stay in a church and be comfortable.

While this response indicates an optimism that God would eventually bring about a change of heart in parents, the potential for anxiety and possible deflection are apparent. So too with this North American respondent of East Asian ethnicity who was interviewed at a missionary conference.

> My parents are a major obstacle. They don't know I am attending this conference. They don't know the nature of this conference. I just came here wanting to participate in mission.

Those involved with motivating others toward mission service also identified family considerations as a potential retardant of missionary involvement as illustrated by this mission mobilizer from Eastern Europe.

> For some people it's their families. We've had a few examples where young people, they were very, very serious about going into missions, but their families didn't want them to leave … their families would rather have them stay home and have a normal life and get married and get a job and build a nice house instead of going to some foreign country.

Spouses

For some of our respondents an awareness of mission was not sparked in them until they became romantically interested in a person interested in mission. Sometimes that person would become their life partner, a non-familial relationship that becomes one. Whether or not the relationship endured, the object of attraction can act as a socializing agent for our respondents with regard to their burgeoning mission interest.

For some of our respondents an awareness of mission was not sparked in them until they became romantically interested in a person interested in mission.

When asked what first motivated an interest in mission, this professor from the United States did not hesitate with their response,

Interviewer: What were the factors that motivated you or inspired you to get into missions?

Respondent: Hmm, it was a crush on (*person's name*) from (*town*)… I was a college student, my dad was a Methodist minister. I'd known about missions. I thought, yes missions is great, that's nice, it's nice that we had missionaries come to our church. Oh it's nice that you're off in Liberia working in a hospital. Oh it's nice that people are off in the Congo evangelizing people. Never crossed my mind at all that I might be a part of that and viewing missions as something separate … that was not my calling *at all*. I had never seriously considered doing this at all until I got a crush on (*person's name*) my sophomore year in college and I got up enough nerve to ask (*her*) out on a date.

The respondent continued to share that this particular date was pertinent because their romantic interest was pre-med and wanted to become a doctor and eventually work in Africa. They went on to tell us, "That night I went home and for the first time in my life I thought, I wonder if I could be a missionary." This potential long-term relationship was never actually realized. The would-be doctor to Africa was interested in becoming a missionary but wasn't particularly interested in our respondent! This brief encounter though was significant in another way, "I never had another date with (*person's name*) in my life but this mission thing stuck and built from there."

We will continue following this narrative because it is also something of a case study for how influential spouses can be with regard to mission interest and service. Although things didn't work out romantically with the aspiring missionary doctor, our respondent did eventually meet and marry another. Both of them by that time had an interest in mission and their story is one of mutual support and encouragement as they left the United States to work in Africa. In this excerpt the respondent clearly indicates that their spouse was particularly instrumental in their initial commitment to Africa and the extension of their time spent there.

> First of all I'll say this, if it weren't for (my spouse) I never would have done it in the first place because I'm a great big chicken. We took psychological batteries of tests, all these different personality things and there was one called harm avoidance. I was over the top. I was off the scale and that fits. Harm avoidance, that's me. But with spiritual development, also with (my spouse), knowing I would be going with (them), that made it easier to go and take off and do this sort of thing.

> But the second thing about that was that our mission had a short-term option and that was a two-year. We signed up for a two-year term, if you will. And so it was like, OK, two years, maybe I can do (that). Right? For wimpy Americans who can't go the whole yards like they did back in the nineteenth century and say I'm going to dedicate my life. I can do two years, knowing you can come back at the end. And so that's what we signed up for, short-term status. We had been there four or five months when (my spouse) said … "I think we ought to move to full-time status." And I didn't have a good argument to say no.

Other people in our study gave similar accounts. Stories in which marriage partners had an interest in mission that sparked interest in their spouse and together they helped one another sustain their mission involvement over time. This represents (co-author) Jay's story of mission involvement. His wife was a key protagonist in his involvement in mission and they have sustained one another through more than two and half decades of mobilization-related ministry.

With regard to the sustaining support of a mission-interested spouse, a missionary from India described their spouse, who shared their mission vision, as a "great support." A missionary in Central Asia from Oceania expressed their appreciation for their spouse this way, "I feel blessed to have a (spouse) who is passionate and who has a vision for cross-cultural missions and is willing to go anywhere that God calls us to go." Overall, data that mentioned marriage partners in our research was generally positive and affirming, revealing high levels of support, shared vision and mutuality in the decision-making processes, and ongoing engagement in mission activity.

In this section we have provided a glimpse of how familial relationships can be a key motivator (and potential hindrance) toward mission service. Although we have only provided representative samples, respondents all over the world testified to the importance for their mission involvement of support from those they loved, respected, and trusted; none more so than family members. The evangelical missions community would do well to recognize this and promote mission service within family networks to future generations. While an important part of our relationship matrix, families are only a subset of the wider theme of interpersonal influences on a person's journey into greater mission involvement.

We all exist as part of a web of relationships. Autonomy can be a powerful illusion for Westerners, deluding with the possibility that you can *make it* on your own. What we have observed is that mission work is never a solo effort, it is something achieved in the context of community. Even so-called *independent* missionaries have

Dr. Christina Baird commented that "member care exists because community doesn't."

to function with some degree of support from the host community, and often the expatriate community around or near them. Relationships are integral to our health and survival regardless of the context or activity. In conversation with (co-author) Jay, Dr. Christina Baird commented that "member care exists because community doesn't," and our data would support that simplified thesis. What constitutes effective missionary-supporting communities could be teased out much more but we did not set out to explore missionary retention. Our primary interest lay with recruitment. Nevertheless, we discovered that *staying on mission* requires a community of support in the start-up phases as much as when in field service. In the next chapter we widen our investigation of interpersonal influences to highlight the types of people that help spur people on in their mission vision.

CHAPTER 15

INFLUENTIAL RELATIONSHIPS

Family relationships aside, all kinds of other relationships emerged as potent influences toward greater mission involvement. Put together, interpersonal interaction, whether with family or non-family, were the largest combination of motivational themes. Relationship-oriented themes were not the most significant in terms of *creating* a desire for mission involvement but they were certainly a primary means of propelling it forward. We will discuss the genesis of a mission vision as our final theme in this chapter, for now let us explore together the various types of influential relationships referenced by our global voices.

Individuals

We meet new people regularly in our daily lives. Some of those people remain strangers, others acquaintances, and a few become friends and part of our personal community. Everyone has the potential to impact us regardless of how much of a relationship develops. The most *chance* of meetings can create significant redirections in the course of our lives. Many of our respondents spoke of seemingly random encounters with people who were to become catalysts of their interest in mission.

For example, this mission leader from Oceania traced their mission involvement back to the most mundane of activities and the stranger that invited them to participate.

> I think it was actually like my very first week in (*North America*). I went to the church that my parents had been attending for the previous year and met a woman who has had quite a significant impact on my life. And she, at that time, was the executive director for a grassroots student movement, mission movement … I think when I initially met her, I mean, obviously she didn't know me at all, but then I think she was, she got me in the door to fold brochures and do something very ordinary, like she was looking for volunteers; and I had time because I couldn't work at that point, I didn't have my paperwork through for working or whatever. And so I was like, oh I've got time, I can come and volunteer. So I came in to volunteer to do something incredibly mundane and in the midst of doing that met these amazing people who had this compelling vision and it just was amazing.

In this example it was not just the stranger who became a long-term influencer that impacted our respondent but the team they became a part of. Often it requires sustained involvement for influence to take hold long enough to create new vision. But sometimes it does not. In our next example an older lady had immediate impact on our respondent.

The power of God resonates through this life-story relayed to us by an Indian minister. We could easily have included this example in the final theme of this chapter but it is a wonderful testament of the obedience of one individual and their influence on the life trajectory of another in a single encounter.

This old, very godly lady was a convert. She called her grandson. She said "Is the church service over, can you call the preacher?" So I went. She asked me, "Do you understand Bengali?" I said, "Sure I can speak as well as understand." Because at that time I was learning Bengali and I can understand. And then she said, she just began to prophesy with her feeble voice. She asked me to come close. I went close to her. She said, "The Lord told me that he has a big plan for you. He's going to make you someone very great. He's going to give you success in winning hundreds of thousands of Bengalis to Christ." You know at that time I was not very sure that God was calling me, but she went on telling many things that I'm doing today and the way the Lord led me in everything she said. And at first I rejected (it), I said, "Old lady you think that my Orissa people will go to hell, that I come and work among your people Bengalis? You must be mad, you are dying anyway. I'm forgiving you." But she just went on for twenty-five minutes telling this is what is going to happen, that is going to happen, exactly. And then she told, "You will get lots of international awards for your accomplishments."

Influence does not need to come from people in such a dramatic and otherworldly way as this though. Inspiration that moves us can be found in sharing life experience with others. In the case of mission, stories of fieldwork realities, their struggles and victories, and suggestions of opportunities can open hearts to new ways of thinking and acting in line with the objectives of mission work. An East Asian missionary illustrates this point,

Usually, the first exposure to mission is to listen to the stories from the ones who are actually involved in missions. People get their eyes opened to what mission is and the fact that someone is doing it. Role models are needed and that can be a pastor, an evangelist, or a missionary who he/she visits the churches. Meeting an enthusiastic mission worker face-to-face would be more impacting than just hearing about mission.

> In the case of mission, stories of fieldwork realities, their struggles and victories, and suggestions of opportunities can open hearts to new ways of thinking and acting in line with the objectives of mission work.

Stories from the real world of mission are eye openers. They help people see the possibilities. But an eye opener can only influence so much. From this East Asian voice we hear that meeting with people face-to-face is more impactful.

Furthermore, it is no small thing that this respondent used the phrase "enthusiastic mission worker." People can be moved by stories of hardship and trial when conveying a life story, but people are more likely to be motivated by someone who actually loves what they do in mission and conveys a sense of hope in what they are about. We will revisit the impact of missionary encounters in the next subsection. We thought this quote was better used here because of the reference to face-to-face encounters with influential individuals.

Remaining within East Asia but a different part, our final example shares some similarities with the Indian prophetess with regard to insistence on the part of the influencer. While this influencer was a friend of the respondent missionary, they used the title of "deacon" as the main referent. This and the fact that the missionary saw the deacon's urgent persistence as "God's sovereign lead" suggests that the respondent greatly respected the deacon's opinion. The deacon, speaking forcefully into our respondent's life, seemed entirely appropriate in light of the preexisting trust levels evident in their relationship.

> I think it was God's sovereign lead. We originally intended to join (that organization) rather than (this organization). A deacon friend of mine introduced (this organization) to me one day but I forgot about it for a while. Afterwards, he strongly and persistently urged me to apply for (this organization). Upon sending my application, the director of (this organization) willingly came all the way to our church to interview us, which was rather exceptional. I interpreted it as God's intervention to expedite our departure process for (*an East Aisian country*). Without knowing much about (this organization), we ended up joining this organization through a third person.

As with all our sampling of global voices we lose a lot of cultural nuance by picking short quotes like this out of our mountain of data and out of their context. In the case just quoted, we know this situation occurred to someone from East Asia in East Asia, and we can be tempted to overlay certain cultural assumptions of power distance, hierarchy, and formality to this example of relationship influence. Do that and the action of the director of the organization the respondent applied to stands out all the more! The humility exhibited by the director's visit had a significant impact on our friend. What may seem a small thing to others can have a big influence on a person open to God's leading. We will explore the affect organizations and staff can have on peoples' mission involvement soon, but before we do, we must first look at how influential missionaries can be.

Missionaries

Missionaries are individuals too. Yes, they are just plain old people like you and us. But their influence toward mission involvement in our data was so obvious they deserved their own category to highlight it. Our hope is that missionaries reading this will be spurred on to be as positive an influence as they can to as many people as they can influence. Who knows what the Lord might want to do with that small turnout to a missionary speaker at an obscure meeting in the middle of nowhere for God's glory across the world. In this subsection we illustrate the impact missionaries have had on our respondents.

> Who knows what the Lord might want to do with that small turnout to a missionary speaker at an obscure meeting in the middle of nowhere for God's glory across the world.

Our first quote illustrates how difficult it can be to separate influences into neat categories or themes. However, it fits here because all of the interpersonal interactions this South American missionary lists were missionaries, even their father-in-law.

> I was influenced by the lives of other missionaries, like my father-in-law, by missions leaders ... who prepared a training plan and would minister to us very closely. This plan included a theoretical training and a practical training in different areas of the church, in other cities, etc. We attended lectures, courses, workshops, etc.

It is worth noting the intentionality in this narrative. There is a strong educational element to it as well. Education is discussed further on because it too had a significant role to play in influencing our respondents. Here we see indications of prolonged influence through the use of educational devices and experiences.

Staying within an educational context, this missionary in Eastern Europe notes that while researching a certain country the missionaries who came to school to speak about that country had a great impact on their mission trajectory.

> And then it was interesting that at that time when I was doing more research on the country ... I had several missionaries come and visit from the country ... and they were speaking to the youth there and the students in that school. And I just felt like that was the place to go to next.

Not all missionaries have as positive an impact. One of our respondents from the United Kingdom held little back about their opinion of missionary speakers.

> I had heard some missionaries in the churches we had been to, although having said that, some missionaries did not and still do not know how to communicate. No matter what country they live in, when they come back to Britain they either bore you or they can fire you up. I can think of some who are dead now who inspired me and gave me an interest in mission. Hearing people like Brother Andrew in big rallies in Glasgow was something that was very significant for me.

"Some missionaries ... still do not know how to communicate," is a sweeping indictment, but to be fair, communicating in their home culture was probably not how those missionaries were best gifted. Mind you, the bar is lifted very high with the reference to Brother Andrew. The point is still made: missionaries do have the potential to significantly influence.

We emphasize this point with the testimony of another voice from Eastern Europe. Here we have strong themes of friendship, stories of mission experiences, longevity of contact, education and educational experiences, all resulting from missionary contact.

> A friend from my home who had been on a number of mission trips—I was close to him and well—I talked with him a lot and he showed me pictures of the places he'd been and what he'd done and that. ... I learned a lot from him about missions. And it had an impact on me. Besides that ... most people ... especially

the missionaries ... I learned a lot from them. And I had a lot of training and trips where I spent quality time with them and I got to know them personally and I saw their dedication and the sacrifices that they had to make.

The lived experiences of missionaries, like the ones who influenced our friend just mentioned, deeply resonated with many of our respondents. Their depth of character and faith often shone through and left a lasting impact. In contrast to our comment from the United Kingdom above, according to our next respondent—a mobilizer from South America, you would have to be dead if stories from experienced missionaries do not move you!

Missionaries do have the potential to significantly influence.

> The presence of the missionary is important. When they give testimonies, it is very touching and it mobilizes people. We have the blessing of having missionaries who are highly experienced, committed, and effective and when they come and tell about their reality in the field. If there is a person who does not feel touched, well, that person must be dead already and it is impossible to move him or her.

The personal witness from this missionary from East Asia echoes that sentiment.

> Well, it was rather the person that impacted me. When (they) came into the classroom, I felt an indescribable aura. That was of someone who lived in a totally different world than mine. That caught my attention. Then, their story about things that are so different from (here) really moved me and made me dream of Africa.

Apparently missionaries can carry an "indescribable aura" so take note if you are a missionary reading this. According to this mobilizer in the United Kingdom, people may want to be like you.

> And we had (*person's name*), from Wycliffe Bible Translators ... come to speak and I remember feeling, "I want to be like him."

Even if you are just "ordinary" someone like you impacted this student of mission in Eastern Europe. You too can encourage people to remain committed to the cause of mission.

> After that, similarly, a few months ago a missionary who had been to Turkey, he encouraged me and I saw his witness—an ordinary man, not with really vast theology, he was just an ordinary man. For a few months he experienced great things with God and it woke this impulse in me. God needs committed people. He doesn't need people with philosophies, but ordinary people, people who feel what God feels. And it made me—that was the second encouragement to keep going.

You may not think so but this missionary from East Asia thinks every missionary should be a mobilizer because you can be a significant influence.

Many of my fellow missionaries say meeting active missionaries made a significant role in becoming missionaries. Meeting a real missionary in person can be an eye-opener. Every missionary should be a mobilizer.

We wonder if the missionary speaker at this girls' camp ever realized the impact she had on at least one teenager in attendance. That young girl went on to be a long-term missionary in India and was one of our respondents.

> At thirteen, when I was at a girl's camp, I felt when a missionary was speaking, she was a missionary who had been working in India, and she said to us ... one day when she was speaking, "If God ever calls you to serve him on the mission field I wonder if any of you would be willing." And I can remember at thirteen telling my Lord that I would be willing and ever since then throughout my teenage years I sought to get to know the Lord better and Christ spiritually; I got very involved in doing the Lord's ministry.

As noted already, chance encounters can have immediate impact but there is something to be said for persistent influence. A minister in Oceania made this observation.

> I think missionaries too, actually, have just had an impact up on me. They're sort of like, you know, the proverbial drip that wears away the stone, they come back for furlough and you get to know them and that, and they just, they form you if you allow them to. I think that ... hugely impressed by (*missionary's name*), just traveling with her in the last days of her life and just hearing something of her initial calling as a young twenty something-year-old and how she just spent herself in that particular calling. Wow that's, that's a good life.

This kind of sustained influence is discipleship in action, popularly known as mentoring these days. This East Asian church leader shared a similar perspective.

> The missionary candidate I met in seminary became a mentor to me. His continuing challenges and encouragement kept my missions flame alive. There were several people who caught the same vision through him, and my interaction with them also was very helpful.

An East Asian church member honored their interviewer, an East Asian missionary, in this way and also shared the deep emotional impact missionary messages and updates had on their desire to serve in mission.

> Missionaries I've met so far, including you, were the strongest influence. The sermons and reports of missionaries who visited our church touched me to tears, incurring a strong desire to go out to mission field.

Jay had a missionary mentor who still deeply affects his mission involvement. One of the mentor's favorite sayings was, "Use them or lose them." Speaking from South America our next global voice would concur. They testified to the fact that their involvement with missionaries was critical to them becoming a missionary themselves. They also mention some practical ways to maintain contact, even at a distance, to fuel a desire for mission.

> What helped me the most was to keep in contact with other missionaries. That contact was done through financial support, and helping them in running through different administrative or legal procedures they needed while in the field, and with their presentations when visiting my country.

We are confident you have got the point by now: missionaries, even ordinary ones, make great influencers toward mission involvement. In case we left you with the impression that only career missionaries can have that kind of impact we will close this section off with an observation from an East African respondent. This global voice mentioned the impact of short-termers on their life and ministry. They are now directing their own ministry in East Africa and they point to their relationship with missionaries (short and long term) as being influential in their spiritual growth.

> So at the point I was becoming a Christian I had interaction with people who had come for one year as part of their short-term missions experience in (*East Africa*), some, three years, and I admired (them). Because talking to them I would get to hear what they do and it was a good experience to learn that these people, out of their convictions of God's call—to leave their country and come and to minister through teaching was quite—I think that was very foundational.

This kind of sustained influence is discipleship in action, popularly known as mentoring these days.

Ministers

The final category of *individuals* identified as influential are the leaders of churches, who our respondents identified as pastors or (arguably more appropriately) ministers. Missionaries as influencers can be relative strangers and their impact can be instant with long lasting reverberations throughout the life and ministry of the one influenced. The minister on the other hand is privileged with sustained influence over their congregants for as long as they are in ministry in a particular context.

Oftentimes ministers are called to serve many, which makes life-on-life discipleship something of a luxury. Their influence is more about helping to define big-picture reality for their congregants Sunday after Sunday and through the church's activities during the week. It should be no surprise to discover that congregants were influenced for mission by ministers who understood and promoted mission involvement as part of helping their congregation to understand God's purposes in and for the world.

This Eastern European minister claimed to have a passive role in this regard, but their response to people in whom they recognized a mission call was far from passive.

> My role in missions is more passive. I don't have the calling or the gift for missions in the sense of leaving the country, but what I can do is to recognize people who

have this calling and to support and speak for them. So that's the way in which I'm involved in missions.

A minister advocating for mission is a powerful point of influence. A church leader in South America confirmed this.

> I do not say this because we did not have problems and because everything is going smoothly, but everything went relatively according to plan and the missionary mobilization has gone from the leadership to the congregation. We can say that we have had a gratifying experience in missionary mobilization.

What a wonderful thing "a gratifying experience in missionary mobilization" would be! If only all ministers around the world were able to influence their congregations similarly. Sadly, it is not always the case, as this church member from Eastern Europe observed from their lived experience of mission in churches.

> And then … I came to (*church name*), because our pastors have a different perception of missions compared to other pastors. So a lot depends on who is the pastor in a church. On the direction he gives to the church. And in our church it's about going out.

Perhaps what is lacking is the influence of ministers by other ministers who have already developed a working understanding of mission and are actively involved. This minister from the United Kingdom tells of a senior minister influencing their perspective over time. This could easily have fit under the missionary as influencer section, but this minister specified the influencer as their former minister rather than a missionary as such.

> In my first church I was an Assistant Pastor in a city center church—a church of about five hundred. And again, we would have visits from various missionaries. Perhaps my view of missions began to change when my old pastor, who was a great guy who I had a great relationship with and who was a terrific pastor and Bible teacher, who went out to (*field name*) for a number of years. The contact I had with him and his coming back into the country put a new angle on what missions was all about and it became very much more alive to me at that time.

This point of minister-to-minister influence could be an effective way to achieve what this South American missionary adamantly concluded,

> The pastor of the local church must be the first one to be "converted" to missions.

However, this global voice's choice of the word "converted" suggests more than another minister's influence or that of something else. As we discuss at the end of this chapter, awareness and understanding of the importance of mission is primarily a supernatural occurrence, reinforced by multiple influences. Conversion is an appropriate word.

With great respect for the authority of ministers, this church member from South America recognized the influence of one of their ministers in undertaking a specific mission activity.

> The work we are performing in (*field name*) was an initiative of one of the pastors of the church. With time and circumstances we felt we had to take on a place and to carry out the task. We try to work under our pastors' authority, obeying their guidelines and advice.

Taking the initiative for mission is a tremendous example for the congregation. Add to that practical involvement and enthusiasm and church leaders can have a powerful influence on mission involvement from their people. A church member in the United Kingdom testifies to this.

> Because the pastor shows enthusiasm, even before he went on his trips, because he was supportive, I had greater opportunity to push world mission within the church both through visiting speakers coming … I did the inviting, I did the administration, but (*the pastor*) pushed it. He effectively endorsed his commitment and enthusiasm for it so that the church people got the message "we are in this together."

Awareness and understanding of the importance of mission is primarily a supernatural occurrence, reinforced by multiple influences.

Enthusiasm and encouragement should not be underestimated. Regardless of cultural or denominational traditions, ministers carry a lot of responsibility for their potential to influence others and affect the ministry potential of their congregants. This mission organization worker in India told of how their minister was emotionally supportive of their mission interest when their parents were strongly against it. The worker was active in mission at the time of the interview because of their minister's encouragement, in spite of their parents' active resistance.

> When I was rejected he was the one who gave me emotional support, and for that support my parents really tortured him. He did not give me physical support but emotional support. He was the leader of that church, that means he would come call me once a while and say don't worry I'm with you. He was someone who said I'm with you because I would feel nobody is with me—that was a big encouragement.

Sometimes the person with an interest in mission can be a great encouragement to the minister. That was the case for this voice from East Asia who went on to become a career missionary.

> During my senior year I was trained by a parachurch organization called (*organization name*), which impacted me substantially. And the pastor of my attending church was a great encouragement in this regard. He would say I was the only real fruit of his discipleship ministry and blessed my commitment. My elder sister also encouraged, supported, and prayed for me.

Imagine being a minister of a congregation where the only tangible ministry result went off and got involved in mission elsewhere! That is dedication from a minister that will likely have impact far beyond their direct influence because of what this missionary went on to accomplish. Notice also the missionary's mention of their elder sister. This is another reference to the importance of family as mentioned in the previous chapter.

If you need more evidence of the importance of the church's minister for accelerating a vision for mission involvement among those under their influence, consider our final voice for this section. A church missions team leader from a church in Oceania shares from their experience.

> You do definitely need the senior pastor to endorse it otherwise you do really struggle because, I mean, it all comes down to budgets and budgets can potentially get squeezed each year if the pastor wasn't really into it. Our pastor, I think he has always been interested in mission. I think sometimes because he's a pastor he focuses very much on the local church, but having said that he has been to (*field location*) a number of times on some healing crusades and he went to (*field location*) last year, and he's been out to (*field location*) to visit our missionaries up there. So he does go on mission trips every few years, which seem to sort of spur him along on the missions track. I mean sometimes you can feel a little bit, when you're on the missions team that, um, I have to be careful what I say ... sometimes you can feel it's a bit, a little bit of a struggle, because he can be more locally focused than you'd like, but I suppose that's also a matter of where your passion is and sometimes it can, sometimes I felt, when I was leading the missions team for a couple of years, you can feel a little bit restrained by the church. But I mean, I guess he's balancing lots of different ministry areas. But generally we've got a fairly good permission from him to do what we're doing in the missions team.

A minister's enthusiasm and encouragement goes a long way toward accelerating interest in mission and costs very little.

This respondent was careful not to overstate things but they obviously experienced some tension at times between their passion for mission and the minister's more local responsibilities. They were very realistic, acknowledging the minister's challenge of "balancing lots of different ministry areas." Any minister of anything larger than a small group will be quick to agree that the local versus global or congregational versus community focuses can create some dissonance. For most churches, resources are scarce and must be wisely distributed. Still, as we have read already, a minister's enthusiasm and encouragement goes a long way toward accelerating interest in mission and costs very little.

Networks

Networks are essentially groups of interconnected individuals. Usually the network exists for a dynamic beyond the sum of its interconnected parts. It is a place from which synergy can emerge and in the hands of mission-interested people, networks can greatly assist with the acceleration of mission interest. We have just closed out our focus on individual influencers with the ministers; we conclude this section about influential groups with a brief nod to networks here and then mission organizations next.

An Oceanic voice introduces us to the theme of networks quite well where they describe a multifaceted mobilization network made up of personnel from a variety of different mission organizations along with other mission-interested people.

> The way I sort of look at the network is we're not an organization where there's a center that works with all these people that report into us. No one actually, if you like, reports into us from an accountability perspective or a responsibility perspective, but the network is more. Instead of having a central core and all lines leading to the center, it's actually a complete web of relationships between everybody.

The significance of this type of decentralization should not be underestimated in our contemporary missions context. Perhaps a mitigating factor against missional anomie could be the missions collaboration that is being spoken of by our respondent from Oceania. The following mission motivator from South America amplified the effect of networks as a point of influence within church circles and beyond.

> Now, this is the work of the network, to present solutions to the pastor, they can suggest training centers, short-time experiences, etc. Then the network becomes an ally, a friend, it solves a problem for him, and gradually there can be an openness for missions, but it always takes time. ... What the network tries to do is to connect the person. The network is connection, links, relationships. So we try (to) connect the people so they can feel encouraged, so they do not feel alone and strange, there are others like them. We connect them in a missionary current where they can be nourished, encouraged, and supported.

This next South American mobilizer would agree.

> Mobilization networks are very important because they make it possible to work in different denominations and this reflects a spirit of unity that benefits the church and mostly the leadership. They don't compete with the church or other networks. It is a complement of the work.

There is a dynamic about the non-aligned, neutral group that can represent mission well to churches and individuals and promote the cause of mission from the collective resources of their group.

There is a dynamic about the non-aligned, neutral group that can represent mission well to churches and individuals and promote the cause of mission from the collective resources of their group. Networks tend to be made up of people with specialized interests and these specialists are a rich complementary resource to the church. However, to be used, the resources need to be seen as relevant to the local church. Ministers who do not currently have an interest in mission can fail to see the benefits of a mission network's resources to their congregation. Nevertheless, those seeking to develop their mission interest and involvement will appreciate a mission network's worth, as our sample voices above did.

Organizations

As we have observed already, missionaries are individuals but they are also most often part of a much larger community, usually in the form of a mission organization. The big difference between a mission organization and network or movement usually boils down to the degree of responsibility and accountability members have to the group. Where networks tend to be loose affiliations, mission organizations are far more intentionally and legally structured with well-defined membership expectations and services. If a mission organization is not legally registered somewhere we suggest the group should be considered more of a network than a formal organization. Movements tend to lean toward being networks over organizations, but movements and networks may develop an organizational body as needs require.

Mission organizations usually exist to help missionaries achieve the vision of the organization; some exist purely to raise funds but even then people (whether or not they are considered missionaries) use those funds for mission-oriented purposes. Every mission organization has its distinctive vision, values, purpose, policies, and practices; and every mission organization experiences its successes and failures. When it all boils down, organizations are just clusters of people who commit to a certain way of doing things for certain reasons.

Every mission organization has its distinctive vision, values, purpose, policies, and practices; and every mission organization experiences its successes and failures. When it all boils down, organizations are just clusters of people who commit to a certain way of doing things for certain reasons.

Organizations that focus on mission were mentioned in various ways throughout our data, and this is one subtheme we will split over the two chapters to ensure we do justice to the potential of organizations as both an accelerant and retardant. Organizations are mentioned here as accelerants mainly because of the positive influence for mission by *individuals* within the organization, but that is not the only way mission organizations influence. In the part five we will explore a much larger body of data that explores the inverse influence of mission organizations, which would too easily eclipse the positives we highlight in this section.

The following examples of positive mission organization influence could just as easily sit in the individual or missionary influencer categories as much as here. The first respondent we quote highlighted this with their emphasis on the people they met once they got involved in the organization that impacted them most. But it was this missionary in Eastern Europe's experience with the mission-oriented *organization* that provided the context that allowed the mission personnel to influence them further.

> How it came about, I think it all began in first year when I was at university and I became involved in (*organization name*) ... and after I got to know the people

there and I got involved in the organization I was challenged to go on mission to another country.

In a similar way, the mission organization created space for this church leader from the United Kingdom to be discipled and influenced for mission. But it was the mission organization's personnel that were the actual influencers.

I only know that because when I went to live in France I remember thinking it would be good if I could find a church but it wasn't like, "My first priority must be to find a church." But God was quite clear he was going to find me a church because on the first weekend—there was one Protestant church in the town I was in and I went to it on the Sunday morning. There was a group from an organization I had never heard of called (*organization name*) and they were leading the service, doing, like, a weekend mission or a weekend in the town, and so they had an event that Sunday night. Because I was new to the town and didn't really know anyone, I went to it. It was an interdenominational charismatic fellowship. Again, I didn't have the language to understand what that was in those days. They took me under their wing and that's when the growth began, really, as a Christian; that was one of my most significant years.

That the mission personnel took this respondent "under their wing" speaks powerfully of intentional nurturing; furthermore, it was at a time when the respondent felt alone and potentially vulnerable. The impact was significant enough for this church leader to look back on that year of mission impact as a highlight of their life.

In contrast to their church experience, a mission organization leader from Oceania credited their experience within a mission organization as developing their interest in mission.

Interviewer: It sounds like your missions understanding grew in terms of a whole discipleship process, it was integrated into them discipling you.

Respondent: Yeah, yeah, because if I'd stayed in the (*denomination name*) church I doubt if I'd grown in missions. So really it was the agency that developed my mission not the church.

With regard to the power of a mission organization to influence and develop the mission perspective of a person, this next East Asia missionary lauded their experience with their mission organization. The more they got involved the more they understood the wonderful fellowship that can be experienced through belonging to an organization with common values and sharing a common goal. More than that, within the organization they learned how to better relate to those they worked with on the field outside of the organization's membership.

My later experience in working with (*organization name's*) international leadership team. It was a foretaste of heaven working as a multinational team in harmonious partnership despite many differences. It made me believe in the practical possibility of working together with national partners without discrimination or condescension. Through it I saw the beauty and glory of mission, the joy of recovery/reconciliation in a real sense. In summary, I learned that missionaries should approach people with a fatherly heart and walk together with them, building up each other; two-way traffic, not one-way.

Staying in East Asia, a mission organization's staff member praises their missions community experience with colleagues in a similar fashion.

Through the (*ministry name*) ministry of (*organization name*) I finally decided to commit myself for world mission. There I met like-minded colleagues, found the joy of being part of such a community, kept affirmed of the call to go, and trained to take missions for granted rather than a special activity.

It is so easy for meaning to be "lost in translation" as we analyze and present our data. For this mission worker we assume that "take missions for granted" means to incorporate mission into the whole of their life as opposed to just some sporadic involvement.

As we mentioned in the missionary section earlier, this kind of enthusiasm for mission and a mission organization is positively infectious and can be a potent influential force. Another East Asian missionary on home assignment recalled the immediate impact on their life of specific missionaries, but they also took care to note the specific organization involved.

When I met (*missionary name*) a member of (*organization name*), who visited (*country name*). Through his challenge, I came to the realization for the first time that there still were so many unreached people groups, so my (spouse) and I made a commitment for world mission right there and then.

So in these few glimpses, where mission organizations are mentioned positively, we can see the potential for organizations to be mission accelerants. If missions personnel enjoy a positive experience with their organization, it better promotes mission to people outside the organization. Mission involvement then becomes attractive. In the next chapter we will hear our global voices speak of how that potential can all too easily fall short.

We have covered a lot of territory in this section as we explored various influential relationships that our respondents highlighted outside of family relationships. Regardless of the context or other surrounding factors, the first three sections of this chapter elevated the life-on-life impact of interpersonal connections as the most significant part of accelerating a person's involvement in mission. But whether the influencer was a missionary, a minister, part of a network of mission enthusiasts or a member of a mission organization, our respondents were motivated by individuals; not their role, title, or whom they represented.

Many of our respondents mentioned immediate impact from a missionary speaker, but most pointed to sustained contact and encouragement being that which best helped develop their understanding of mission. Where revelation can come from something that immediately impacts, a broad understanding of mission leading to involvement can take time to acquire. It has to be learned and learning is a process. All of our respondents were people who have sustained their mission involvement and they all indicated being discipled in mission in one way or another. The value of taking the time to come alongside and coach a mission novice should not be underestimated. However, there are many ways for people to be educated in mission and multiple resources for the mission discipler to take advantage of to develop understanding. Our respondents mentioned a variety of educational resources and we move now to look at the various ways our global voices encountered education as they developed their mission understanding and involvement.

But whether the influencer was a missionary, a minister, part of a network of mission enthusiasts or a member of a mission organization, our respondents were motivated by individuals; not their role, title, or whom they represented.

CHAPTER 16

EDUCATION

We introduced education earlier as a mobilization ideal-type. There we identified education in a variety of forms as means often used by mission recruiters to lead people into greater involvement in mission. We expand on the educational theme in this section through the perspective of our global voices. We detected many references to educational devices throughout our data and grouped them into categories or subthemes under the overarching theme of education. Education rightly belongs in this chapter of mission accelerants because according to our data it is clearly a key factor in promoting mission. However, we will also note where education fails to meet the expectation of accelerating mission interest.

Education is only as effective as students want it to be. "You get out of it what you put into it," as they say. Another popular Western saying is, "You can lead a horse to water, but you cannot make it drink." In the context of this section that means education is most effective when there is a desire to learn. If the desire is there, any number of educational means, models, methods, or mechanisms can enhance a person's mission understanding and involvement. As we did in the mobilization ideal-types section, we look again at education with very broad strokes, starting with more formal means of education and then on to informal and promotional ways of educating.

Academic Institutions

For many of the missionaries we conversed with in our study, training and education was an assumed process, either through attendance at a Bible college or taking a mission-oriented course. Study in theology and/or missiology as a prerequisite to service was described positively by many of our respondents as necessary preparation for the work they went on to become involved in. Although challenging for some, the experience of educational preparation was beneficial on a number of levels. A missionary from the United Kingdom was "a little put off" by the idea of formal training at first but they soon saw the value of it.

> It seemed a long time to be preparing; even the training itself, we were a little put off to be honest because it is so long. But since we've got to the field, every little bit we've needed and has been incredibly important. So many times we've been out in the middle of the jungle and words come back to us—things that we learned on our training and it's just been invaluable, so we would do it all again.

A church leader from East Asia ministering in the United States expressed that mission education helped correct their understanding and pursuit of mission. The fact that mission-experienced people were teaching them was also a significant factor.

> But studying missiology at (*school name*) made me realize how narrow my perspective was and how wrong my understanding on church growth was. Learning and reading about missions were influential in my case. Lectures by professors with rich mission experiences as well as sharing of various missionaries taught me the spirit and purpose of mission as well as its biblical basis. My paradigm eventually shifted from local church perspective to that of world mission.

Also revealed in our interview data were secondary benefits from more formal courses of study and the environment of educational institutions. One East Asian missionary spoke of their experience in a formal education setting as being instrumental in their spiritual development and future calling, "I asked myself how specifically to serve the Lord. God led me to missions through the influence of a campus ministry." A minister, also from East Asia, was deeply influenced in a similar way even though they did not attend a Bible college as a student but as a teacher on a temporary basis. They told us, "Spending one full year teaching there convinced me that I could be involved in mission in a meaningful way." They described this as the "most crucial impact" in the forming of their understanding and conviction for missions.

From India, this missionary spoke of the influence of a Bible college context for their mission vision.

> I applied to attend the Bible college of (*location name*) because I wanted to spend two years studying the word of God deeply and I applied and I was accepted by the Bible college. After two years in the Bible college, in my second year, through many Scriptures and many challenging messages, I heard the Lord make it very clear to me that his call was on my life to come to India.

Besides being in a place where you can hear the voice of the Lord, other benefits resulting from a Bible college experience were shared with us by this mission mobilizer in the United Kingdom.

> It was the context, the fellowship, it was the opportunity to grow as a disciple, that was the crucial thing of Bible college; growing to maturity as a believer, starting to integrate my faith with my life. So, that was really, really very stimulating, very encouraging. I got lots of opportunities to develop there so one of the nice things about Bible college, and I think it is often the case, that you get the opportunity to start to develop your giftings wherever they are, there are often ways of doing that.

While most spoke encouragingly of their theological education and the way it accelerated their mission vision, some expressed concerns, the focus of which centered on the curriculum. This mission organization worker in Oceania lamented the inadequacy of the intercultural element of their postgraduate course at a Bible college (in the United States the institute providing a qualification at this level would be considered a seminary).

> **Respondent:** I'm very grateful that I studied, did the MDiv program. However, the intercultural component of that, which was my major, has actually proved to be less than helpful.

> **Interviewer:** Why?

> **Respondent:** Because I realize now what I didn't know then, which was that the curriculum, the people, perhaps with one exception that I remember really quite clearly … were very much what I would call "old school." It was from a previous era of mission. It was the way things were done, you know, and that's good to understand, the history of mission, but not when the history is taught as the present reality. To be fair, I mean, I've been out, I've been in (*field location*) for little over nine years and things have changed in nine years. The preparation you need is how to stay up with what's the current reality. It's not modules from ten years ago, even today's modules, because in ten years from now, those are going to be out. So you're looking for the timeless principals and I don't feel like that was necessarily what I received during that training.

This mission mobilizer in East Africa recognized a similar problem with institutional curricula in their experience. Their emphasis is on the training of future church leaders, but their concern for what it means for mission resonated with the voice from Oceania.

> We may have to trust God for change of heart, in fact, a divine interruption of the curriculum in the Bible schools and the seminaries because, ideally, the graduates from these schools are the ones who are running the churches, the emerging urban churches who are well endowed with human and financial resources. But, as you say, if they did not develop biblical convictions of missions there is no possibility that they cause this to happen within the thousands that they control. And to me they are controlling God's people, the church, which exists primarily for missions. So in the short term and medium term, perhaps it is to trust God to interrupt those curriculums. I have talked with a number of professors who are involved in missions; they can see it, but they are in a curriculum which is fixed, given, it's like this is the truth. It exists like this, we have never seen it before that way. And of course it comes with the challenge of who will write the books, and I say there are no new books being written. It is to reorganize the existing materials perhaps inject more of missions and also alter the philosophy of education for it to be more of a discipleship experience than an academic exercise.

Another East African, a researcher at a theological school, was critical too of the perceived status of the faculty in some Bible colleges, "You know there are professors in theology who are not even Christians, professors who are not practitioners; they are not engaging the real things. We need to rethink theological education." And although somewhat less forthright in their critique, one church leader from the United Kingdom, when asked about the quality of the missions curriculum in their college experience, summed things up by saying, "It wasn't brilliant." A church leader from East Asia spoke of there being a complete absence of any mission component offered by their institution, "The seminary's role? Well, it's difficult to answer, as my seminary had no input about global mission."

It is appropriate to pause briefly here to discuss formal theological training with regard to mission. These few quotes represent a much larger undercurrent of frustration concerning theological institutions' lack of mission intention as perceived by those passionate about mission. Many of our respondents saw the potential for these places to accelerate mission interest and involvement, but it was not realized. There are many reasons for this, some of which are evident in the quotes above. Power politics get involved with staff wanting to preserve influence and aging lecturers wanting to teach what they have always taught. But also many training institutions exist to teach abstract theology or applied local ministry rather than mission studies as such. Would it not be unfair to expect them to teach a specialization that is not part of their vision or value system?

Mission enthusiasts have developed a theological understanding that integrates mission. This can cause them to struggle to understand a Christian academic institution's lack of overt cross-cultural or intercultural training as part of its curriculum. At the beginning of the twentieth century, systematic theologian Martin Kähler laid claim to mission as "the mother of theology" and this has been used to argue for a mission flavor to infuse all theological training (Bosch, 1991, 16). Most Christian colleges and seminaries would testify that their training does, in so far as all theological training, have a place in the "real world," but mission specialists tend to view mission with greater definition and applied theology can fail to meet their expectations.[1]

> At the beginning of the twentieth century, systematic theologian Martin Kähler laid claim to mission as "the mother of theology" and this has been used to argue for a mission flavor to infuse all theological training (Bosch, 1991, 16).

Unfortunately, there is only so much resource available to educational institutions and they need to invest where the demand is greatest. Mission influencers may want these institutions to be contexts where students with no prior interest in mission are exposed to mission thinking, but if the students were attracted to a school for its abstract theology, pastoral, or youth ministry training it would be difficult for the school to add "superfluous" material to its curriculum at considerable extra cost—difficult, but not impossible.

Thankfully there is specialist mission training available in many parts of the world and there are many fine Christian institutions providing robust contextual theology and cross-cultural or intercultural training for those with a prior interest in mission—and access to it. However, we can understand the desire of mission influencers to see all Christians equipped with a thorough comprehension of God's mission to frame their Christian perspective of the world, its history, and its future.

---

1   For a very helpful historical overview of the missiological foundations of theology, see Gailyn Van Rheenen's article in missiology.org. In it he claims, "Theology was done in missional contexts in response to missional questions as Christian ministers planted new churches and nurtured existing churches to maturity." You can read the rest of the article here: http://www.missiology.org/mr-21-the-missiological-foundations-of-theology/.

Church Education

Many of our respondents noted a general lack of mission knowledge in their experience of Christian community. From their observations we conclude that it is because mission is largely missing from the Christian education congregants receive within their churches. Although most of our respondents made mention of it in a negative sense, we mention general Christian education at this point for the same reason we put formal education in this section—because it is not exactly a retardant of missions service; on the contrary, it has great potential to be an accelerant of mission interest. The fact that many of our respondents lamented that it was not indicates this potential. We saw hints of church education's potency for accelerating mission interest in our section on the influence of ministers.

We hope you can see some logic forming in our presentation here. General Christian education happens in the local church and is taught by leaders of the local church. If those leaders are formally trained at all, chances are it was in academic institutions such as those referred to above. If those institutions are not teaching mission, we should not expect the ministers or other church leaders to do so. Nevertheless, our respondents clearly wanted them to.

From our data it was very apparent that our mission-involved respondents were concerned about the omission of mission from their experience of church. They articulated a disconnect between a Christian's understanding of the Christian life, directly related to what is taught in their church, and the convictions of missionaries, mission workers, and mission organizations. For example a mission mobilizer in Oceania told us flatly that, "When it comes to overseas mission most people really have no idea."

An East Asian mission leader spoke of a situation that many mission recruiters in the West would love to have—"many knocking at the door"—but this respondent was wise to the fact that future missionaries need to be well prepared and the local church was not providing a good enough example.

> The struggle is there are not many people we want to send while so many are knocking at the door of (*mission organization*). Many of them are either lacking in preparation or improperly prepared. Most prominently, their perspective in mission is very weak. Instead of thinking deep about the nature of mission, they simply pursue doing what local churches have been doing. Often times, such people make more trouble than contribution on the mission field.

Similarly, a number of the people we spoke with directed their concern for the lack of mission knowledge at the local church. A church member in South America told us, "I personally think that pastors don't have a clear vision of missions and its importance. Therefore, the congregation is not aware of the reality. There isn't any teaching about missions." A different church member in South America expressed frustration at their church leaders' inability to apply mission knowledge even if they have some.

> The leadership shares the mission but they do not know how to carry it out; how to send and to support. There is no training, no vision lines expressed with clarity, because people who should do it are not qualified.

This sentiment was repeated a number of times. From East Asia a minister shared this opinion of the situation in North America.

> Most (*East Asian*)-American churches lack the knowledge and know-how of missions, so they tend to lose out potential human resources such as the (*short-term experience*) participants who return to their local churches, warmed up and committed to missions. They don't know how to handle or follow up missionary prospects and candidates, these precious human resources are eventually wasted.

Also from an East Asian perspective, church leaders hindered this church member's zeal to resource mission well from within the church. Thankfully they felt their persistence was finally starting to pay off.

> I've personally had problems working with elders as they really don't know much about missions. I wanted to build data and do various things related to missions, but elders would say the only thing our church should do is to send out short-term mission trip teams. But now, finally, some elders are interested in missions education.

If a church does not provide adequate mission education for their congregation those who sense a draw toward mission involvement may satisfy their felt need elsewhere. That could happen in a formal academic environment but this mission mobilizer from the United Kingdom identified a more common route as that of the parachurch organization.

> What comes first the chicken or the egg? If the local church was doing what it should be doing in terms of teaching, I think that is the key, (but) the parachurch has to play such a role because the local church is not doing it.

Another mission influencer from the United Kingdom expanded this idea further from their experience. They identified "movements" as providing opportunities for mission-oriented education and service. In this case movements differ from parachurch organizations in that they remain connected to denominations or within defined church structures rather than outside of those structures altogether. The respondent saw some advantages to these movements, but they would still rather see local churches taking up responsibility for mission education.

> I think both in the new churches and in the old churches, there is still a failure to understand the centrality of mission to the purpose of the church. There are movements in denominations in the UK which have grasped that and it's exciting to see. But I do feel that the structural problems are normally because mission is no longer seen as being what the church is about. It sometimes isn't taught that way, sometimes the teaching is that mission is central but the reality doesn't line up.

From East Africa we heard similar complaints about mission education at the local church level. This voice calls for a change, starting with the church leaders.

> **Interviewer:** You are talking about many people not understanding missions, so that still makes me wonder where is the missing link, is it teaching in church or what is it?

> **Respondent:** I think they need to, church education needs to take place, so that people, starting with the leaders, the pastors, they need to understand what missions is.

The longing for better mission education in the church, encouraged by leaders of the church is obvious in our data. That lack of it was clearly expressed by our mission-active respondents as frustration. Such frustration will not be readily eased because the idea of mission can threaten the comfort levels of a congregation. As we noted in chapter two, Christians can resist being inconvenienced and mission involvement has a tendency to interrupt this world's wonderful plans for your life. Nevertheless, as the East Asian promoter of mission persisted with their elders, we encourage others to gracefully persist with encouraging a better understanding of mission, via appropriate training, within their Christian communities.

A need for *appropriate* training was evidently desired by missionaries, mission agencies, and mission recruiters seeking to facilitate prospective missionaries into mission service. One South American missionary told us, "We both desire and promote a lot the training of young people with a missionary calling," but as our voices above pointed out, sometimes the training provided is not adequate for the tasks the trainees find themselves doing. They can too easily end up unhelpfully involved in mission in ways the East Asian mission leader described as "more trouble than contribution."

It is in the best interest of the evangelical missions community to ensure that mission training is relevant for the global context in which missionaries find themselves ministering and appropriate for the competencies needed for mission today. We have seen how academic institutions can struggle to adapt to contemporary needs and that churches can too easily ignore teaching about mission altogether. Christians also receive mission education in the context of courses and conferences. However, if that is the only education future missionaries receive should we be concerned? Should we keep the East Asian mission leader's voice echoing in the background, "Such people make more trouble than contribution"?

Courses and Conferences

A number of our respondents spoke favorably of specific courses utilized by various mission organizations. The most prominently mentioned were versions of the *Perspectives on the World Christian Movement* course (using the official US Study Guide designed and edited by Ralph Winter and Steve Hawthorne, as well as a modified South Pacific guide, popular in Oceania among other places) and the much more condensed *Kairos* course (developed by Max Chismon) originally derived from *Perspectives* material.[2] Other courses specific to an organization or church were mentioned at times as well.

A mission mobilizer from Oceania who teaches the South Pacific version of the *Perspectives* course described it as "way ahead" of other mission-oriented courses and in their experience it produced a life-change in many of the students who have gone on into career mission service,

> A lot of them came in without any real interest or desire, but just thought it's a course worth doing, and have gone further on; and it's taken them, you know, just wherever God wants them in the mission realm.

A mobilizer from the United Kingdom told us that the *Kairos* course, which they described as "the old condensed *Perspectives* course" was becoming "increasingly important." They described *Kairos* as "a course thinking about mission in a slightly more reasoned and filled out way" and likened its style and format to that of the *Alpha* course but with a mission emphasis. These examples indicate the potential value of preservice training and education, at an exposure level anyway. Courses such as these provide an opportunity for awakening Christians to their mission-related responsibility and some awareness of the opportunities available for them to engage in mission service.

While mission courses can be effective catalysts for mission involvement they can suffer from lack of demand. Those who run the courses still need to attract people to the course, whether through clever promotion or the recommendation of enthusiasts who have had their lives changed by the course. This leads us to what we consider to be *the mobilizer's dilemma;* how do you capture Christians' interest in such a way as to reorient their view of the world and God's purposes for us in it for the cause of mission? The courses mentioned seek to achieve this in different ways, but the overwhelming majority of our respondents pointed to a different experience as being far more effective at birthing an interest in mission—the Christian conference.

The mobilizer's dilemma; how do you capture Christians' interest in such a way as to reorient their view of the world, and God's purposes for us in it, for the cause of mission?

The rest of this section will explore the conference phenomenon. As we do so, we are conscious of the relationship between the conference effect and the final theme of this *Accelerants* section. As with all our data, themes easily interact and overlap. Nevertheless, the volume of comment regarding the ability of a conference to incubate and enhance a desire to investigate mission deserves special attention as an educational subtheme.

---

2   For more concerning the *Perspectives* course see their official website: http://perpsectives.org. Jonathon Lewis' three-volume *World Mission* manual was the basis for the original versions of the *Kairos* course, however Lewis' material and approach was largely drawn from Winter and Hawthorne's work. Source: http://www.kairoscourse.org/about-kairos.

Its impact belies the length of time invested. As we saw above, taking people through a systematic course can be influential, but the conference experience seems to have a different level of dynamism.

We launch our exploration of conferences by considering why people attend, what is the attraction? Here is how one mission mobilizer in the United Kingdom described why they ended up at a mission conference, and the unexpected impact it had on them.

> There was a mission conference, and there was a (person) I liked and (the person) was going to this mission conference so I decided to go because (the person) was going. I never saw (the person) the whole of the conference but that was a minor detail because by the time I got there, there wasn't anyone other than (the person) and I who were under twenty-five. Everyone else was about thirty-five to sixty. But it felt like (a hand in) glove. I got on so well with everybody, what they were saying, what they were thinking and it was exactly as I was thinking, how I felt in terms of commitment: it was all or nothing. It was the ethos, and it was the value of prayer and obedience and sacrifice; these were the things that spoke a lot to me and that made a connection with me in regard to mission. I remember thinking—this is amazing, this fit just like a glove. I had never felt so at home, it was just incredible. I had only been a Christian for a couple of years and the thought of going to a mission conference where there were mission organizations of all sorts was strange, but it was interesting. I just loved it. That was the start for me.

Obviously not everyone attends a conference chasing a romantic interest! Our point is there are all sorts of weird and wonderful reasons why people attend conferences that have some degree of a mission component. Large gatherings have their own appeal and power to influence. As we explore the impact further, perhaps all we need to do is record this response from a missionary, also from the United Kingdom. They seem to sum up what many others observed about conferences (also called conventions or congresses). We will of course triangulate this concept with multiple voices but this testimony speaks for many of our respondents.

> I went to a Bible convention in Northern Ireland in a place called (*location name*)—(*location name*) Mission Convention—and it was there that I remember in the missionary meeting, the Lord just got a hold of my life. I was just really challenged by the reports that had been given in that meeting. I remember at the end of the meeting just praying and saying to the Lord, "My life is yours, wherever you want me to go, whatever you want me to do, I'm available." I came home from that convention to (*the UK*) and, just in my own quiet time I was reading in Jeremiah chapter one. I remember saying before I read that, I was basically praying saying, "God my life is yours but I'm only fourteen, so I'm still really very young," imagining that at some later point in life God would make his will known where he wanted me to go. Really saying, "I'm young now; show me in a few years time." That night I read Jeremiah 1 and it says "Say not I am a child,

for behold I am sending you." There are so many Scriptures but that particular chapter spoke to me; the Lord confirmed it to my heart—I knew that night that I was going to be a missionary.

Among the many remarkable things about this experience is the age of the respondent at the time—fourteen years old! The impact of the encounter they had at that conference was so significant that it set the very course of the rest of their life.

Our two United Kingdom respondents present different views of the typical age range of mission conferences and we acknowledge that there are a lot of variables involved with each of their experiences. Nevertheless, if you can get them there, the mission impact of conferences on younger people seems significant. Mention of the influence of a mission conference on teens was not limited to the United Kingdom. A South American missionary hit on it straight away.

Interviewer: What events, programs, etc., influenced you?

Respondent: Since my teenage years, the missionary conferences.

Another South American missionary shared similarly,

In my teenage years, when I was defining much of what I believe and did later, the key elements were the missionary conferences and evangelistic campaigns.

For others, an awareness of mission emerged at conferences during their late teens or twenties, most often while they were in a context of higher education. Let us hear from some in succession.

- During my junior year, I had a chance to attend an international (student) conference where I experienced the beauty of multinational worship for the first time. A friend of mine, who later became a missionary, influenced me toward mission. During my senior year, I attended Mission (*country name*) conference where I learned about the need and fact of world mission, and especially through the exposition of Colossians I decided to invest my life in what God wants—i.e., a value-driven life rather than what I want. *Mission Mobilizer in East Asia.*
- During my MSc I attended one mission conference and in that conference lot of need in the north was projected. The tentmaking concept was so much applicable to me and I felt that God called me at that time to be there as a tentmaker. So in that three-day mission conference I decided that. *Missionary, India.*
- So God actually called me for missions when I was at teacher's college … I went to a (student) conference and there were mainly mission speakers throughout the whole conference. *Missionary from Oceania.*
- When I was a second year student I went for a conference … organized by FOCUS (Fellowship of Christian Unions) in 1997 and the theme was, "Who can but speak?" And as the issues were raised as where you can speak, how you can speak. I remember one of the sessions by (*a pastor*) speaking about speaking out in the urban poor, he called it the jungle, and very challenging issues raised

for the need for involvement. And given time to reflect on what had been going on this afternoon, given time to investigate what is the deeper calling? Why has God called me? —to serve as a student. I had just been elected as a (*student ministry*) treasurer at that time; and then we went home because of a strike, but I managed to come to attend the conference and it was very challenging—that I have a responsibility to speak—and that changed how I lived. *Ministry Director in East Africa.*

- I attended a missions conference in my first year in university, and it was the decisive point of my life because in that conference I was exposed to issues in missions. Many issues, which nobody had really told me about: Christian life. So that exposure to mission issues, but specifically as a student, I was challenged on how I could see my life as a student as God's calling for me at that particular time and how I could effectively use it. *Christian Educator from East Africa.*

While it could have been placed above, as an example of the potential impact of courses, we have chosen to place this next quote from a South American missionary here because they express something that is more often experienced in a conference setting—"vision and seeds of passion for Jesus."

The seminars or missionary conferences with "workshops of awakening." It is true that a workshop does not make a missionary, but it will if the vision and seeds of passion for Jesus are sown, and this teaching tool is used with ability and good purpose. It should focus on those aspects more than in covering a lot of information or theoretical knowledge.

We like the term our interviewer translated as a "workshops of awakening." Awakening expresses well what other voices experienced in a conference setting. One of our East European voices testified to this sort of awakening at a mission conference. As a result, they are now actively engaged in promoting mission.

Four years ago I went to one of these conferences for the first time. To be honest, I'm almost ashamed to say this, I hadn't heard of these conferences until then, although it was already in its fifth year I think, or the sixth, if I remember rightly. And for me it was extraordinary to hear the information, to realize what cross-cultural missions actually means, what it means to invest the resources God has put in me—what God has invested in me—to invest that in his kingdom. I think it was the key moment of motivation and of challenge for me to find out and to offer myself for missions, and to pray for missions. At least that's all I could do at that point.

> Awakening expresses well what other voices experienced in a conference setting.

Awakening can also be described as the emergence of a vision, which is what this missionary in Eastern Europe spoke of regarding certain mission conferences.

There's been lots of missionary conferences. The Pentecostals for about four years had a partnership with the (*European country*) Pentecostal church and they did pastors' conferences for like four or five days. They had lots of high-powered foreign speakers and some (*Eastern European country*) speakers that came in. And I know that a few pastors caught a vision from that and went back and started implementing things.

A missions-promoting churchgoer in South America described their commitment to running mission conferences as a way to challenge people afresh. This could also be considered "envisioning."

> A missionary conference is organized as a special event every year where new projects are presented; we have first-hand news directly from the missionaries, people are challenged to commit with the new missions both praying and giving and getting involved as workers.

Another South American, a minister, saw such worth in these sorts of conferences that they listed them among the most significant thing their church could do for mission mobilization.

> **Interviewer:** What processes, activities, and events are significant to mobilization?
>
> **Respondent:** Carrying out missionary conferences, missionary congresses, and missionary training workshops

This is further confirmed by this missionary from South America.

> **Interviewer:** When did you make a commitment?
>
> **Respondent:** At a missionary conference where I received the calling.

And this minister in East Asia.

> Then I attended Mission (*country name*) Conference in 1992 which made me to commit myself for world mission.

As with all of our themes much more could be said but we will conclude this subsection with this voice from India who was challenged at a mission conference about their priorities in life. While it could seem a relatively small thing to others, God used a challenge of tokenism to arrest this person who went on to give themselves to lifelong missionary service.

> In one of the mission conferences in (*location name*)... I received the call of God, I know this is the voice I heard. That, "I'm not interested in your token ministry," means, you know, when we go to hotel or restaurant to eat and after eating we give some tips, the Lord said, "Whatever you have done so far is like a tip, I want you." So I responded to the call of God.

Literature

Not everyone has the luxury of access to a course or is able to attend a conference. Courses require a significant investment of time and resources to run and conferences can be even more resource-dependent to hold. But education need not be limited to life-on-life interaction, whether as a discipleship process or as part of participant learning alongside others. The desire to learn can lead us to follow myriad paths and along the way we can happen upon less personalized material that still speaks to us in holy ways.

In this section we will briefly highlight examples of non-personalized educational material that our global voices spoke of as being significant to them. You might be surprised that some of those things we mention are considered educational, but every means of delivering information has the power to add to our body of knowledge and understanding if we are willing to expose ourselves to it. The onus is then on us to discern what is relevant and what is not, and sometimes that depends on timing.

> Education need not be limited to life-on-life interaction, whether as a discipleship process or as part of participant learning alongside others. The desire to learn can lead us to follow myriad paths and along the way we can happen upon less personalized material that still speaks to us in holy ways.

For example, these two South American voices spoke concisely about the impact of non-personal information on their mission interest.

> **Interviewer:** People who influenced you?
>
> **Respondent:** My pastor, spiritual advisers, materials about missions that I started to read. *Missionary from South America.*

> **Interviewer:** What processes, activities, and events are significant to mobilization?
>
> **Respondent:** Missionary conferences, visits from missionaries, workshops, the constant preaching, and printed information so that each person can have it at home. *Pastor in South America.*

Books

Books mentioned in our data that most often influenced our respondents were true stories of missionary adventures, but other types of non-fiction were mentioned as well, particularly those that influenced people with a more strategic mind. Here are some examples.

> I could say that I began preparing before leaving in 1996—I read Hudson Taylor's biography and about the work of George Müeller and it affected me a lot. I wanted to see God at work in my life like he worked in their lives. *Missionary in Eastern Europe.*

> In some ways, being exposed to different missionary biographies, I realized God wanted me to get involved in missions. The biography of Jim Elliott was a tool

that got used for me to get involved in missions. *Another Missionary in Eastern Europe.*

Back when I was a student I was training at university doing a degree in land surveying, and during those years just a real strong sense, two or three prophesies, but really something developing inside … I was absolutely taken every time I read anything by Brother Andrew in a book. I don't read much, but every time, still the same thing applies, every time I pick up one of his books I'm consumed I can't put it down. And just, in his terms I guess, a heart for the suffering church. And then just a sense of maybe being able to outwork that somehow in the nations. *Former Missionary, now Mobilizer from Oceania.*

I think that mostly I was motivated by books. I read about pioneer work. Even when I was young I read missionary biographies and I, I think that motivated me from when I was very young. *Mission Mobilizer from Eastern Europe.*

I was very blessed through reading the Amy Carmichael book called *God's Missionary*, and she spoke about missionaries who came. Some of the early missionaries used to be very official, think they were very special and they used to put Indians at a distance, and she spoke very clearly that we should not do that, we should be one with the people and love the people and move with them very freely. *Missionary in India.*

I was hospitalized for six months. There I came across this small booklet titled *Pineapple Farm*, which directed my sight to world mission for the first time. That booklet turned out to be God's clear call to missions. Thereafter I've never looked back or doubted about my commitment to world mission. *Missionary in East Asia.*

I've also read lots of books about missionaries who went to dry places. One of the books I read was *Afghanistan—My Tears*. It made me see people's need for God. And see this through their wild behavior. *Missionary from Eastern Europe.*

Interviewer: Who, what, or which, was the factor that influenced you in your commitment to missions in general and then to your current ministry?

Respondent: It was God's dealing with us through the book *Prioridad Uno*. This was the beginning of our ministry. *Missionary from South America.*

I listened to missionaries, I read books about missionaries, I studied strategies, etc. *Missionary from South America.*

God put a burden in me, but when I was (about sixteen) there was a team from the OM ship who came to my school and my church. On both occasions I was very challenged by the young people who had evidently given up a lot to follow Christ. George Verwer's book *Revolution of Love* really challenged me. *Missionary in the United Kingdom.*

Magazines

Mission magazines were also influential, non-personal sources of information for some. The next respondent, a missionary from Eastern Europe, shared a particularly powerful and tragic example of the importance of magazines to those with little access to other mission training material and service opportunities. The follow-up by those referenced in the magazines could have been a little more positive, and unfortunately this missionary's story is unlikely to be an isolated case.

> Give me materials, a magazine, something! I want to go but I don't know anything. I don't know how to start; I don't know what to do. Nobody in my country is helping me, nobody knows anything. And they sent me magazines, and brought them for me from England. Someone brought me a load of magazines. I looked, and I started to write to all that I saw there. "I want to go to Africa but I don't know what to do … tell me, can I go with you? Can you help?" And only two or three answered. "We're sorry, we're merging with others. … We can't do anything at the moment. The Lord help you."

What follows are some other examples of magazine use.

> I became involved in missions because of some information in (a) magazine which is about involvement in world mission, and I got information from there, information about the mission school, because I was interested in missions. *Missionary in South America.*

> I used to read a lot of magazines published by (*organization name*). I began to have a burden to pray for missionaries, to raise funds. Most missionaries struggle for even basic needs because they are not paid well by missions. So that is how I started to get a burden where I need to do something for the missionaries; that is how I got into missions. *Minister in India.*

> And I enjoyed reading periodical magazines published by mission agencies such as (*organization name*) and (*organization name*) which further directed me to mission. *Missionary from East Asia.*

> My (spouse) had been receiving monthly publication by (*organization name*) since 1985; a Christian colleague used to encourage me to consider Bible translation; and I was deeply impressed by editor's columns of (*organization name*) monthly magazine. *Missionary from East Asia.*

We conclude this brief mention of magazines with quotes from two different mission mobilizers ministering in the United Kingdom. The quotes did not specifically deal with the outcome of magazines for mission, but they did indicate the potential that mission recruiters see in magazines to cross-pollinate stories that can make an impact for mission.

> My biggest issue is how can I help the churches who are not connected with us and have got to work with other networks, which are more church networks, to

actually see the fantastic stories that there are; and I would like to see magazines like (*magazine name*) going into every single Christian's hand in this country, possibly with better stories of how churches are doing things, not just how agencies are doing things within the missional lifestyle.

We advertise (*course name*) in our magazine, so people who already feel that they identify with (*organization name*) are reading about that course. We try to advertise it a lot in the magazine and make a big thing of it so we get people who are already interested or praying and try to draw them in further, using that.

Promotional material

The previous quote serves as a bridge between sections. Non-personal information is rarely neutral. Books and biographies are more often than not published to promote the work of a particular organization through the life story of its founder or some other impactful example; and magazines are produced to promote the work of a specific organization or network, or to promote the ideas of one particular way of looking at mission. One way or another missions publications involve advertising. We touched on marketing techniques in our chapter on "Creating Mission Momentum" and the effects of those techniques are illustrated next by a few diverse examples.

Note the variety in means of promotion, whether real or desired, referenced by our global voices: email, word of mouth, electronic documents (PDFs), printed booklets, etc., as illustrative of the relational mobilization ideal-type. We include this Indian missionary again because they also mentioned a few promotional devices.

Awareness is definitely a must. To build up awareness, we need to use technology, teaching, writings, the visual media. (But) it's hard-core spending of time with people for nurturing into direct mission work … that's what we need to do for people who are willing to give their lives to missions. *Missionary from India.*

Interviewer: How do people hear about this? Is it again through the churches?

Respondent: Yes, we send out invitations to all the email contacts we have; we talk about it in presentations; we try to get people through the contacts we have in Bible schools and in churches to put up posters so people can read about it. People talk about it and tell others. In 2006 when we organized it we did very, very little about making it known basically. We sent out this invitation to all the email contacts we had. There was no advertising really done in any magazine or anything. We had twenty-five participants, paying participants because it's not free. So that was very encouraging. *Mission Mobilizer in Eastern Europe.*

There is a lot of literature on theological training in missions but so little practice. A digital publisher should be developed in order to distribute materials in PDF format created by "anonymous Latin Americans" who are working in missionary mobilization from local churches. There are unknown fabulous things that would be very good to share. *Mission Mobilizer in South America.*

But also I was working as a secretary in the (*organization name*) Hospital and they'd produced a booklet and it gave an outline of all the different mission organizations and the kind of people they were looking for and I went through it because I had this idea that missionaries were doctors, nurses, and teachers and that was it. And I also had the idea that most missionaries were old people, you know, very old fashioned idea because our church wasn't into missions. Then I went through that booklet and it was almost like every mission organization or about fifty percent of the book they were looking for people skilled in office work—secretaries, and I just couldn't believe it. It blew my mind. I went through the book and I circled every one. *Missionary from the United Kingdom.*

They were doing a weekend outreach in (*location name*) in evangelism, person to person involvement, and we boarded the ship; we had some time with them, we ate with them, they showed us some videos, and in one of the videos they showed us, I can't even remember the title of that video, it basically was speaking of the needs of the world, what is going on in the world, the people who are in needy places; and as I listened to that video something broke in me and that night I wept out my heart and just rededicated my life to the Lord. "God what would you want to use me to do with the area of missions reaching these people who were not yet reached?" So in that ship I bought a map of the world and I bought cards … to seventy needy nations and majority of them were Arabic countries but there were some that were not necessarily from Arabic countries, countries that were considered, so to speak, closed countries. *Minister in East Africa.*

> Artificial coloring of the narrative in promotional material or brightening the shadows (omitting important negative details) can establish unrealistic expectations in the reader and lead to much disappointment with their mission experience.

Interviewer: You've been involved in cross-cultural ministry as well; do you think that the marketing out there is an accurate representation of what missions is like?

Respondent: No. Um, I think often our marketing is too, um, self-absorbed. It's hard because you are trying to connect with your audience, but at the same time there's some realities on the ground, so bring those two together I think can be really, really difficult. And then I think often what connects with the people that we're trying to mobilize isn't actually the thing that's going to help them reach the least reached. But it might get them started. *Mobilizer in Oceania*

We deliberately closed the promotional material section with the above cautionary quote from a former missionary and current mission mobilizer in Oceania. While we agree that mission promotional material is important, the temptation to inflate stories to accentuate the positives of missionary service is great. Perhaps we should call this temptation *mobilizer's license.* Artificial coloring of the narrative in promotional material or brightening the shadows (omitting important negative details) can establish unrealistic expectations in the reader and lead to much disappointment with their mission experience.

Missionary reports

Mission promotional material is not the only medium prone to the temptation of artificial elaboration. It can happen in missionary reports as a way to encourage giving. Thankfully, most of our respondents viewed missionary reports as a positive accelerant of mission interest and involvement. Like this minister from South America who was thrilled with reports from their church's missionaries and saw them as motivating future mission interest in the church, "We have two people in different countries. And their reports are encouraging, motivating, mobilizing."

We heard this in our mobilization ideal-types exploration, but it is worth hearing again from this minister in Eastern Europe who felt that missionary reports (that show results) actually breathe.

> So there is that "breath" that comes through reports, that "breath" that comes from results. I'd say there is a very strong connection between the church which supports spiritually and materially and the people on the mission field who communicate things to the local church; concrete things, precise things, moments when they saw that the hand of God saved them—let's say—from the intention of being kidnapped, or other plans against them, very precisely at the moment the church was interceding.

We suspect the missionary reports that this missionary from East Asia responded to did not include such drama as a kidnapping or near-loss-of-life experience, but the impact was quite dramatic for them.

> I think I received the calling in two stages. The first was when I heard a missionary's report and got a burden for Africa.

These final few examples harken back to the impact of the missionary as much as the reports sent by those missionaries.

> I think that the mobilization carried out by the missionaries is the most powerful one. In fact, our strongest challenge came from the missionary's life and not by the missionary conferences we attended! Visual reports are very good and regular and fresh news too. *Mission Mobilizer in South America.*

> I can remember hearing folk coming back on furlough and talking to us about different things they were up to and how God had been working and what God was doing across a global perspective. So I suppose that I started to get an awareness and an interest in what goes on out there and how different the church might be, what God might be doing in different countries and continents. *Church Leader in the United Kingdom.*

The monthly letters of missionaries have to be shared with the congregation so they know how to respond to them. Not only the missionaries who are far away do the task, we also have the workers who work in the extension projects inside the country. *Minister in South America.*

This brings us to the end of our short survey of data that references literature as a means for educating people about mission. Books, magazines, sundry promotional material and missionary reports were the most frequently mentioned references to literature, but they represent most kinds of printed material promoting mission.

We think this is the best place to note that we were surprised by how little the Internet was spoken of by our respondents beyond the occasional mention of email or electronic documents or incidental mentions of website use. There were not enough common references to the Internet across our interview groups to make up even a microtheme. There could be a number of reasons for this, chief among them being the fact that most of our interviewers did not specifically probe the use of technology for promoting mission and educating people for mission. Instead, our aim was to invite the respondents to discuss whatever seemed relevant to them. We cannot say much more about this without speculating, but it provides a great opportunity for further research into the effects the Internet and other electronic means of education might have with regard to accelerating mission awareness. Perhaps this voice from South America will inspire further research. The late Ralph Winter would rejoice. It will help dramatize this quote for you if you add Latin linguistic flare and cultural passion to this mission mobilizer's accent.

I am a fanatic and I am very convinced in marketing. Young people today are used to see and to have everything at hand with the TV, the radio, the email, and the Internet. So we have to use all the means we have at hand because we have to reach the young. They are swimming in this world, and if they do not find anything while they swim, we lose them. We have to introduce things in this river of marketing that will be useful for them. But if they do not find it in their world, like the Internet, if they see a black and white leaflet, it will not be attractive to them. They are used to another level and we have to improve and do everything to impact them through our materials and what we can offer.

Hardship

Before we move on to the final major theme in our exploration of accelerants, we feel we must make mention of a remarkable means of mission education and mobilization that took us by surprise. This is somewhat parenthetical because this theme did not appear often in our data as an accelerant. Nevertheless, these quotes leave us with much food for thought. We are confident you will agree. They are accounts of mission learned from difficult experiences, in contexts of hardship and trial.

Our first example is voiced by a missionary from Eastern Europe speaking of doing mission under the weight of communism. The resistance they experienced only served to spur them on to engage in more mission activity.

> We did good things with our money and we were treated as if we'd done a bad thing. We went to do mission. And the spirit of adventure, the fact that … maybe if there had been freedom and they'd left us alone, maybe we wouldn't have gone, but the fact that there were restrictions fired us up, it encouraged us more. And that spirit. … it was the only thing good.

Then this church planter from India tells of their perseverance in the face of much opposition. They too were motivated by the struggles they experienced, in which they learned much. Not to be deterred they remained faithful to their calling and lived to tell this story of hope and fruitfulness born out of hardship.

> So through all these difficult times, hunger, rejection, I've been rejected back and forth and from every angle. Of course today's scenario has changed because I led all of them to Christ and I'm well respected in the family, but I went through all these struggles. So the call of God in the student conference, struggling, pain, rejection, hunger; and the third thing is ministry of winning people in the college campus and through the Bible correspondence course and in the slums of Calcutta, mobilized me. It gave me enough impetus to be motivated and to know that God has called me to do his ministry.

If mission promoters are tempted to add a little too much gloss to their stories of mission, let these voices remind them that sweetness is not the only flavor pleasing to the palate. As any chef will testify, bitter ingredients add a world of possibility to the culinary experience, tantalizing the taste buds. In keeping with this metaphor, God is the master chef of mission, mixing all manner of ingredients together to produce the most wondrous of dishes, the fruit of Christ's kingdom purposes. To God we now (finally) turn our attention.

VOCATION

Throughout our entire discussion so far God has remained somewhat in the background. We have spoken of God and God's mission, people have referenced God's influence in their lives, but it is now time to bring the triune Person to the forefront.

To this point we have only explored the machinations of men and women when it comes to promoting mission. We have acknowledged the power of personal influence from family members, individuals, missionaries, ministers, mission organization staff, and friends within mission networks. We recognized the many ways people could be educated for mission through academic institutions, courses and conferences, a variety of different printed matter, and even through hardship and trial. But our data shows that these things do not germinate, generate, initiate, or ignite a passion for mission in the hearts of those who would become involved.

Regardless of the theme in which we quoted our respondents, whenever they referenced their first awareness of mission they acknowledged God as the one who brought it about, not the means, model, method, or mechanism. Furthermore, respondents identified such moments as hearing the voice of God or the call of God or some other sort of revelation that did not originate in this terrestrial realm. God spoke. They answered.

> These things do not germinate, generate, initiate, or ignite a passion for mission in the hearts of those who would become involved.

So we arrive at the apex of our study. The most significant finding among all is that of an initial irresistible personal *calling* to pursue involvement in mission in the lives of the vast majority of the people we interviewed. From this sense of calling we have chosen our (English) title for this theme, *vocation*. As many will know, vocation is derived from the Latin *vocare*, which means *to call*, which has its roots in the word *vox*, meaning voice.

While this title may suggest a fully formed sense of calling, what we noticed in our data was that the call expressed by our respondents was always *nascent*. In other words, it was initially undeveloped with regard to the logistics of how such a call would come to pass, and yet perception of God's voice held great potential for future service for our respondents when they heard it. It was this genesis sense of call that propelled our respondents to search out ways to fulfill their call; to educate themselves, to expose themselves to the many accelerants already mentioned, to satiate a desire to pursue the fullness of what God seemed to be hinting at, a deeper purpose for their lives.

This nascent *calling* can be seen as a raw, pristine conviction or desire to embark, somehow, some way, on a journey of mission involvement indicated by some sort of encounter with God. At its point of origin (or conception) this calling is most often not defined in terms of the timeframe or direct course of action necessary to achieve it. We see something like this in the life of Isaiah.

Isaiah speaks about his calling arising out of a powerful vision of God, followed by a conversation with God. God asks, "Whom shall I send? And who will go for us?" to which Isaiah responds, "Here am I. Send me!" So God commissions him, "Go and tell this people" (Isaiah 6:8). We are not certain how much time passed before Isaiah commenced his commissioned task but we do know that he received this particular calling the year that King Uzziah died (Isaiah 6:1) and the event immediately following his commissioning was when Uzziah's grandson Ahaz marched against Jerusalem (Isaiah 7:1). For reasons best debated among theological scholars, one whole generation is skipped. For us, this suggests time spent developing his calling.

> This nascent *calling* can be seen as a raw, pristine conviction or desire to embark, somehow, some way, on a journey of mission involvement indicated by some sort of encounter with God.

From the very start of our research project we desired to listen to voices from around the globe and hear their diverse opinions about what helps people become interested in mission. More importantly we wanted to know what *worked* for them personally. Our voices testified to the One Voice as their biggest influence and we must not take this lightly. When we look at Scripture we see only one clear *strategy* for sending out laborers into the Lord's harvest fields. God's voice cannot be commoditized and marketed, although some try. God's voice cannot be replicated in such a way as to influence people into mission. God's voice cannot be manipulated into speaking—or can it?

Isaiah's call resonates through Matthew 9:37–38 and Luke 10:2. Matthew records Jesus as saying,

> The harvest is plentiful but the workers are few. Ask the Lord of the harvest, therefore, to send out workers into the Lord's harvest field. (Matthew 9:37–38)

Those seeking to influence people toward greater mission involvement know these verses very well. Yet we so easily fail to see the way Jesus expects the Lord of the harvest to be encouraged to speak (as indicated by Isaiah's sending experience) and send, cast, throw, thrust, catapult out workers. We do not for a second believe we can manipulate God to do anything, but on several occasions (Matthew 9:37–38, Luke 10:2, Luke 11:5–12, and Luke 18:1–5 for example) Jesus certainly points to persistent prayer as an effective way to gain God's attention toward action.

It is worth mentioning that while most of our respondents pointed to an encounter with God as being instrumental in their first awareness of mission, prayer, or asking the Lord of the harvest to send out workers, was not notable as a means of mobilization in our data. Because of that, we cannot explore it further as an accelerant. This is not surprising though. It is notoriously difficult to research the direct affect of prayer. As historians of revivals are wont to do, it is easy to look back on effects and point to prayer as being instrumental. But to scientifically *prove* that prayer in *this* way manifests results in *that* way is not something that we are aware has ever been successfully undertaken, especially with regard to mission mobilization. We are *not* saying "prayer does not work." We are saying prayer is more the stuff of faith than science. Furthermore, if Jesus said ask, we probably should be asking.

While we cannot tell if prayer specifically influenced them, the different accounts illustrating a nascent calling suggest that their awareness of a calling was a significant formative marker in the experience of our respondents. Even if it transpired while participating in a mission-oriented activity, this point of origin for their mission interest transcended the intervention of professional mobilizers, missionaries, educators, or other external influences intended to accelerate the flame of mission passion. One East European minister even observed that "some people mobilize themselves." From the context of the interview we think the minister was observing a nascent calling emerging in others. We are not suggesting that a calling is only ever an independent supernatural event, but rather that the mechanics of an institutionalized mobilization process with its plans, systems, strategies, and devices are not, first and foremost, the mechanisms though which people are awakened to mission.

Having set the scene, it is now appropriate to hand over the stage to a sampling of our respondents and allow their voices to speak of their experience of a nascent calling.

Calling—Everyone, Wherever?

There were some conflicting perspectives regarding mission involvement that are not easily reconciled. While not explicitly referring to a call, it is implied in the references below. These global voices see mission through a very wide-angle lens and maintain that whatever a Christian does, or is called to do, is mission, and they should do it for the Lord with all their heart (cf. Colossians 3:23). The inference in these quotes is that a special calling is not necessarily required. Rather, the assumption seems to be that all Christians are called by default, as a byproduct of their following Christ, and that you will find God's will if your will is to seek God's will.

> You will find God's will if your will is to seek God's will.

This minister from the United Kingdom begins our exploration in this regard.

> There is a display board outside which talks about the world mission that we've been involved with in recent years, but the point which is made on there, that alongside this, everybody is a missionary, every Christian is a missionary, but not necessarily by getting in a boat or getting on a plane to go somewhere. We try to do both. Whether we succeed in that is a matter of debate.

In spite of referencing the need for mission organizations to assist with cross-cultural mission, this Indian mission mobilizer also believed that everyone ought to be involved in mission and mission is wherever they are.

> At least right now my own understanding is evolved over the years where now I believe that every Christian has to be involved in mission, every believer must be involved in mission. We need mission organizations because we need to help people when they move cross cultures, but I think always that the mission is whether (you're) in your own place, in the market place, in a work place, in a study place, you need to be involved in missions.

A church member in South America reiterated this sentiment; although, during the interview, they also hint at mission requiring some sort of active engagement further afield as distinct from the local setting.

> I think it is necessary to remember that all the members of the church are missionaries and that no one is exempt from the implications of this responsibility.

In contrast, another South American church member sees Jesus' command as encompassing everyone, as a command to go, not stay.

> He commands everyone and it is an order, "Go." It doesn't say, "Those who have the calling, go," or, "Those who want to go, go," but says, "Go," and whoever understands that, can go.

A concern for going

With due respect to our passionate South American friend, Jesus' command was to make disciples. The going aspect is best translated on the way or as you are going, more of an assumption than a command. Yet the idea that all are called to go persists in some mission circles, especially among mobilizers. If all are called, then all that is needed is to convince people to obey. It simplifies the mobilization task immensely. This deserves a bit of a sidebar discussion.

Back in 1984 Melody Green, wife of the late Keith Green, released an album of Keith's material that popularized the idea that, "Jesus commands us to go, it should be the exception if we stay" (from the Keith Green song, "Jesus Commands Us to Go"). Is that really true? There is plenty of biblical precedent for going or *leaving* to follow a call of God, and Jesus certainly expected his disciples to be on the move in one way or another. But if the wandering pilgrim way is supposed to be the default for all Christians there are billions who appear to be disobedient. Billions.

A recent way to try and harmonize the reality of settled Christianity with Christ's expectations is to emphasize that the *going* part is incidental. The main thing is the *doing* and whatever the doing is, it is mission. Our sample voices referenced above, prior to the final word from South America, seemed to be saying something like this.

What then are we to make of the supernatural convictions of those who claim a special call beyond that which is common to all Christians? They seem to line up more closely with the biblical precedents of the likes of Abraham, Joseph, Moses, Samuel, Isaiah, and each of the disciples who heard (or *envisioned* in Joseph and Isaiah's case) God call them to go or leave for a purpose yet to unfold. Is a dramatic supernatural call a prerequisite for specialist mission service? Is a nagging conviction sufficient? Is a cognitive understanding of the theological rationale enough? These are important questions to keep in mind as we develop the concept of vocation as it applies to mission in the rest of this section, allowing other voices to weigh in on the subject and discuss their nascent call experiences.

Calling—Overview

Once again we have only selected a sampling of voices to illustrate the phenomenon of a special or specific calling. This subsection will cover the broader territory and the following subsections look more briefly at some of the finer aspects of a calling to mission that stood out. We group the voices loosely under common microthemes. First, we note some respondents connecting their calling to full-time service. For others their calling was a gradual process as their sense of purpose unfolded over time. And yet for others, their calling was quite sudden and definite. Then we will hear from some voices that describe calling in terms of receiving specific supernatural direction. For all of them the calling was quite distinct, and it disrupted and influenced the course of the rest of their lives.

A full-time commitment

Our first contributor summed up what many of us traditionally think about a "Christian vocation," some sort of full-time ministry. This concept is now being challenged, with Christians encouraged to consider the potential of being called to all sorts of nonreligious or marketplace activities, as illustrated in our introductory subsection for this chapter. This idea is not new. Pete Hammond, et al., even compiled a book that lists books that discuss the reality of Christians in the mainstream marketplace at the turn of the century (Hammond, Stevens, and Svanoe, 2002). Nevertheless, the call to some sort of dedicated Christian ministry, set apart from the mainstream, remains strong for our respondents, as this church leader from the United Kingdom exemplified.

> I think coming back to the question that you asked me about, formulating my thoughts about where my calling might be, that was an interesting journey because I think that from fairly early on, having had a relatively dramatic conversion, I just sensed that the Lord was going to be calling (me) into some form of—I hate the expression—full-time Christian work. And so I had a second year at university as a Christian, had my third year in France when a lot of spiritual growth happened and then I came back. Entering my final year, I started thinking about what next? I realized that I had (it) still, in spite of the fact that it wasn't quite clear, that my foundation story was grace, grace, grace. There was part of me that was aware

there was a call upon my life and I knew that I had to do something about it otherwise God's not going to be pleased with me.

Several other respondents made mention of a leading toward full-time ministry in mission. This mission-interested church member from South America had been waiting a long time for that dream to be fulfilled, and at the time of the interview it was finally coming to pass.

> We have been married for thirty-three years and we knew that God was calling us full time for his kingdom since we were single. We understand that we are in the right place and time now. We depend on him and leave everything to follow him among the people of (*location name*). We are convinced of what he is expecting from us so we are looking for God's time.

Another church leader from the United Kingdom was living proof of the fulfillment of a calling that our South American friends were hoping for. This voice spoke of it as something like a dream come true.

> The Lord started to talk to me and really confirmed that there was something more he wanted me to do, but then I ran my business for two years because it just paid the bills. I really felt the Lord was going to call and when the Lord called I didn't want anything to hold me back. I wanted to just be able to close the door and go. And that's what happened but certainly there was that leading and guiding. That desire was there. I thought it would never happen yet the Lord does exceedingly, abundantly above all you ask or think. And so that's where I'm at today.

An Indian mission organization worker also referenced a call to full-time ministry and explained that it could be something unexpected and a gradual thing that unfolds as desire for a ministry grows.

> I didn't have any clue about missions at all, and I never dreamt that I would enter God's ministry full time and that it was a good fellowship to be part of, the (*group name*), and (I was) faithful in the weekly Bible study, prayer fellowship, and so on. But then, gradually, that was the Lord's doing absolutely, the desire for witnessing came. Nobody told me to go and witness. It was swelling in my heart. I went to some prison ministry. I myself went, witnessed here and there and started printing some tracts and distributing. So at some point of time whereas the burden was so clear, the call was so clear, I had to resign my job. I was teaching in a college at that time. Then I joined full-time ministry, so, it was a slow but steady process over a few years and that's how I ended up (in mission work).

A growing awareness

The gradual realization that dawned on our Indian friend was uncommon in our responses but not a completely unique experience. Here a mission organization leader in Oceania describes their awareness of God's purpose for their life as something like an ongoing revelation. We felt this sat comfortably under the category of vocation/call even if the respondent resisted defining it as such.

> I think there has always been, well since (the time of my conversion) anyway, just a sense that (pause) I knew that God was calling me to something. I didn't know what it was and to some degree I still don't know exactly what, you know what I mean? It's a journey that unfolds over time. But I think there was very much a sense of responsibility that was there from when I was young and I don't really know what brought that about. Then, maybe it's gifting, maybe it's, I don't know what it is, but I felt responsibility to my friends, and I felt responsibility to do what I could to be a positive influence. And I think one of the things that was apparent even then was a sense of being able to sort of see perhaps what needed to happen and being frustrated that other people weren't making it happen and so then making it happen, if that makes sense. Kind of the stepping in to fill a gap. Even though I wouldn't choose to do it, I kept thinking that there's got to be someone else to do it. But regularly finding that there actually wasn't anybody else so I would sort of end up filling a gap, whether or not I liked it or felt called to it, well not necessarily felt called to it, but felt gifted for it, you know?

Another Oceania respondent with a passion for promoting mission expressed the fulfillment of their calling more as an unfolding narrative, yet with a strong foundational sense of God's call.

> So yeah a number of influences, and then I think that in my teenage years there was a very strong overlap, a very strong call of God to mission. Whatever that will be, whether that is going or staying, facilitating others to go, we're still working through that one. But that's been a growing phase.

A sudden conviction

For many of our respondents the call to serve was a more dramatic and obvious affair. A cluster of responses from South American missionaries reads very decisively. The direction of call for the first missionary took an unspecified number of months to become clear but that is still a relatively short period of time.

> I made a deliberate commitment, surrendering my life to Jesus forever, making a lifelong commitment when I was fifteen years old; in the following months he showed me what he would do with my life and the nations.

For the other South American missionaries, it seemed quite a bit quicker. For these missionaries their calls were clear, personal, experiential, and direct. They were interviewed separately but each missionary was responding to the same question from the interviewer.

> **Interviewer:** What was your motivation?

Respondent 1: The Great Commission, a clear calling from God, and the certainty of the need of Jesus among European young people.

Respondent 2: The vague information I had about the need of the nations, and a personal word from God in my life about what he wanted for me in the future.

Respondent 3: A specific spiritual experience that I had as a calling from God to the missionary task in April, 1986.

Respondent 4: Through a direct calling of God to my heart.

An East Asian missionary expressed their call as coming in a compelling vision, another way of describing a sudden conviction. This was something they could not shake; it had to be fulfilled.

I was just an ordinary youth back then; life seemed to be so dull, and I vaguely thought my life would be just like any other … getting married and so on. However, after getting the vision for Africa, I couldn't think about anything else because it was so vivid and the yearning in me was so strong. I didn't know how, but I knew God would lead me to Africa.

An East Asian minister shared a similar experience. They described it as an inexplicable 180 degree turnaround orchestrated by God.

My heart was not really opened to missions. But suddenly one day, God poured a strong burden in my heart. It's very hard to tell how and why, but all I can say is it was God who gave me this heart.

This mission influencer in Oceania also experienced a sudden and compelling awareness of God's intention for their life that radically changed them and their family when they returned home (gleaned from their wider interview context).

So it's like a worship service, about four thousand people from around the world. Somewhere in the middle of that, I like to think it was in the middle of the song "How Great Thou Art," but I can't actually put a time on it; somewhere in there God just took me, "So what are you going to do about it?" It was as simple as that, and then followed a wrestle because I came home a different person.

Supernatural direction

Like so many of our themes, subthemes, and microthemes, there is considerable overlap so it is tough sometimes to determine where best to let our voices speak on a subject. This is one of those categories where quotes could be used elsewhere, but they shared a specific trait. They all illustrate quite a specific direction or leading that they attribute to God calling them. For example, this narrative from a United Kingdom respondent who became a mission mobilizer after following some very clear but supernatural direction to attend Bible college.

About a year after that I was lying in my bed. I had only been a Christian for about a year up to this point. I was lying in my bed and the words come to me about going to Bible college. I had no idea that Bible colleges really existed, none whatsoever. I was going nuts. I was hearing things and all kinds of stuff. Anyway, I never told a soul; I thought I'll send away for information. But then I went to the pastor's mid-week Bible study and asked him, "Is there such a thing as a Bible college?" For me, college was scary. I mean, I was dyslexic, though then I hadn't been diagnosed dyslexic, but I was remedial in reading and writing up until the age of thirteen and I think that was just due to the family background. It was all about survival, not about study and all that. All I could think of was Bible college—but was this right and stuff like that—books and reading, I didn't want anything to do with that. I went back to the pastor and said, "Is this possible, is there such a thing as a Bible college?" and he said that for the last six weeks he had been praying that someone would be called from the fellowship to go into full-time ministry. Well I said, "That's interesting because it's six weeks since I was in my bed and heard this voice."

> In our experience of the evangelical missions community it is quite common to hear missionaries say something to the effect of, "If you don't have a clear sense of call you'll never make it on the mission field."

This minister in East Asia has difficulty specifying how they received a call to mission but they clearly saw it as God's leading.

I never had a chance to contact a mission agency or to attend a mission-minded church. I cannot quite pinpoint, but what I can say is mission is directly related to God's call, and thus I have been led by God himself in my awareness of mission.

Another minister, from Eastern Europe, testified on behalf of someone they know concerning some very clear direction toward mission service, from a television program no less.

Respondent: For those going long term, I have seen a common trait. Firstly, there is the call of God, a very personal calling.

Interviewer: How does that manifest itself?

Respondent: God spoke to them personally. In (her) case, she had studied languages—French and English. She was studying French to get into university, and while she was watching a French television channel, she saw a program about (*country name*) and God spoke to her directly, "You are to go there." So it was a revelation from God for her, after which she began to prepare herself for it. She came to university, studied French; then she told us about this vision.

Calling—Sustaining

These clear and directive convictions are wonderful testimonies of God's divine intervention in peoples' lives. According to these next respondents such a call will hold call-recipients in good stead. In our experience of the evangelical missions community it is quite common to hear missionaries say something to the effect of, "If you don't have a clear sense of call you'll never make it on the mission field." By that we assume they mean some sort of supernatural confirmation that you are meant to be there, presumably because the mission field is hazardous. This was confirmed by our data such that it warranted hearing a sample of voices under its own specific subtheme.

We present this perspective from a senior mission leader in the United Kingdom first because in their experience prospective missionaries need to have a deep conviction about serving in mission to even make it through the pre-field screening process, let alone go the distance in cross-cultural ministry.

> **Interviewer:** You say, looking back on it now you wonder how you ever stuck it. Do you think this is something that would be off-putting for people, if they thought that level of preparation was required for someone to get into mission was too much? Could that be a real barrier to effective mobilization?
>
> **Respondent:** Yes, I do think it would be off-putting although I have to say, that's one of the great things, that you have a sense of, "God has spoken to me about this and is encouraging me in this." There is a sense in which you can take an awful lot if there is a conviction that this is God's place for me. Whether you express that in terms of a call, or in a sense of having got somewhere, having a sense of peace and knowing this is God's place. If you have got that I think it's amazing what ridiculous hurdles you will jump over because you recognize that that's God's place. Which is sort of nice because that, for me now in a senior role in missions, helps me to realize that we can really mess up the way that we deal with candidates, but the people who have got the real genuine call will probably find their way through it.

The "conviction that this is God's place for me" is echoed by this mission promoter in South America, helping them persevere.

> The main influence in my life to keep me going, despite difficulties, is to have a clear vision of what God wants to do with our lives. Being clear about God's calling for my life and about what is my ministerial calling to which God called me. Another very important thing is to know who called me and who sent me to the work and ministry. Knowing my God, Holy and powerful, more each day is what allows me to keep going.

Again from the United Kingdom, a missionary expressed the sustaining power of a "that's where you're meant to be" sense of call.

> You do need a sense of call because in the mission field—as probably in every type of Christian work—there are times when you feel like packing it in. There are tough times but if you have that sense of, "This is what the Lord has for me to do at this point in my life," that can carry you through all kinds of problems because you know that's where you're meant to be.

From East Africa we have a similar perspective as seen through the experience of a mission organization staff member. Reminiscent of Jesus' example in John 10:11–13, the ones who are called have a great deal more staying power through the difficult times than those who are hired.

> The other area is people coming into the work as a result of a call rather than an opportunity to earn a living. Those who come as a result of a call do appreciate that God has called them, they are willing to persevere and when they feel that God is calling them to something else, they will move on and move on well, in the sense that they will go through the right procedure and they are confident that this is what God is calling them to. And they are able to transit through. As opposed to that, those who come for an opportunity to make a living come and when the challenges come, they are already looking elsewhere. So they are ever on transit, there is no commitment or there is very short-term commitment.

Calling—Youth

The fact that a deep conviction of God speaking sustains missionaries and ministers in service is evident in the number of respondents who were active at the time they were interviewed as adults and spoke of receiving a call in their youth. We saw this illustrated in some of the examples of the impact of conferences. Aside from our first voice, all the other sample voices speak from India because it was such a common occurrence in that group of interviews.

This evangelist from East Africa was a young person when they felt called, and they were not even following the Lord at the time! Needless to say, it was not long before the desire to evangelize others led them to commit to following Jesus himself.

> It's interesting because I am one of those people who tell individuals that I received my call before I became saved. Many years ago, a pastor came moving around in the little town where we were staying. And he was preaching. And that is the first person I ever heard talk about salvation. I had never heard anyone talk about salvation at all. And I was so impressed by his preaching that although I was a young man and was a Catholic, going to the Catholic church, and we didn't speak salvation those days in the Catholic church. So when I heard him preaching, I said, "If I become saved, I want to be like this one." And I think a desire began developing in my heart.

Now let us hear some remarkable examples from the soil of India. Similar to the East African evangelist, the first Indian narrative is from a minister who also sensed a call to ministry prior to their awareness of a need for salvation.

> **Interviewer:** You said you knew of the calling beforehand; can you tell us a bit about that. How did you know?

Respondent: I think about my calling, (pause), I knew about it quite early in my life. Even before I made a personal commitment to God. I say this because I guess more or less in my faith in my thinking I was a Christian, although I didn't make a personal transaction with God. Going to church, to Sunday school, learning the Scripture, the stories, more or less I was living the life of a good Christian. In school, even my teachers liked me. Around the time I was in my third standard (primary school), our family was large, about six brothers and two sisters. We'd sit in a circle for reading the Scripture together; each one of us would read verse by verse and do a whole chapter. So around the time when I was in the third standard, I had not been reading, I was too small to read so my father said, "Now you're in the third standard and you can read, you should read, you have difficulties your brothers will help you." That day when I started reading with my family, the chapter was Jeremiah chapter one and when my turn came it was verse five. I knew when I read it that God was speaking to me, because I knew the stories, I knew how God speaks to people, I knew about the ministry—I was going to a good Bible believing church, so when I read it, I knew that God was saying something to me. Although I did not understand everything in that verse, whenever I read anything in the Bible, I would look at that verse, but when I committed my life to the Lord, I was in the ninth standard (high school), the first thought that entered my mind was that what had happened in the third standard, what had happened and how I felt the Lord calling me to be a preacher of the word of God. So that was settled.

This next missionary in India was a child when they sensed something of a call, evidenced by the burden they carried to bring people to Jesus.

I had a longing to be a missionary because I had a burden for bringing souls to Christ so it was in me from a small child.

Calling—Interconnected

Rarely is a call an isolated event. Unlike Moses at the burning bush, a calling tends to interconnect with the context in which it happens and there are usually other influences around. Some people can track elements that converged to create a calling, for others it was more of a sudden awareness. Here we highlight some factors that appeared to be intertwined with the respondents' awareness of a calling.

As illustrated above, it is not uncommon for a calling to ministry to coincide with a commitment to Christ. As this Indian mission worker testified,

Then one day when I attended my church in the evening service there was a gospel preached so at that time I felt God was calling me for ministry as well as that I should commit my life, confess my sins, surrender my life to Christ. So I accepted Jesus on that day.

It is only right to acknowledge once more the impact of family members on a calling to mission service. Growing up under missionary parents helped develop the calling of this missionary to South America.

> I got involved because I had the calling to missions since I was little, through a specific word of God to me, and through the example of my parents, who served as national missionaries in (*country name*) in the 80s.

We have also already explored the potent effects of unrelated missionaries on the mission involvement of others. Here another missionary voice out of South America described the impact of other missionaries and mission awareness alongside a very certain "divine calling."

> **Interviewer:** What was your motivation?
>
> **Respondent:** The certainty of a divine calling. The example of other missionaries. Knowing the reality about the unreached peoples. Being in the missionary field and seeing how God works.

Rarely is a call an isolated event. Unlike Moses at the burning bush, a calling tends to interconnect with the context in which it happens and there are usually other influences around.

Sometimes though, a supernatural call is connected to an unexpected supernatural occurrence. This missionary from East Asia, not given to fancies of supernaturalism, was deeply impacted by a vivid dream.

> The other factor may sound rather strange, but I had a dream about (*East Asian country*). I am not a kind of person relying on dreams, but while being trained by the (*organization name*) I had a very clear dream, like Paul's Macedonian call, in which a poor (*name of country*) family implored me to come and help them. That's how I began my journey to missions. So I started with spiritual formation by the (*organization name*), taking discipleship training and practicing it, which I think was foundational for my future missionary work.

The Holy Spirit

At the start of this section we promised to turn your attention to God, to bring the triune Person to the forefront. We hope you at least saw God's fingerprints on the testimonies of calling experiences we chose to include. God loves to reveal themselves to us (yes, we are using the plural pronoun for God too, following some the Old Testament examples). Along with most other Christians, the World Evangelical Alliance and its Mission Commission commonly believes in the triune nature of God in three persons as: Father, Son, and Holy Spirit. So it is appropriate that we conclude this section on vocation by providing examples that specifically mention the One doing the calling.

To avoid muddy theological debates, we will unequivocally say that God calls in whatever way God chooses. However, many of our respondents specifically referenced the Holy

Spirit as God manifest in their particular experience so we grouped a sampling of those voices into this final subtheme.

Our next respondent, a minister in Eastern Europe, is another of the rare ones that referenced prayer in connection with mobilization. We could not pull together a subtheme on prayer but we are certainly glad that those that mentioned it are able to voice their experience of the Lord through prayer in this section.

> It was amazing to see that the Spirit of the Lord laid it on the heart of someone in the church to call people to prayer. Sure, we've had situations that have really encouraged us in this way. And that mobilizes the church. There is a communication of the Spirit, which encourages, which mobilizes the church.

A missionary from Oceania also referenced prayer, not directly connected with their calling, but it undoubtedly contributed to their openness to hearing from God. Their experience of the Spirit of God with regard to mission awareness came while participating in a mission-oriented course.

We will unequivocally say that God calls, in whatever way God chooses. However, many of our respondents specifically referenced the Holy Spirit as God manifest in their particular experience.

> Then I was involved in a prayer group and at a study, the *Perspectives* course, which really I suppose opened up my mind to the whole mandate of missions from the Scriptures and also the awareness of the less reached areas of the world and unreached people groups and the 10/40 window and just God's heart for all peoples. You know, Abraham was blessed to be a blessing to the nations, so it was just, it was sort of like the light switch went on. I'd had all this background before but maybe it was just the Spirit of God, maybe just woke me up, to the reality of it.

The Oceania missionary's experience of God's revelation would not be surprising to this next minister in South America. As far as they were concerned, such encounters with the Holy Spirit are just "Jesus' style."

> The best way to mobilize is to wait for the Holy Spirit to show the appropriate time. Not before or after. We have to do it in Jesus' style.

Waiting for the Holy Spirit to move is the default expectation of this mission organization staff member in Eastern Europe. They believed a Holy Spirit conviction was important to mobilize the young people they were involved with.

> The Holy Spirit is the one who convicts. I helped them to do this short-term trip with that conviction—in his gentle way the Holy Spirit will break through and convince them. I am especially involved in mobilizing young people in missions.

The Holy Spirit is not only credited with influencing people to move, but also influencing people to support. This local church mission team member in the United Kingdom recalled the guidance of the Spirit in encouraging their church at the time to adopt a missionary.

Well, purely under the guidance of the Holy Spirit (I) thought, "Oh yes that looks interesting—I'll send them an email and introduce myself," and say, "I'm developing a world mission activity within, whichever church it happened to be, and we'd like to adopt you. Do you send out newsletters or prayer letters? When were you last home? Who's your main supporting church? How can we get in contact with you and when are you coming home again?"

> Whichever way you choose to define or explain it, remaining connected to God is clearly a prerequisite for people who desire to be fruitfully involved in mission.

Lastly, from their experience, a missionary from East Asia recommended regular experiences of renewal by the Spirit as a necessary part of sustaining oneself in mission service.

I would not call it a second baptism or Spirit baptism, but to experience the presence and renewal of the Holy Spirit day by day, moment by moment, I think, is the most important impact that makes you a true missionary. That and that only enables you to do the work of mission as a humble servant, spiritual power supplied from above.

Whichever way you choose to define or explain it, according to many of our global voices remaining connected to God is clearly a prerequisite for people who desire to be fruitfully involved in mission.

PART FOUR: SUMMARY

Seeded throughout the record of our global voices were their lived experiences that fairly clearly pointed toward dominant themes. Regarding our particular concern for what promoted mission involvement, two very obvious themes emerged: the prominence of interpersonal relationships and the positive effects of education on respondents' awareness of mission.

As data became apparent for what was to become chapter fourteen, it was a surprise for some of us to see familial relationships feature so notably, but we did not have to think long about our own spheres of mission to confirm how influential families actually were. As with so many of our themes, the influence of family overlapped with that of missionaries and other mission-related influencers. The benefit of a family relationship is that it can provide a context for prolonged exposure to mission. A family that already has an appreciation for mission may be a great incubator of mission interest, but it will also provide tremendous support as that mission interest grows and flourishes. We saw this effect particularly with spousal influence.

Outside of the bounds of family, other influential relationships were identified in chapter fifteen. The most potent seemed to be the mission-interested individual who came alongside others to encourage mission interest, inviting novices to deeper involvement. Missionaries could be particularly inspiring through their faith, commitment, and testimonies of God's faithfulness. People who remained exposed to missionary communications were likely to grow in their appreciation of mission. Ministers who released people to pursue mission interest were also influential, particularly those who were able to recognize the potential for mission in others and encourage them to persevere.

To a lesser degree, networks could be helpful for promoting mission awareness and interest. They were seen to have some potential to influence other influencers (ministers, for example) and also provide resources to add fuel to mission's flame. Mission organizations could do that too, and once an inquirer had established a relationship with a mission organization, caring personnel were known to provide great support and inspiration to potential future missionaries (closely related to the individuals and missionaries as influencers subthemes).

The educational theme explored in chapter sixteen incorporated multiple aspects of mission promotion, the common element being the way the educational devices facilitated learning. Academic institutions could foster mission interest, but some also were considered to be bastions of out-of-date thinking about mission, or omitting mission studies from their curriculum altogether. The local church was also deemed to be an obvious context for learning about mission, through church-based education. But many of our respondents were of the opinion that churches failed to realize this potential. Nevertheless, even the negative responses revealed how a local church could accelerate mission involvement if it so desired.

After a brief exploration of some sample mission courses that were considered to be effective in mobilizing for mission, we noticed that many of our global voices held conferences in high regard. We connected this with our final accelerant theme and noted the dynamic influence that a big event can have on a person's openness to God's voice with regard to mission service.

Since the invention of the printing press, literature has been used to influence the mind of the church. Printed matter has been no less influential from the birth of the modern mission movement, and until very recently information has been most easily disseminated in printed form. Information carries ideas and ideas can influence. We listed a whole string of literary devices along with sample quotes from our data. Worthy of particular note is the missionary biography or other narratives from the place of mission. These can be as potent as a personal relationship with a missionary in influencing people toward mission. At the end of the book we will discuss the power of mission-related stories again, to recommend them as potent accelerants. To lesser degrees magazines, promotional material, and missionary reports were mentioned. We also note that the Internet was not often mentioned as a means of information dissemination and mission education, and we posited some thoughts regarding this.

Before we launched into the climactic chapter of our book we took a brief look at the curious educational worth of tough experiences as a mission accelerant, propelling mission interest against the tide of resistance that some respondents faced.

In chapter seventeen we unveiled the primary influence toward mission involvement according to the bulk of our respondents. Unequivocally, the ignition of mission interest, the initial accelerant, was the voice of God calling people in and on to some form of mission involvement. Where other accelerants helped boost the flame of mission interest, the call of God was clearly the spark, the catalyst that set people on a path toward greater involvement in mission. While some respondents argued that all Christians have a call by default (whether they realize it or not), the majority of our respondents articulated that it was instead an unusually powerful occurrence or supernatural influence in their lives.

> Unequivocally, the ignition of mission interest, the initial accelerant, was the voice of God calling people in and on to some form of mission involvement.

We noted that the call does not often come fully formed, but is most commonly nascent. It requires further development, which other accelerants can definitely assist. The genesis of call is experienced as something other, outside of a person's normal realm of experience, so much so that it is identified as an encounter with God that has dynamic potential to be quite directive regardless of how formed it may or may not be.

We looked at the attributes of a call in general and then the sustaining power of a call in mission service. Age seemed to pose no barrier. We observed many respondents receiving a call in their youth or as young adults. Some experienced a sense of call before they had even committed to following Christ, and we observed how the call is often connected to many other influences previously identified.

Chapter seventeen and this entire section concluded with an encouragement to turn our eyes to God and acknowledge the Holy Spirit's influence in all that we call mission, particularly in leading us to greater involvement in mission and providing the impetus to pray for mission.

Questions for Reflection

1. What aspects of our dominant themes stand out to you as major influences for mission in your context? Which ones have influenced your mission journey?
2. How would your preference for a particular mobilization ideal-type affect your prioritizing of mission accelerants described in this chapter? What can you learn from our global voices to strengthen the mobilization aspects of your ministry?
3. What areas of mission education can you influence for improvement? Consider the issue of attendance. How would you attract people to some sort of mission education context (e.g., a conference, course, small group study, etc.)?
4. Did the concept of a call resonate with your experience? If so, in what ways?
5. The recognition of a nascent call in our data raises a lot of potential questions. Here are some you might like to reflect on:
   - Is a specialist calling necessary or just extra helpful?
   - In what ways could a deep sense of conviction to some sort of mission involvement help missionaries remain resilient in their contexts?
   - Does a call expire? If so, could that explain why missionaries leave mission-oriented ministry? How else could the transition from active service back to normal life be explained?
   - Have humanitarian ideals and easy access to mission fields made it easier for people to go without a call?
   - How do you think the genuine nature of a call can be effectively assessed? Are there learned ways to discern whether the talk of a call is a convenience or a conviction?
   - In what ways can we equip local churches and mission organizations to train congregants and applicants to better understand the phenomenon of a call?
   - What could it suggest if mission organizations do not have mechanisms to assess an applicant's call as part of a selection process to evaluate their suitability for service?
   - If a call is the surest way to influence people to become involved in mission service, how should a mission mobilizer best invest their time?

PART FIVE: RETARDANTS

Do not put out the Spirit's fire. (1 Thessalonians 5:19)

The metaphor enveloping our presentation of global voices has been one of fire. In many cultures fire is poetically connected with deep emotion, with passion, whether positive—an intense desire for something or someone, or negative—a violent rage against something. Fire is similarly used in the Bible as a means of God's wrath (e.g., Deuteronomy 32:22) or holy purification (e.g., Matthew 3:11–12).

Considering the supernatural manner by which our respondents were called into their mission involvement and the work of the Holy Spirit implied by that, the verse from First Thessalonians quoted above stands as a stern warning. We ought not intentionally quench the Holy Spirit's fire.

Although the objective of our research project was to explore why people *became* involved in mission service, the nature of the research method was such that our conversations developed in organic ways to reveal themes the respondents were passionate about within the overall subject under discussion. Therefore, not surprisingly, our data revealed a lot about what retarded the fire for mission along with what accelerated it.

Discussions around the subject of money were easy to collect. These are discussed in chapter eighteen. Some of our data was encouraging but the bulk of the comments directed the subject of funding to our *Retardants* section. Respondents had a variety of different opinions on the subject, ranging from problems with too much money to problems with not enough. We deliberately conclude the chapter with encouraging evidence of God's wonderful provision.

The next most popular subject that seemed to create barriers to mission service was that of the mission organization. In chapter nineteen we will find again that the responses ranged from too much of something to not enough. In this case it is organizational infrastructure. Apparently it is difficult to strike a happy medium of screening, selection, systems, and support. Respondents, particularly from traditional sending nations, expressed frustration with policies and practices that hindered mission advance. We are also surprised by mention of mission organization personnel contributing resistance to people trying to engage in mission. At the other end of the infrastructure debate were voices from new sending nations that commented on the lack of support structures in their contexts. The chapter concludes with a commentary regarding the commercialization of mission promotion.

A popular idiom in the English-speaking world refers to "the elephant in the room." This means that something is obvious to everyone but no one wants to talk about. Usually, if tension is tangible enough at a gathering some brave soul will venture, "OK, so, shall we talk about the elephant in the room?" in the hope that the thing creating tension can be discussed and resolved. Chapter twenty on gender does just that. Throughout our data, gender bias was a significant elephant in the room and we dared to go there. Understandably, a lot of our data is from a female perspective. This is the one chapter in the book where issues of power and control in mission are explored more overtly.

> Gender bias was a significant elephant in the room and we dared to go there.

Chapter twenty-one deals with discouragement from where we normally least expect it, the church, and then touches on various frustrations arising out of our sending contexts, which in some ways brings us back full circle to Bosch, since the issues of secularism, individualism, prosperity, and time resonate with the factors that manifest as a crisis in mission.

The final chapter of this section lifts us above our circumstances once more. The voices in chapter twenty-two help us realize that whatever retardants we are wrestling, they are not of this world. This chapter mirrors chapter seventeen, which concluded our *Accelerants* section, in reminding us that mission is God's domain and that Lord of the harvest will ensure the harvest comes in.

CHAPTER 18

FUNDING

Can you be a missionary without any money? No you cannot. We all need some form of income to survive. As we have already encountered, there is a belief that you can be a missionary anywhere, including the business world, but even there you are raising funds, you are just using your marketable skills to do it.

Some might argue that a subsistence lifestyle does not need funding, but those limited to a subsistence lifestyle rarely have the luxury of engaging in what many of us would consider to be mission work. For those desiring to be self-supporting in mission it can be difficult to find time alongside their income generating activities to engage in mission activity, even if the location of that activity is their workplace. The days of Paul working and possibly ministering from Aquila and Priscilla's tent repair center are long behind most of us. Making a living outside of our native boundaries is a very difficult and complex exercise, particularly if permanent emigration is not intended. There is one model of mission without money that is considerably more prevalent in the New Testament than tentmaking and that is imprisonment, but we are unlikely to mobilize many for that method of mission.

> There is one model of mission without money that is considerably more prevalent in the New Testament than tentmaking and that is imprisonment, but we are unlikely to mobilize many for that method of mission.

Current evangelical philosophies of mission are still predominantly still linked to a colonial paradigm, but the *modern missionary movement* that points back to the Moravians and William Carey draws on a much more ancient tradition of sacred service assigned to set-apart specialists. It is popular and right to play down the false dualism between sacred and secular these days, but to deny the possibility of consecrated service is to throw the baby out with the bathwater. There is rich biblical and historical precedent for a special commission that is supported by communities of faith. It is beyond the bounds of our study to explore that further but it undergirds the principles of missionary funding we will discuss in this chapter.

Finance is a vexing subject for mission and ministry. The gospels record Jesus saying much more concerning money than he did about sexual infidelity.[1] Everyone has their

---

1   Scott Bssenecker writes,
"Jesus warned against the corrupting power of wealth and possessions in the gospels five times more than he addressed the issue of sex outside of marriage. I count seven passages in the gospels where Jesus warns against sexual infidelity. I believe these warnings to be appropriate and critical to our spiritual

own opinions about the source and use of money and we cannot address them all here. Instead, we have selected some voices that represent opinions that were well supported in our data.

It is for good reason that the issue of funding is discussed in the *Retardants* section. So much of mission's potential rests on the wise application of finance. If it is lacking, or if it is misapplied, mission suffers. Thankfully our global voices spoke of wonderful provision as well as woeful poverty, and many of them saw the two extremes hinge on the generosity of the local church.

Churches

What image does the word *church* conjure in your mind? For most it will be something institutional even though many of us want to believe it is much more communal, organic, and body-like. At base, a local expression of church is a community of people *called out* to worship God together, to love one another and to support one another as we love our neighbors. Every community of Christ-followers is a variation on this theme with many nuances of difference.

It should not be surprising then to discover variety in our references to churches regarding the use of money. Christians pool funds for the common good in churches, and then distribute those funds according to a mutually agreed value system—at least in theory.

Generosity

We were delighted to hear reports of churches that were very financially supportive of mission. When a community of faith catches a vision for the wider world it is remarkable what resources can be found to bring that vision to fruition. These South American ministers affirm this.

> **Interviewer:** What about people, finances, and prayer?
>
> **Respondent 1:** If the question refers to people inside the church, I say that people respond to the ministry and to the vision if we involve them with transparency and respect.
>
> **Respondent 2:** People respond partially and gradually, but progress can be made. If the projects are good and if we can sell them, the finances can be obtained.

Do not be put off by the reference to selling. Every leader who casts a vision effectively has to sell it to their followers. It involves creating a desire that will illicit action toward

---

health. But Jesus' concern for his followers' spiritual health was most often and most clearly expressed when he warned them about their relationship with possessions and money. The love of money is infidelity toward God. You might say that Jesus was more concerned about how his disciples misused their coins than how they misused their loins. Fidelity to God and his kingdom is best measured in our affections for the material world." (Bessenecker, 2014, 80)

a goal. In the marketplace that is the goal of transferring goods or services for money. In ministry and mission, the goal is usually something with eternal value. Our next voice, a South American mobilizer, must have a compelling vision because their church has been very generous. Their experience encouraged them to mention another topic that is important for us to consider.

> A local expression of church is a community of people *called out* to worship God together, to love one another and to support one another as we love our neighbors. Every community of Christ-followers is a variation on this theme with many nuances of difference.

It is always thought that there are no finances for that kind of ministry or that it is necessary to turn to our Anglo-Saxon benefactors. Personally, I have devoted at least fifteen years of my ministry to mobilization and my own church has paid the bill, and other churches from (*my own country*). In a few words, it is possible.

Along with the ministers, this mobilizer shares the belief that it is possible to raise money for mobilization and mission from within local contexts outside of the "Anglo-Saxon" (or Western) world. We will look at this from an educational perspective in a moment. In the meantime, a minister of a mission-supporting church in Eastern Europe would agree that raising funds within one's own nation is possible, but they added a dose of reality from their perspective—it is not easy.

Financially, of course it hasn't been easy. But neither have there been big obstacles, which would make it necessary for us to bring the missionaries home. Yes, God has provided and we've had lots of these kind of experiences. Once when certain missionaries needed more money than usual one month, we told the church. I was desperate. I didn't know for sure whether I would find the money. I told the church and there were people who made donations immediately. "OK, no problem, we'll give." So there haven't been financial blockages.

We imagine this East European church would struggle if such requests were to be a regular occurrence. This missionary from East Asia was sent from a church that was not able to provide a lot of financial support, but that is not the only kind of support missionaries require.

My (spouse) took discipleship training at this church during (their) high school years and both of us served this church from our college years. We had established an intimate relationship with this church for ten plus years, so missions partnership came very naturally. Being a small church, they cannot support a lot financially. But since they know us intimately, they have supported and prayed for us faithfully for many years. We try to be very careful not to put a heavy financial burden on them. Several other churches have come alongside, sharing the financial responsibility.

Thankfully they have enjoyed the support of multiple churches who together share the financial responsibility. This was the experience of a South American missionary as well.

Financial support for our family came almost exclusively from churches in (*South American nation name*). Which means that this is possible to do. We were never left in lack of something. Even when we had to go through surgeries and unforeseen situations, new offerings would cover the expenses we had. God is faithful. But I can also say that the (*South American nation*) church was faithful.

The emergency health needs of a missionary, the desperate needs of the poor or some other crisis can motivate people to give spontaneously. This is a type of vision casting that can be relatively easy to respond to. God's people can be very generous in times of need. A church leader from the United Kingdom observed this but warned that it can be something of an excuse against committing further.

> **Respondent:** Inevitably, looking at the congregation as a whole, there are some who are happy to pray about it, some who dip their hands in their pockets, but actually it's the thoughts or the sense that they might be the ones who are sent out that is far from their minds. I think one of the things that is an ongoing challenge in Christian ministry is that often it's the easiest thing in the world to put our hands in our pockets and assume we've done our bit, but the harder task, and I would say the more rewarding task, is to actually go out there and take a more personal interest in what's going on.

> **Interviewer:** How do you make decisions about giving financial assistance to people that want to engage in mission? Do you have a system by which people get a certain amount in proportion to what they need, or depending on their circumstances?

> **Respondent:** Until about a year or so ago, it was very ad hoc. We hear that so and so would want to go to wherever and we would come up with a figure. Now, in an attempt to try and formalize it a bit and to try and be more predictable, and I suppose more financially manageable, we say to any of our people who go to write to the leadership giving details of what they are doing, why they are doing it, and what they are looking to receive from God in it, and how much it costs. We will then, as a leadership team, decide how best we can help them alongside pointing them to other local charitable trusts who may be able to help. We can probably cover the cost of most people's requirements.

Being *flush* with money can come at a price, even when it means you are able to send out many missionaries.

That a church can "probably cover" the entire costs of most people's mission vision would be something of a wonder to many of our respondents, but not all. As we will see next, being *flush* with money can come at a price, even when it means you are able to send out many missionaries.

Danger money

The flipside of churches having money is seen in the way money can be applied inappropriately for mission. An East African mission trainer and mobilizer shared their concerns about churches that may have money to send out missionaries but lack the infrastructure to care for its missionaries. In this respondent's opinion it was therefore irresponsible to send them.

Okay, two issues are at the foundation. One is the structure, both the sending and the support structures which perhaps combine with the second one, which is finances. But we also are having incidences and cases of people who are now being sent out by churches where there is money for example, so financially there is no issue, but we can tell the structure is not adequate enough (for example) to provide member care, the whole spectrum of necessary support. So money really is just part of it. So even if we solved the question of money and people are approaching it as a financial issue, we still have to come back to the issue of structures, support structures.

Obviously we would rather see better support infrastructures develop than for a church to stop sending missionaries, but this next East African minister would argue that the right sort of missionaries need to be sent (and supported), those with a genuine call not just those who can afford to go.

One of the comments that I have made before in some other circles is that the commercialization of missions has done a great harm to us. Missions has been commercialized in that the monied are the people who go for missions. Those who can pay for it are the ones who go for missions. It's no longer the calling. Your call is determined by your money. So if you do not have the money, your call is doubted. And I think that approach to missions has done a great harm to missions.

Remaining in East Africa, this next response comes from a mission mobilizer who ministers among students. Their frustration echoed the East African minister with regard to only those privileged with funding being able to participate in mission-related activities.

(Regarding student attendance at mission conferences). We have been challenged because sometimes we would love (to have) strategic students come, but because of finances, it ended up to be almost open-ended; if you have money, then you come! When you look critically, I think that is not the best way to mobilize because I think there are students who are missing out basically because of money. From poor backgrounds or those who are having serious responsibilities. And if you go back to their sources of money, sometimes it applies to churches, from their relatives. I think there is the bit that I think churches are yet to realize—to invest appropriately. You know, generally, churches in (*their nation*) would rather spend buying comfy seats or organizing one event as opposed to saying, "How can we invest because these students come from these churches? They come from our congregations." Are the churches willing to support the students? It's a real challenge.

If these East African voices seem to be taking a hard line, then these next two mission leaders in East Asia will be even more sobering. Later, we will hear from those who struggled with a lack of resource supply for mission; here we hear more about problems with having plenty.

My subjective and rough evaluation is only half of eighteen thousand (*nation name*) missionaries are qualified and the rest are dubious in their motivation. A Christian friend of mine said to me, "There are more than two hundred (*nation name*) missionaries in the city of (*name*) alone who are not virtually doing anything but are supported well by (*name of nation*) churches." I hope it is not true, but— (significant pause).

When you have it to spend it is easy to send, and apparently it is easy to send the wrong people to do the right things in the wrong way. This other East Asian mission leader spoke about it in terms of missionaries lacking humility, and they associated this pride and inappropriate triumphalism with the sending church's wealth.

God sure has blessed the (*nation named*) church with human and financial resources. But we have failed using it humbly for God, but rather with much pride and triumphalism. Church planting, for example, tends to be nothing more than transplantation of (*nation named*) church in foreign soils, just as a secular company expands its territory by branching out overseas. So I guess we need humility, to put missions in God's perspective, to treat people out there as our equals, to serve them rather than dominate.

Perhaps that is why Jesus' personal attitude to money was so dismissive, "give to Caesar what is Caesar's and to God what is God's" (Matthew 22:21). The trouble is, many controllers of the church's purse act as if they were God's accountants.

The abundance of wealth creates a power issue on many levels. It is difficult to avoid because with great wealth comes great responsibility. It is a very delicate balance to maintain. Unfortunately, a lot of manipulative control hides under the guise of "good stewardship." Perhaps that is why Jesus' personal attitude to money was so dismissive, "Give to Caesar what is Caesar's and to God what is God's" (Matthew 22:21). The trouble is, many controllers of the church's purse act as if they were God's accountants.

Sole control

To be fair, it is very difficult to discern where to invest funds for kingdom purposes. To whom does one listen? Most church leaders juggle a lot of competing priorities and it is easy for outsiders to look on and critique. Nevertheless, our voices have spoken and we need to represent them honestly here, as we just did with our East African and East Asian ministers. This next voice, speaking as a missionary *and* church leader from East Africa, shared something of the money-handler's predicament.

Let me give a practical example. We say we have a missionary who needs a motorcycle, and from the pulpit we have two people sign up for that, and what, to give towards that and ask how much does it cost. So you say it's (US$1,300). Then you have money for two motorcycles that you need, and you ask (yourself) can we use this money to build a missionary house, to put a roof, all that kind of thing (pause)? I don't think I have ever struggled, but you know as in any other church, when someone gives that kind of money, it should have been in the offering basket. So that really interferes with the church budget; so you can see the designated funds for projects that we have spoken is very well funded, but the general giving (is) going down. This does not go down well with the church administrators. Yet it's really money coming from (one) pocket to another. So those are the kind of things we need to explain to the congregation, that this is not an offering, but giving for mission is over and above the normal offering. But when you speak about this issue so passionately that someone says that maybe this is what God wanted me to give towards… but there are other dynamics. But speaking from the pulpit, for example, one time we needed a water tank and in a matter of two days I had the money for the tank. But it's the same scenario, just money from one pocket to the other. But that has been my experience in the short time that I have been around.

Having established the dilemma in East Africa we now fly all the way down to Oceania to hear from a well-experienced missionary and mobilizer who has their own solution to the problem—don't give the church any money.

I guess my comment would be that I think that, generally speaking, a lot of Christians don't think through the whole issue of giving and supporting, particularly of missions. I personally believe that they've been hoodwinked into thinking that the local church is the sole right for all their sources of giving. My challenge, even to pastors when I speak to a group of pastors, is for them to find any verse in the New Testament from Acts onwards, Pentecost onwards, where giving went to any other source apart from the poor and the needy and the mission band. And I think if Christians understood that they actually have a responsibility before God for their giving rather than just simply writing a check or dropping some money in the offering plate and saying, "I've done my bit," and they are not really taking any interest in to how it's used or where it goes and so on—I think if more Christians seriously took that into account then missions support and giving right across the board wouldn't even be an issue, wouldn't even be a problem.

All right, so maybe they weren't going as far as saying not to give to churches *at all*, but they came very close. Our Oceania friend more clearly suggests that there is an education issue at the heart of funding for mission, and other respondents echoed that.

Giving Education

Our first contributor to the subject of educating Christians about faith and giving is a minister from South America (who actually verified their observations with concrete evidence! It is the nature of our research methodology that we draw out narrative opinions to work with, and it is difficult for most people to recall specific data in a conversation).

This minister knew their church's history so well that they had no problem being specific about percentages.

> People start giving with time. The teaching and motivation to give by faith makes people to respond individually. Besides, when the church assigns a small percentage in the course of time this can increase. We started with less than one percent of the church's income, and in the course of the years, we managed to obtain forty percent of it for the missionary task.

The point made is that giving is a learned discipline and learning takes time and intentional teaching. The effort obviously paid off for this church (and the recipients of their mission fund). This was a rare example of a church teaching its congregants about giving to mission. The next two voices discuss learning about giving to mission, somewhat incidentally, through some courses we met earlier in the book. First up is a mission sender/supporter from Oceania (who inadvertently illustrated how difficult it actually is to recall statistical information on the spot).

Giving is a learned discipline and learning takes time and intentional teaching.

> We felt God was calling us to be senders and we were very impacted by the statistics we heard about how of all, I can't remember the exact statistics now, but of all Christian giving only a minute percent, like point zero one percent, goes to missions or something like that, or zero point one percent, and of that zero point one percent only point zero one percent went to the least reached. And so we thought, well you know, we've got good jobs, we earn well and God seemed to have placed us in a position where we felt we could give a lot more to missions. So that is kind of the big outcome that came for us out of *Perspectives*; that instead of tithing to the church, and I know that some churches do teach that you should tithe to the church, but instead of doing that, what we've felt we should do is actually give the bulk of our giving to missions. We do give to our church, but by far the bulk of our giving goes to missions. And (*Perspectives*) helped us work out where we would strategically give our giving as well. And we worked out, I don't think we ever wrote it down, but we worked out in our heads that we felt that we should be giving to overseas mission, we wanted to focus on least reached areas. And so it's a combination of supporting missionaries, supporting people in home base, as well who are working towards—you know like, if we are wanting to give to the least reached we also feel that it's important to support the people at home base who are trying to send out people to reach the least reached. It kind of crystallized what our vision was, for where we would focus our giving and it hasn't really changed a lot. When we think about and pray about new opportunities to give, we think about it in those sort of terms.

The next mention of a mission course that taught people about mission giving comes from a missionary now in Eastern Europe. In this instance the lesson learned was more about fundraising than fund-giving but the principles will be similar.

By then I had done the *Kairos* course and this time I'd taken it seriously—I can't say I had a hundred percent attendance, but nearly. It gave me a different perspective on world missions, on the needs, on the way in which they should be viewed. And I think what I learned on that *Kairos* course about fundraising is very important. I was very nervous and I think fundraising is a great obstacle for those who want to go into missions. We received teaching that argues from the Bible that fundraising is as important as any other work for the Lord, preaching or church planting.

It is very difficult to fundraise when the principles of giving toward God's kingdom-advance run against the grain of a culture. Others spoke of this in various ways and we will touch on it again later, but in this instance a mission organization staff member from East Africa recommended that their culture needed to be "developed" toward giving for missionary support as an act of worship to God.

> It is very difficult to fundraise when the principles of giving toward God's kingdom-advance run against the grain of a culture.

We also need to take into consideration the culture we have and the culture we would like to develop in the sense that we don't really have a giving culture. We haven't developed the culture where individuals support missionaries, but we need to move to that where missionaries can actually raise personal support and continue in the field, rather than depend on salary. We need to develop that culture where we see supporting Christian work as being of benefit to us, not just the person we are supporting; that we are worshiping God by what we are doing, we are not just having sympathy on an individual somewhere.

We understand our East African friend's reference to "salary" as meaning organizational support from funds raised, probably from outside the local context. Dependence on foreign sponsors or *patrons* to supply can be a humbling experience, but also one that is too easy to get used to and too tempting to pursue for some. Harmonizing with many voices from new sending nations, this South American mobilizer understands that foreign subsidies can be helpful if managed well, but does not think they are necessary.

It is *very* important that finances originate locally. One of the worst things is the foreign subsidy because it causes dependence, comfort, and *submission* to those who give. We have also seen cases in which well-managed foreign help has been beneficial, but the great challenge is to develop our own national resources. It takes time to achieve it, but it is long lasting.

We interpret this mobilizer's use of the word "develop" in a similar way to our East African friend. Giving to mission is a concept that needs to be developed through an educational process along with developing local sources of funding, and indeed it can take some time to achieve.

It is also important to note the mobilizer's mention of *submission* to those who give. As we touched on earlier, there are a lot of power dynamics at work in the transfer of funds and often there are expectations on the recipient by the donor that are not always obvious at first. This next contributor, also a South American mobilizer, believed that there were funds already available within their continent, but what was lacking was an understanding of the blessedness of generosity toward mission, which is something that can be taught. It also helps reorient the giver away from claiming power and control.

> I think that we have to have a balance between looking for finances (outside) and (inside) our continent. I am very sure that there are funds and people who can provide them, but it has not been taught, it is not a habit—the proper conviction that it is more blessed to give than to receive.

By Faith Alone?

A thread weaving through our funding narrative is that of humility. Abundance of funds can foster a sense of superiority, and control of supply can generate a power imbalance. One way of avoiding submission to the power and influence of money controllers is to not apply or ask for assistance. For over 200 years the modern mission movement has had a philosophy of trusting God alone for supply, giving rise to the term *faith mission*. The concept was born in an era where patrons, landed gentry, and wealthy business owners financed many social and recreational pursuits and supported the arts and charitable work. Many founders of today's older mission organizations were from the educated class of that era with connections to patron families. They did not need to make their needs known because their needs were known. It may have taken some time, but eventually word got around. It was a much smaller world back then.

> Faith has very little to do with communication methods and everything to do with whom you view as the supplier of your needs. Business people can require as much faith as the far-flung missionary, trusting God for their income. There is one Provider, just different means of supply.

That is not to dismiss their wonderful example of dependence on faith. Faith has very little to do with communication methods and everything to do with whom you view as the supplier of your needs. Business people can require as much faith as the far-flung missionary, trusting God for their income. There is one Provider, just different means of supply. One benefit of the business world is that there is an expectation of asking for that supply, in exchange for the goods and services provided. For missionaries it can be a much more personal (and awkward) affair.

There are a variety of reasons why missionaries prefer to not ask for funds. Most often it is articulated in the theological language of faith. That is admirable and we take it at face value, but there are usually many additional societal and psychological factors involved. This United Kingdom missionary speaks for many of our respondents regarding the social stigma attached to overtly seeking charity. This is one instance when we left country identifiers in to ensure the contrast is conveyed.

> In the Northern Irish context, some of the churches that (we) are from, you don't normally talk about money. I think it's different in England where they

are more business-orientated or something—you can talk about finances and how much you need more easily. But here, that's not talked about. People know you need it, but they rarely ask and they don't expect you to present a need. I think our folks over in England don't understand that, that the way our churches think in Northern Ireland is quite different. Having said that, our home churches are doing something to support us and help us and a wider support base of individuals and family, etc., have been really faithful which is tremendous. Now and then they will ask, "How's your support going?" and then you can tell them, but they don't like you to initiate that. They look upon that in a kind of suspicious way. It's not the done thing. So that's a little bit different. Now maybe in the US it's different; you can tell a church, "This is where I am, this is what I need," and people will say "OK" and respond if they are in a position to do so. But that's not the way it works here.

The Northern Irish are not alone in experiencing great discomfort in making known the fact that they are in need of generosity. The colonial cultures *Downunder* share a similar sentiment. From Oceania, this missionary was attracted to their mission organization because they would not be required to ask for funding.

I knew it was a faith mission and I liked that idea. I liked the concept that they didn't have their hand out left, right, and center like so many other organizations do. I didn't understand that you were not allowed to talk about your needs unless asked. And I think that point is something that I don't feel a hundred percent in agreement with, although I'm willing to accept it if that's the rules of the game. Personally, I think the way the Lord works these days, it's not the same world as our (mission founder's) day, and there's an awful lot of people who are keen to give and are asking the Lord who they should give to, but they are asking by what pamphlet turns up on their desk or what person walks through their door and explains their needs. And I think that God works in that way just as powerfully as he does with people who just trust.

For many in these cultures, joining a mission organization that does not permit you to ask your network of friends, family, and churches for supply is a convenient relief. Asking for money when you have nothing tangible to give in return is a humbling experience. Our Oceania friend spoke of something like a mid-way point where making the need known could be permissible "these days." Even that level of vulnerability can be distasteful to some in mission who prefer to neither "just trust" for miraculous provision nor ask individuals for help. Those ones prefer to generate their own supply to avoid the humiliation. But by doing so, they can also miss out on the fruit of faith that we explore at the end of this chapter.

> Asking for money when you have nothing tangible to give in return is a humbling experience.

To the contrary, this next voice, a missionary in India, expressed their belief that the Lord would honor faith and that the fruit of a work of faith will be met with adequate supply.

One of the things is we will not solicit funds. But we will make known to the believers what the Lord is doing in us and through us. We will project our proposals and to the people. But we will, directly or indirectly, will not solicit funds because Hudson Taylor's biography influenced my life all through the years. He never appealed for funds. I said, "Lord, if Hudson Taylor was able to do that during that time, even today you are the living God and I will do it." So the Lord honored my faith.

"According to your faith will it be done to you" (Matthew 9:29). Whether you just trust, make needs known, ask overtly, or transfer goods and services, they can each either be a faith-filled exercise or a feeble excuse. *Just trusting* can be *just laziness*; only making needs known—conflict avoidance; asking overtly—an unhealthy sense of entitlement; business transactions—pride and unbelief. There are no right or wrong means to expressing your faith. It is *your* faith. Others will express it differently.

> *Just trusting* can be *just laziness*, only making needs known—conflict avoidance, asking overtly—an unhealthy sense of entitlement, business transactions—pride and unbelief

Faith comes by hearing the word of God (cf. Romans 10:17 KJV) so whatever your expression of faith, it should be rooted in God's revelation to you, and we should add, confirmed by your faith community. That carries conviction; like the conviction of this South American missionary.

Another condition that I set was that I wasn't going to ask for money. Ever.

Another South American missionary and mobilizer had the same mind-set and explained how their conviction worked out in practice.

I never took decisions on the basis of finance, but on the basis of what I had to do. From the beginning I did not have a fixed financial support. Similarly to other friends, I would look for an extra job every now and then to cover my basic needs. I do not recall having gone to any church with the intention of raising financial support, but to teach or organize some event, and as a reward I was given an offering.

We close this section of our chapter with a final voice from the faith mission perspective because many share this North American missionary's conclusion. Regardless of the means of financial supply, "If God wants you there, he'll somehow provide."

Once we were accepted, or in the process of being accepted in the mission, they explained that we needed to raise money, and they sort of had some basic guidelines. I mean they told us specifically, "You are not supposed to ask and say we need to raise this amount of money; you can respond to people if they ask you." And some other things about—you know, you sort of put the need out there, this is what our plans are—and, you know. There's also a theological basis for it too in a sense. That's the faith mission part; that is the faith mission way of doing missions. I now realize it's shifted and changed on different terms from the past one hundred years, but their basic idea was you sort of say and you should believe it, also that if God wants you there, he'll somehow provide. That's what we really believed, or said, "OK, we want to believe this," and then lo and behold it happened! And that was the blessing part, that it really did happen, and that we didn't, as far as we know, create a lot of angry people who threw tomatoes at us because we were wanting to find money.

Found Wanting

"Lo and behold it happened!" was similar to the lived experience of many, and we will complete our chapter by hearing more from those who experienced it; but some global voices shared times in their mission experience when financial supply did not happen. In this section we discuss the clearest evidence of finance being a major retardant of mission. One missionary in East Europe puts it succinctly.

> I think it was in '93 that I nearly went to (*country name*), but I couldn't get the money so I gave up.

The fact that they identified as a missionary when they were interviewed indicates that they tried again with more success, but this particular experience clearly hindered their mission involvement at the time. A mobilizer in Oceania shared similarly.

> I guess I've alluded to that already as an example, and I would guess that the finance issue is one of the biggest hindrances or biggest, not hindrances, as so much as (pause), delay things, if that's the right word. I'm quite convinced that it shouldn't be, but it tends to be.

Our data clearly confirmed that finance could hinder mission. The unfortunate corollary to that is that people get hurt in the process. Their dreams are dashed, their faith is questioned, and as this South American mobilizer observed, they can feel dishonored.

> The reality is that finances are limited for this kind of ministry. The ones who invest many hours a week to spread the kingdom of God are not being honored; sometimes they invest more time than a pastor in his church that pays him (a salary).

Our data clearly confirmed that finance could hinder mission. The unfortunate corollary to that is that people get hurt in the process.

Quite possibly the most tragic story we heard from our respondents was shared by a missionary from the United Kingdom. Our research project did not specifically probe issues related to missionary care or retention. If it did we may have received far worse stories than this one, but this is sad enough. It would be easy to lay blame on the mission organization from this brief glimpse into the story, but we have enough collective experience of mission infrastructure to realize mission policies are notoriously difficult to manage to everyone's satisfaction.

We came back on furlough and had our health visit back at offices in London. At that point (*our mission organization*) apologized for the way they had done things and they said they would look to see if there was a way of funding us, without the salary, by providing other funds. That could keep us out there—funding (my spouse's) work, funding hospitality. Because we were based in (*city name*), we picked up everybody from the airport, they stayed with us, we moved them on to where they were going, we took them round, etc. We needed some sort of hospitality budget, which we didn't receive before that. Then we met again later on during our furlough and it was obvious there was no funding forthcoming, so we agreed to go out for that year in order to end properly, but that we would come back (home) after that.

From what we gather that must have turned out to be a temporary setback because this respondent also identified as a missionary at the time of the interview. Anybody who has been in a situation of need and at the mercy of others in mission will be able to identify with this story and the heartache it implies. Apparently the organization could not resolve the lack of supply so their mission involvement was retarded, at least for a time.

Mobilization can be one of those types of home-based ministries that struggle for support.

A former missionary and mobilizer in Oceania could identify with funding struggles holding back mission involvement due to organizational policies, and they considered it to be the rule in mission rather than the exception.

So we struggled getting support. Most people seem to—even those who are with organizations who are quite happy to send out a lot of letters around the place. Heard numerous stories about people being held back for quite a while because they had eighty or ninety percent or whatever the organization said they needed to have before they left.

If missionaries find it difficult to raise sufficient funds, it can be even harder for mission workers in their home country, as this home-based missionary from Eastern Europe confirmed.

Now, at the moment, it's hard for me financially, because we don't have financial support. And it's hard when you are only supported financially when you are actually on the mission field because that makes you feel like people only see you as useful or as a good Christian when you are actually doing something.

From the interview context we know that the missionary was "doing something;" apparently just not what supporters in their country expected mission work to be. Mobilization can be one of those types of home-based ministries that struggle for support. This church minister in South America believed the answer was in self-funding through training meetings.

> There are no finances for mobilization now. It is very difficult to get resources, for the mobilizer is not considered a worker. We should work towards self-funding by organizing training meetings to obtain funds. It is also important to work with local pastors as for the need of affirmation from the worker's local church.

Our interpretation of this quote is that the minister expects the mobilizer to raise support by charging participants to attend mission-training meetings rather than relying on the church to provide them with support, or a salary. We do not know the context well enough to say whether or not it is possible to make a living that way, but South American mobilizers previously quoted suggest it can be.

Another South American minister agreed that funding is scarce but provided this example of how they strategize around that.

> Finances are always difficult in missions, for training, for sending, for orientation, for everything. The practice I have had is to work hard for every event to be self-funded. I always had the premise of not having anything so the only way forward was to generate resources. That is why we worked carefully with budgets according to our means. Maybe we could have chosen this or that hotel or this or that material, but our reality would not allow it.

This minister from East Africa would agree that budgeting according to means is an important principle. They also strongly argued against following the default expectations of Western missionaries.

> I think (in) Africa we live simple lifestyles, and perhaps missionaries need to think of simplicity. How do we avoid copying the Western missionaries who come with a fridge, four-wheel drive car, who come loaded with their laptops—they are basically transporting Western world back into the mission field. How do we avoid that by trying to do simple lifestyles? And perhaps if we adopted simpler lifestyles we may be able to make much more inroads, and the funding levels may be lower funding levels. Recently my church has been thinking of sending a missionary to (*location name*). We have sent teams already to (*location name*) and we surveyed the area. And then we sat down with one particular congregation and began looking at what would it take for us to send a missionary. This congregation that we were hoping to partner with sent to us a budget of what they think it would take. And we looked at that budget and we said, "This is outrageous!" One of these budgets you look at and you know that even the bishop of the church cannot be able to live in that level of standard of living. So I think these are some of the things we may have to reduce so that we do not copy the Western model.

From the context of the interview we cannot tell if the congregation referred to was local or overseas, but the point is well made against the Western model as they have experienced it. However, living according to more basic standards can also hinder mission involvement. As this Indian church member and writer explained, "Talking about a young person's perspective, you know, missions do not pay a really decent salary so it's more like a tough life."

The expectation of "a really decent salary" differs from place to place, but whatever the levels, the desire for a good income remains a hindrance to mission service. A mission mobilizer based in Oceania discussed the phenomenon of a decent salary and ministry pay from their context.

> And it's difficult now, because the mind-set is often within (*our country*), that you need two incomes to, around the middle class anyway, you need two incomes to break even, would be somewhat what some people would say, certainly to get ahead. Yet as soon as you enter into ministry, whether that be church-based ministry or a particular mission-based ministry, the mind-set is that you're on one salary. You are on a one-person salary, it's not, you know, "You're not both working? Really? Surely not?" So I think that that could be a financial hindrance for people stepping out, that they might go from two incomes down to one mediocre income, and so they are not able to invest in the kind of security that others are naturally investing in because the reality is the social systems change and we've got to work within that system.

The contrast between this observation and the perspective of those with more of a faith orientation is quite marked. This mobilizer speaks for many though. Income levels are seen as a means of security against future need.

It is commonplace and convenient in our globalized marketplace to believe that those who are in need are in need because of some fault of their own, whether as a result of vice or unwise decisions. Choosing ministry or mission involvement is too easily seen as an unwise decision, and that impression unfairly creates a sense of shame in otherwise godly people. A mission mobilizer in Eastern Europe considered this sense of shame a major hindrance to mission involvement with their organization, but was confident that the shame would leave once people understood faith-based living.

They can also experience a wonderful dimension of worship of a God who promises to remain with us to the very end of the age of want.

> I think the main issue, the main hesitation for most missionaries is the fact that we're a faith-based organization so it means they raise their support. And at first that's quite a step for a lot of people. So they see that as a difficult thing. Maybe sometimes they see it as a shameful thing, which it isn't, but that's the way sometimes people see it until they learn more about it.

When they learn more about it they can also experience a wonderful dimension of worship of a God who promises to remain with us to the very end of the age of want.

Organization Complications

Interviewer: How did the fundraising policy of your agency or current ministry influence or help you in making your decision or choice?

Respondent: It had nothing to do with it. I do not believe that the fundraising policy should be a decisive factor.

This South American missionary's attitude to their mission organization's funding policy was admirable, but as we have just seen it was not a common view. Many of our respondents expressed some level of discomfort with their mission organization's financial policies, attitude toward fundraising, and use of money.

An East Asian church leader in North America was perplexed and strongly critical of mission policies they had seen in action. They expressed well what others have experienced. There is a Western proverb that says, "The squeaky wheel gets the oil." That could be the case here, where missionaries who are most frequently seen get the most support.

And I've found this irony that while those who are working hard on the mission field tend to have a poor financial support, those who spend too much time outside the venue of their ministry tend to get a better support. I have a hard time understanding missions policies. I also want to raise the issue of financial cost. Sending (*East Asian*) missionaries demands lots of money, especially as many of them are involved with unqualified expensive projects. Hearing about the problem of spending too much money on the mission field through mission-related seminars troubles and confuses me. And I think it is (the) church and mission leader's responsibility to come up with healthy mission strategies. Our church is the largest (*ethnicity*) church in (*city name*), supporting more than sixty missionary units—monthly US$200–300 per unit. But I don't think we are contributing as much as our potential. I can give forty points out of a hundred.

> It is extremely difficult to establish funding policies especially within multinational organizations.

This minister seems to be aiming for the same as the South American minister whose church contributes forty percent of their income to mission, but this one clearly wants to see value for the money. Applying business metrics to faith enterprises is a contentious subject in many parts of the mission world, but with the East African minister calling for more simplicity in mission, this minister seemed adamant that excess expenditure was unhealthy.

Who can be trusted to determine what level of funding is appropriate for each faith-based enterprise? Should it be centrally controlled? Is it one-size-fits-all? Do we run with the lowest common denominator? Shall we sacrifice health and well-being on the altar of frugality? Will we allow each missionary unit to spend what they get however they want? What does charity law in this sending country say? How can we reconcile it with charity law in that sending country? So much complexity and so many complications to consider, which brings us back to the money-handler's predicament with the realization that it is extremely difficult to establish funding policies especially within multinational organizations.

Furthermore, funding policies can change; and as this missionary from the United Kingdom observed, policy change can be a hard sell.

> I suppose the major change from our point of view over the years has been (*mission organization name*) used to have a pooling concept so all monies sent in were shared among the missionaries in the field. I think it's a biblical principle actually if you go back into Acts 2 and Acts 4—it's that sharing, but it was hard to sell to the support base and I think that's why it got changed. I think in particular the American support base—although maybe I could broaden that out and say Western. People wanted to feel that what they were giving was going to their missionary and that kind of thing. So (*mission organization name*) has changed its policy and that pooling isn't a significant factor anymore. So you have to raise a certain amount and if you don't get the amount that is expected or paid (although it's somewhat flexible, you determine what you are going to try and raise), if it's short, then you will be on a lower income the following year to compensate. It's very much more a tailored approach as opposed to a pooling approach and I think (*mission organization name*) lost something there; they've lost, in my opinion, like I say, something that had a biblical basis, and I know they had to do it because of the support base and the way people think these days. You don't support the mission you support the missionaries, so maybe they had no choice in the matter. I feel something was missed out on here.

In our experience people generally give to people, or projects with a vision that captures a donor's emotional investment. Because of this, mission organizations the world over are suffering from a cash flow crisis. At the time of writing, the International Mission Board's (IMB) plight was a prime example. However, the greater point being made by our missionary is their concern about a potential loss of equitability (fair distribution) as a result of the change in organizational policy, and their concern is worth noting.[2]

Our final voice cuts through organization complications and returns us to focus on "what God wants." Mobilization and money make very uncomfortable bedfellows so it is best to leave it out of the mobilization equation until a solid call is confirmed. At least, that is what we understand this Indian mission leader and mobilizer to mean.

---

2   We point to the 170-year-old International Mission Board and its organizational reset in 2015 as prime evidence of organization complications. According to the official online report, last updated February 26, 2016, since 2010 the IMB's spending has exceeded its income by US$210 million. Like many mission organizations, they were able to use reserves to cover consistent shortfalls, but the IMB directors decided to make some radical changes to curb such losses going forward. The most public change was calling for the voluntary resignation of at least 600 missionaries. The last update, before this book went to print, revealed 1,132 field and home staff were leaving. Source: http://www.imb.org/updates/storyview-3490.aspx#.VoRmpjawObI.

I strongly believe that attracting people with money is not the solution. Attracting people with career in the missions is not the solution. What I normally do is help people identify what God wants in their life in the perspective which God has for them and then encourage them. I have seen that many times when we increase the salary because people wanted money, and obviously you increase and take people into missions, and when somebody else offers a better salary they quit. So that is not the solution for mobilizing. Mobilizing people is to help them identify what God wants in their life, and to identify what God wants in their life we need to have a good prayer life. So when we challenge them accordingly they are mobilized and challenged.

Jehovah Jireh

There are few, if any, voluntary Christian activities that test the faith of the believer more than mission work. A possible exception is persecution, but that is rarely voluntary and neither is forced migration or the like. No, becoming a missionary exposes you to unfathomable stress and seasons of utter dependence. It also provides moments of ecstatic relief and wonder and worship due to God's undeniable divine providence. Stress and stretching become strengthening, and we grow in maturity until the next time the testing of our faith starts to develop perseverance afresh, and so the spiral turns (cf. James 1:3–4). This must be the faith paradigm of all Christians, not just missionaries, but without this perspective it is extremely difficult to make sense of the challenges missionaries face.

> Becoming a missionary exposes you to unfathomable stress and seasons of utter dependence. It also provides moments of ecstatic relief and wonder and worship due to God's undeniable divine providence.

To our readers who were deeply wounded by their mission experience or are currently going through all kinds of trials, you have our empathy and we pray for God's divine providence to be made manifest in your life as evidence of the Spirit's presence with you through your particular *valley of death* experience. Remember, for the joy set before him, Jesus endured the cross, scorning its shame (Hebrews 12:2b). So we want to close out our chapter on a note of hope, trusting that it will be an encouragement to our readers, promising great joy ahead.

Our God provides—in spectacular ways. The treasurer of a mission organization in South America testified to that fact on behalf of those they serve in mission.

> I am talking as a treasurer of a missionary agency and we can see God's provision for our missionaries in a spectacular way. The missionary never has money to throw around but they never are short either. There we can see the hand of God in a supernatural way. Some fields are very expensive, but our missionaries receive monthly what they need where they live and money comes from unexpected places, and we are very thankful to the Lord.

Thanks be to God! This missionary to India responds similarly with gratitude to God as a result of the Lord's faithfulness and miraculous provision.

I would like to say also that our ministry is a pure faith ministry. When God called me to India he called me to come out on faith; that means completely trusting him for my needs, and from the day I stepped on the shores of India till today the Lord has proved absolutely faithful. You are sitting in this building today and you see it's the provision of God in a miraculous way. We had no money to buy ground, this land, but the Lord guided, and just miraculously how he provided and even put up this building as a miracle of God. And our ministry now is running with how many staff? Four hundred staff, more than four hundred staff and we are looking to God every month for (US$120,000) really to run the ministry in faith.

Wow! God is good. But the miraculous cannot be measured in monetary terms. Trusting the Lord for a single missionary salary can be as challenging as trusting Jehovah Jireh for four hundred, and it is just as miraculous when it is provided. This missionary from East Asia confirms Hudson Taylor's belief that "God's work, done in God's way, will never lack God's supplies" (Guinness and Taylor, 1894, 238).

Interviewer: Are you fully supported?

Respondent: Yes, with some fluctuations, but the needs are met when I see it annually or in two-year terms.

Furthermore, God loves to supply through the generosity of the people of God. We end with two examples from Eastern Europe, as part of the European continent it is less wealthy than most. From two different East European missionaries we heard two contrasting examples of God's marvelous provision but the same heart is revealed in each, the heart of a Father who cares for his children.

My fundraising was strange because I was aware that the donors in the church were known by all. The people that were likely to give had already been approached by members of the team, and I thought that I can't put another burden on their shoulders, and I tried to raise money from non-Christian friends among my acquaintances, and the Lord did incredible miracles. I received almost the entire sum I needed from a single businessman with whom I hadn't had that much contact and who I approached under, I don't know what, with what courage, but it was an awesome experience.

I remember a handicapped girl, a family with five children of which three had muscular dystrophy, being those who supported mission the most. I was talking with *(person's name)* and he was saying that they have nowhere to give from except their own benefits. And so you realize, that is, I was encouraged that God will do his work if he wills it.

Now to him who is able to do immeasurably more than all we ask or imagine, according to his power that is at work within us, to him be glory in the church and in Christ Jesus throughout all generations, for ever and ever! Amen. (Ephesians 3:20)

CHAPTER 19

MISSION ORGANIZATION

It is a pity that we must continue with our exploration of retardants after leaving the previous chapter on such a high. We hope you took some time to reflect and worship God for the ways the Lord has been present in your times of need as well as times of plenty. Paul "learned the secret of being content in any and every situation" (Philippians 4:12) by realigning his priorities away from circumstance to focus instead on the eternal realities he knew to be true. Commentators suggest that the learning came through revelation rather than concentrated endeavor or disciplined austerity (Martin, 2007). That revelation was intimately connected with Paul's relationship with the Christ and his will and rule. The author of Hebrews encourages us all similarly, to "fix our eyes on Jesus, the author and perfecter of our faith" (Hebrews 12:2a).

We begin this chapter with such encouragement because it leads us toward the perspective on circumstance that allowed Paul to remain at peace when all around him suggested otherwise. If we dwell too long on the imperfect schemes of humanity we are sure to despair. So, having set our eyes on things above, we can now listen to our global voices as they share their frustrations concerning mission organizations and the potential of mission organizations to retard passion for mission.

> The perspective on circumstance that allowed Paul to remain at peace when all around him suggested otherwise.

Prerequisites

At times in the previous chapter we heard voices from different parts of the world critiquing the types of missionaries they saw serving in mission. There were claims of lack of qualifications, misapplication of funding, and buying their way into mission service. But missionaries typically go through *a screening process* before they are selected for mission service if they do so with a larger missions community; assuming, that is, that such a process exists in the sending context at all. It is not uncommon to hear experienced missionaries lament the low quality of new recruits. Sadly, it is almost a rite of passage for new missionaries. In the eyes of the experienced, it seems new missionaries are rarely prepared well enough to join the ranks of the elite forces already deployed. But they will never be prepared enough. At heart, missionary service is one that requires on-the-job training—apprenticeships if you will.

As with funding policies, mission organizations also face challenges with recruitment policies. How high should the bar be? What competencies are non-negotiable? What pre-field training is required and for how long? How can expectations be massaged to match reality? What types of back-up support need to be obtained? How is adherence to the organization's purpose, policies, and procedures assessed? How much is just the right amount of psychological dysfunction to do mission, and how much is too much? How can you *really* tell what baggage and bad habits are hidden away in their emotional closet? Because it will all manifest itself in mission sooner or later.

How much is just the right amount of psychological dysfunction to do mission, and how much is too much?

We labor this point about screening, presenting it as evidence for the mission organization's defense, because the voices we present next argue that many organizations' standards are a bit high. In the interest of full disclosure, and as stated previously, our research questions leaned much more toward "how can we get more out there" (recruitment) than "how can we keep more out there" (retention), which probably had something to do with the negative bias we will hear here.

A staff member with a mission organization in Oceania simplified the situation for us.

> I think of the mission agency side, there is perhaps, that we've made things too difficult for people to go. And that we expect a lot of stuff from people who want to go and you know—I mean, going back to what we talked about earlier, it was (*mission name*), you know, one of the reasons why (*mission name*) has been and still is such a raging success at getting people is that they make it easy for people to get involved.

"They make it easy for people to get involved," and we can hear all the field leaders and member-carers crying out in horror. That sort of simplicity brings with it complexities in other areas of mission and the respondent was quite aware of that. Nevertheless, in a similar vein, this mission mobilizer in the United Kingdom argued from their experience that the selection process had become far too choosy.

> They might not have been the best nurse or the best doctor or the best engineer, they might have been a bit too young and wet behind the ears, but, wow—and then suddenly we had all these procedures you had get through to get passed. We stopped sending some of these people and some of that was right, I am not saying it was wrong not to have done that but it did change. There was a sense of adventure with God. I wonder if we have lost some of that, almost delight in it, and that sense of adventure, sense of fun, sense of being on the edge. I think we have lost a bit of that and I wonder if that is why some younger people do struggle with old traditional missions because there isn't that sense of adventure. If you look at Hudson Taylor or whatever mission it was, what that sense of adventure was, there isn't that spark now.

Loss of edge, adventure, fun, and spark all speak of losing something dynamic and attractive, but is it mission reality? This mobilizer seemed to be saying that holy risk taking and jumping through procedural hoops are mutually exclusive. Maybe they are. Maybe they are not. Restrictive procedures do tend to be a retardant though. This mission leader in East Asia wondered if having high standards (and by implication, a requirement to assess candidates according to those standards) dissuaded people from even knocking on their mission organization's door.

> I don't know if it should be regarded as an obstacle, but sometimes (*organization name*) is perceived as a high standard organization. So some people don't even try to contact us simply due to their low level of English. In a sense, (*organization name*) has a good screening system, but it tends to discourage people away, and I feel bad about it.

We cannot afford to get started on a discussion concerning English proficiency requirements. That is the stuff of another research project!

Staying with the choosy theme for a moment, this mission mobilizer in Oceania observed that high "cream of the crop" standards, restricted resources, and a narrow focus can deter people, especially young people, from engaging in mission.

> I think that the whole strategy at the moment that revolves around taking the cream of the crop because of lack of resources, because of focus, is a deterrent. So we're not getting as many people through, the young. "I'm intentionally engaging in mission"—we're not getting as many people through that phase. Certainly for some people who I've tracked with, the agency process is not helping to fulfill what God's wanting for them, and I think that more often than not it's an underlying mind-set, that once you start tracking with me and my organization you're locked into me and my organization. And I think that some people like that, but I think more people now don't like it.

The mobilizer concluded with a comment that is worth noting about the assumed exclusivity of mission organizations. Inquirers can feel very shy about talking with mission organizations, perhaps for fear of getting "locked into" the wrong one.

Remaining in Oceania, a missionary commented on their reluctance to commit to a specific organization, especially when so many variables remained unclear. It is not uncommon for mission organizations to require completed applications for membership before they will allow an inquirer access to their field information vault, but for them it was a retardant.

> But it just wasn't right. For us it wasn't right because we were saying we want to go and work with (*a particular people group*) and the (*mission name*) were saying to us, and I don't know whether this was policy or what, but at the time they were saying to us, we can't guarantee anything, you have to join us first. Just join us and then we'll work out where you're going to go. And we couldn't swallow that. So we said, "No we want to know where we're going, we want to know options." It was like, "No you've got to do this," or something else, "and then we'll work it out." And as much as we respected and appreciated the rep and the people and the agency, we just could not get over that.

The Oceania missionary found their place and was still in mission and leading their own organization when we interviewed them, but their experience did not make it easy for them to get involved in the first instance. While listening to the previous voice, you might recall our earlier mention of a related comment by a senior mission leader from the United Kingdom, talking about how a deep sense of call could carry you through hindrances such as these. If not, here is a reminder.

> I have to say, that's one of the great things, that you have a sense of, "God has spoken to me about this and is encouraging me in this." There is a sense in which you can take an awful lot if there is a conviction that this is God's place for me. Whether you express that in terms of a call or in a sense of having got somewhere, having a sense of peace and knowing this is God's place. If you have got that I think it's amazing what ridiculous hurdles you will jump over because you recognize that that's God's place. Which is sort of nice, because that, for me now in a senior role in missions, helps me to realize that we can really mess up the way that we deal with candidates but the people who have got the real genuine call will probably find their way through it.

"Ridiculous hurdles"—they said it, not us. But how is this for ridiculous? A missionary in East Asia described their convoluted prerequisite dilemma in this way.

> I spoke with my pastor; he accepted me and encouraged the church to pray for me. But from there it did not go straight to being sent by the church. I approached several mission agencies but none seemed to be right, as I sensed they required an approval from my denomination (but) my denomination wouldn't qualify me as a missionary unless I had gone through an approved process.

They obviously broke the impasse somehow to become a missionary, but that sort of multilayered complexity has potential to be a significant retardant.

Practices

Closely related to prerequisites and other pre-service requirements are mission organization practices, which include policies and procedures. Every mission organization develops its own organizational culture and like every culture there are some who adapt easily, those who adapt eventually, and others who emigrate.

One of the talents of an effective mission recruiter is to assess quickly whether or not an interested contact is likely to be a good fit for their particular organization. Like beauty, the suitability of an organization can be in the eye of the beholder. What one person thinks is delightful another person can consider disastrous. Enthusiastic novice recruiters may think their job is to get as many people as possible through the organization's system and involved in mission quickly, until their member care colleagues suggest otherwise. A wiser recruiter will be careful to ensure an inquirer's values resonate enough with the organization to help them adapt to the internal culture. Otherwise they may inadvertently send someone out to do mission work like this missionary from Oceania who thought there was something a little *off* with the organization that originally trained them.

> It was a great (*mission name's*) school, we had some really awesome speakers, but I just felt that there was, just some things happening there which just seemed a little bit kooky.

While it is important for new recruits to adapt to the organizational culture, organizations can also adapt. As we saw earlier, change is a delicate process and organizations can adapt too quickly to the perceived demands of their sending context and upset their existing missionaries. This missionary from the United Kingdom illustrated this from their perspective.

> (*Mission name*) don't seem to be as interested, as it were, in long-term missionaries and maintaining contact with them, at least not in the central office. I hope that doesn't become a trend, but the impression, it's just an impression, I get is that the concentration now is on short-term people, gap people, etc. I sympathize with them because there is a lot of work involved in getting those folks ready to go off, even if they're only going for a couple of weeks or a couple of months or whatever. But I wish that there was a little bit more come and go between the career missionaries and the home office as it were.

Every mission organization develops its own organizational culture and like every culture there are some who adapt easily, those who adapt eventually, and others who emigrate.

In this case the organization was probably taking the ineffective path we saw earlier, of trying to gain more long-term recruits by offering short-term *taste and see* opportunities.[1] The missionary correctly observed that this strategy is extremely resource heavy, was compromising a focus on long-term mission, and causing the care of long-term missionaries to suffer.

The thing with mission organizations, like many other complex institutions, is that they create their own center of gravity and see themselves as relatively autonomous, cut off from others, leaving the decision makers to pursue their vision for the organization via policies that seek to fulfill the tenets of their mission statement. From the inside it is difficult for the organization's key change-makers to fully appreciate how their choices might impact those on the outside. A minister in India shared from their outside perspective in ways related to this theme. We recommend that every mission decision maker listens carefully to this voice and takes serious note.

---

1   As we mentioned earlier, the pool of research into the effectiveness of short-term mission for long-term recruitment is growing and finding very little correlation between the two. Most long-term missionaries have engaged in some sort of short-term mission, but the data shows negligible influence the other way. The conclusion is that people believe their involvement in long-term mission should be accredited to reasons other than their short-term experience. Our data certainly confirms this. Short-term mission was not a noticeable accelerant. Eleanor Chee's Hong Kong study found something similar (Chee, 2014), as did Hibbert, Hibbert, and Silberman's in Australia (Hibbert, et al., 2015).

They don't take church into (their) confidence; they don't involve the pastor, bishop, or the church leaders in their mission societies. They want only two things—prayer support and financial support. They set up prayer groups and through that prayer group they motivate to give money for mission societies. They take everything and do (it) on their own. But in that process they don't involve the local sponsors and supporters much, especially in decision-making policy. So it becomes like a club. This mission society is only for this group of people. They don't give their responsibilities to others.

The thing with mission organizations, like many other complex institutions, is that they create their own center of gravity and see themselves as relatively autonomous.

We certainly appreciate how impossible it would be for mission organizations to consult with every stakeholder in its ministry, but this church leader implied the organization(s) in question enjoyed a high degree of partnership involvement with their churches, which would be enhanced by more cooperation. If more humility was expressed by mission organizations, and churches became more involved in the missions objectives, perhaps that could lead to exciting new mobilization potential. It could not be any *kookier* than firing out more short-termers on their adventure of a lifetime as a way to accelerate long-term mission interest.

Personnel

You would be forgiven for thinking we are treating mission organizations as if they were sentient entities divorced from human control. They are not of course. As stated earlier, organizations are just clusters of people who commit to a certain way of doing things for certain reasons. Mission organizations do things for mission reasons, but at the end of the day they're just a cluster of missionaries working together according to an agreed purpose, policies, and practices.

Sometimes it is just individuals and their prejudices within mission organizations that become the retardant to mission involvement. Imagine you were this long-faithful supporter of mission from Oceania seeking to invest a term of service on the mission field, and you received the sort of response they did from mission organization personnel (from the interview context we know the "friend" was a senior leader with a mission organization).

My heart was set. I wanted to go on the mission field. But I was nearly 65 and 65 is the cut-off date. So I decided that the only thing that I could probably do was to go and be a teacher in a missionary school. So I went to (a friend) and said, how about me going to (*school name*) and he said, "Oh rubbish, you couldn't do that, you don't speak French, it's much too hot for you, just forget about it." But I didn't forget about it. And then I heard that there were some kids that were going to a school in (*location name*). So I made inquiries and found that it was run by (*organization name*) so I wrote to them. They never really wrote back because the lady was on furlough that I wrote to, but eventually she did reply and it was very negative. She said I had no cross-cultural experience, that it would be much too high altitude, that I had no missions background, and I don't know how she knew this, but she said I was too heavy! (laughs.)

At least they can now laugh about it. From the rest of their interview we know that the respondent got to serve for a number of years and they felt it was a wonderful experience for all involved.

Prejudice rears its head in many forms. Above, it was age, health, and weight. More common, according to our research, was age-old racial prejudice. It is ironic that mission organizations can be so dismissive of people that do not fit their missionary profile because of race or location. We have heard this Eastern European missionary's story already but it bears repeating in this context.

> Give me materials, a magazine, something! I want to go but I don't know anything. I don't know how to start; I don't know what to do. Nobody in my country is helping me, nobody knows anything. And they sent me magazines and brought them for me from England. Someone brought me a load of magazines. I looked, and I started to write to all that I saw there. "I want to go to Africa but I don't know what to do—tell me, can I go with you? Can you help?" And only two or three answered, "We're sorry, we're merging with others, we can't do anything at the moment. The Lord help you."

It mirrors this East African minister's experience.

> So I wrote this man and said I really want to see the possibility of being involved in (*location name*) and he responded to me, and I think from his response he also had this idea that this is an enthusiastic young man. So he sent me a response and said, "Well if the Lord opens a way for you, you can come to (*location name*)," in other words, "My hands are clean, I am not getting involved, if you are able to come on your own, just go ahead and get involved on your own." Down the road, a few years when I began going to (*location name*) and I have been in (*location name*) many times and have had some wonderful ministries (there). I met with this gentleman and I thought to myself, well finally I am in (*location name*), and more people are now in (*location name*), and the place is now open to the gospel, and the great work that is going on within (*location name*), and the church is growing in leaps and bounds. And so even the Western agency that had better structures was not open to Africans (becoming) involved."

Considering that there are now more missionaries from new sending nations than traditional sending nations (Johnstone, 2011), and a nation like Brazil is (debatably) considered the second largest sender of missionaries by number, with Palestine as the largest sender of missionaries per million church members (Johnson, Bellofatto, Hickman, and Coon, 2013), it should be considered shameful that mission organizations so quickly dismiss enquiries from outside traditional sending nations. The experiences recorded above happened a long time before the respondents were interviewed, but in our experience the situation has not changed much.

We realize there are all manner of reasons why mission personnel dismiss the potential mission involvement by people who are different from them. Some of them are legitimate reasons, like logistical complexities. We just want to note here that being too hasty to deflect inquiries does mission involvement a disservice; it is a mission retardant.

Props

Building on our Eastern European and East African voices just quoted, we turn now to another subject we cannot hope to deal with as adequately as it deserves. The subject is that of mission infrastructure, or inversely, the lack of mission infrastructure available in new sending contexts. Most of what we have already discussed as hindrances to mission involvement is infrastructure related, but this brief section is particularly focused on organization support mechanisms, those things that *prop up* missionary service.

It should be considered shameful that mission organizations so quickly dismiss enquiries from outside traditional sending nations.

The lack of props, or support mechanisms, was mentioned frequently enough by voices from new sending nations that it earned a place here among mission organization retardants. Interestingly, if respondents from traditional sending contexts complained about anything, it was too much infrastructure. Here, respondents from new sending contexts lament the lack of it.

For example, this missionary from Eastern Europe would like to have seen more investment in the processing, sending, supporting, and ongoing development of missionaries from their nation.

> Because (*nation name*) didn't have opportunity to send out missionaries, basically ever, there isn't really an infrastructure developed to develop missionary candidates, to send them out, to care for them, to link them with foreign agencies that might be able to come around them and support them on the field in ministry there. So, we've seen that it's possible to motivate a lot of people, and it's possible, now we even have some training things happening that didn't exist ten years ago. But you can get people motivated and people get trained, but then how can they go unless they are sent? So there's a breakdown at the sending level, that churches don't have the mechanisms to do that. How do you pay the guy's salary, what do you do with insurance, taxes, working documents? And all those questions are hard to resolve.

So even though people are interested and willing to go, the lack of a means to send and develop them is a significant retardant.

A mission-oriented minister in East Africa also experienced difficulties with the lack of infrastructure. The main area of lack for them was the means to support missionaries.

I do not think I have enough structures to support our missionaries. We might have the financial resources, plan, and all that. But one thing I know about long-term missionary work is the missionary coming back. I know (the church) will need to provide the care the missionary needs because of the realities of the mission field. But right now I think we don't have the systems and the structures.

Our next global voice talked about infrastructure problems from a different angle. Without much mission organization presence or visibility in their country, the thought of becoming a missionary did not seem to occur to people, which is an obvious retardant. Speaking from East Asia, this missionary eventually found their way to mission service but it was not easy.

Actually, the calling to be a missionary was the last thing that came. That's because you cannot just be a missionary if you wish, the idea is not common, especially in (*nation name*). I hadn't gone to a seminary and was completely off the track to be a missionary from my denomination.

A church leader in East Asia's response confirmed the difficulty.

We are very weak in forming and utilizing infrastructure. Most of our missions operation is individualistic, yielding ineffective results.

Another East Asian missionary, referring to their sending nation, lamented a lack of accountability that good organizational infrastructures can provide. Here too we can see an individualistic style of mission involvement being critiqued.

> For mission involvement to thrive, determined effort needs to be made to find the right mix of support and constraint to help missionaries thrive.

Any type of *mission* is being justified as long as people doing it have strong zeal. It's like running a train without providing rails. Without rails, the train cannot move toward the right direction nor can it run a long distance.
But (*nation name*) mission in general doesn't seem to know or understand this infrastructure.

Without rails (or supporting props) mission struggles to move in the right direction and go the distance and mission involvement is hindered. As we saw previously, with too much infrastructure mission is constricted, which also retards mission involvement. Somewhere in between mission organizations need to find a fulcrum point, a balance, between too little and too much infrastructure. It may be a shifting point as needs require, but for mission involvement to thrive, determined effort needs to be made to find the right mix of support and constraint to help missionaries thrive.

Pitches

Regardless of how well or badly it manages to prop up its missionaries and mission work, a mission organization needs to present itself as positively as possible to its stakeholders for its own survival. In the world of sales and spin this is known as *the pitch*.[2] Like all other organizations, especially those that depend on donated funds, the degree of investment in them is determined by how much confidence their target audience have in who they are and what they do. It is the business of persuasion.

It may seem deceptive or distasteful, but mission organizations need to actively manage their public profile because fulfilling their vision and objectives depends on them looking as positive as possible. So it should not be surprising that they work hard to present themselves in the most positive light. This necessity has increased as options have increased. With prospective missionaries having more organizations to choose from, each mission organization now has to quickly establish what makes it stand out from the rest in order to keep recruiting or raising funds or do whatever it is they exist for. Where organizations are few, such as we discussed in the *Props* subsection, this is not such an issue, but where a plethora of mission organizations are represented, all doing the same thing with slight variations, marketing can make the difference.

> Mobilization ought to be more about promoting God's heart.

It all makes perfect business sense, but some of our respondents felt that mission was becoming far too commercialized. This mission mobilizer from South America confirms how distasteful business methods seem to those who put their "whole life on the grill" for mission.

> **Interviewer:** How do you see marketing in mobilization? How do you compare it with your reality?
>
> **Respondent:** I don't know if the word I like best is marketing because it gives the Great Commission a business and institutional sense. Those of us who mobilize others and ourselves are setting our whole life on the grill. More than promoting mobilization programs, we promote God's heart-urgency and the opportunities he has for us.

They took issue with the interviewer's suggestion that mission involves marketing in a "business and institutional sense." The point is well made that mobilization ought to be more about promoting God's heart.

A mission mobilizer in the United Kingdom would wholeheartedly agree. They seemed to be experiencing considerable dissonance about the way mission promotion was being conducted.

> I think the biggest barrier is mission agencies (who) think that it's their own work that they are doing and they haven't understood what it means to be part of God's mission. I think they are too much into self-promotion, they are too much

---

2   *Spin* is the way Public Relations (PR) specialists present reality. This skill is technically a form of propaganda, but propaganda has negative connotations so PR and sales people call it spin, which is itself spin—a manipulation of reality (usually via some sort of media) to present a biased perspective with intent to persuade.

into, "This is our mission, aren't we good at it?" type publicity, and I would like to see a much more selfless understanding of mission in the agency's theology. That is quite a strong statement. I have thought about it a lot the last couple of years since I have been in this post. I get very concerned about some of the literature that is out there, talking about what *they* are doing all the time and almost think that it's *their* mission and not God's mission they are involved in. That causes me concern. Therefore, it becomes very competitive.

This observation is loaded with critique. Their main point seemed to be that the way *other organization*s pitched themselves was lacking in a robust understanding of the mission of God. However, their concern became a little clearer as they continued with their response. It seemed that it was not exactly the competition that was the problem, but rather what the competition represented—too many mission organizations. They continued,

> As far as I am concerned we have too many mission agencies in this country. I think some have become ineffective because of the way they are functioning, because they are too small.

Perhaps the United Kingdom-based mobilizer speaks for many who believe that since there is one mission there ought to only be one mission organization. We could say the same about denominations and local churches. Mission leaders and administrators would care to differ. There are good reasons why different organizations exist. However, some of those reasons may no longer be applicable or viable and we are starting to see more and more amalgamations as mission organizations seek to use their resources wisely for future mission advance.

We will continue to have the issue of choice of mission organization in many parts of the world for a long time yet, and with that, the positive promotion of mission organizations' differences and opportunities. Our caution to marketing, sorry, *mobilization* departments of mission organizations is to be careful that you present yourselves accurately, not just positively. This mobilizer in South America believed that honesty was the best policy.

> Many who believe that since there is one mission there ought to only be one mission organization.

> If there is some kind of marketing, it should be absolutely honest and challenging although not always attractive. It seems that missionary mobilization today has elements to attract customers with this message, "We are going to an adventure, but safe." That may mean, "An experience to enrich my spiritual life," and nothing more. Today's reality is that people come to missions and arrive with a wrong concept of what (involvement) in the missionary field means.

How closely does our promotion of mission opportunities resemble a Disneyland brochure or a safety-conscious packaged tour to appeal to the cautious? How much of it looks like a Red Bull commercial to attract the daring? How much of it resonates with 2 Corinthians 6:3–10 to call the faithful?

An Indian minister believes we should be much more challenging in our call to ministry and mission.

> Those days I used to hear many challenging messages about committing life, joining full-time ministry, etc. That commitment only helps us today to stand in mission ministry. Nowadays how many preachers are giving those challenging messages? That challenging message is missing in the mission and also in the church. That is the saddest part. They challenge people to give, they don't challenge people to come for work. So that challenging message is missing these days; that should get revived. Consciously, preachers need to challenge in churches as well as in missions societies.

Back in the United Kingdom, another mobilizer's voice was heard from the perspective of trying to promote the cause of mission among all the other activities on offer from churches. If it is difficult for mission organizations to be differentiated from other mission organizations, it seems almost impossible for a mission organization to "get its head above the parapet" amidst church-based promotions.

> For me, symptomatic of (mission marketing) is the exhibitions we find ourselves in, where the laws of the market place drive the whole interaction with delegates to the conference and the various stands. And so the more money you pay, the more contacts you have. It's all about selling stuff, because Christians effectively have had this idea modeled to them that the church exists as a sort of giant marketplace and they can sell stuff to their fellow Christians and buy stuff from their fellow Christians and there is this inherent message that that's a good thing. I don't think it is, but I know that I am little bit of a voice in the wilderness and a lot of missions are, because the rules of the marketplace mean that the church becomes quite self-obsessed, becomes quite financially driven by just selling to itself and buying from itself and that tends to lead to a misunderstanding of missions. "They just want our money," which is on the whole not the case, although clearly mission needs finance to exist. It marginalizes mission because mission, if it is not operating in the marketplace, doesn't have the resources, sometimes doesn't want to use the resources it needs to make itself seen; to get its head above the parapet.

The keen observation of this mobilizer reveals a deep underlying problem with the evangelical church (and its expressions of mission) and we do not believe it is a Western problem alone. It is the free-market paradigm. It is the assumed belief that free-market business models, methods, and metrics automatically apply to ministry and mission situations. It is far too large a subject to explore here but it needs to be observed for the sake of mission continuance. You cannot spend money to create more missionaries; they are called not cultivated. As we have shown, you can do all sorts of things to accelerate interest, but it is the Lord of the harvest who sends out laborers.

The free-market paradigm was perhaps no more obvious than in this response from a missionary speaking about returning home to their sending church in Eastern Europe, which was led by a minister who had lived for many years in North America. As we finished the last chapter on a high, this ending should make us want to cry.

We weren't able to work with that church for long because of the (*North American*) mentality by which a missionary is seen as a "convert-factory." It's automatic; you insert the dollar, out comes the convert. If the convert doesn't come, you stop putting in dollars. It was very difficult. After the first seven months—the most difficult months—we paid our first visit home. When we were met at the gate, the first words were, "You didn't send a report." Not, "I'm glad you've come," "I'm glad to see you well," but, "You didn't write my reports, what are we to do?"

> You cannot spend money to create more missionaries; they are called not cultivated.

CHAPTER 20

GENDER

Issues of funding and various mission organizational dynamics create significant hindrances to mission involvement. They tend to be external factors, system, and structural designs that create internal frustrations. We touched on some underlying assumptions in our discussion so far, but for the most part we did not delve into philosophical roots. We cannot avoid it in this chapter.

Issues relating to gender—specifically gender disparity—run deep and permeate the way we view the world. Noticeably, when asked to comment on potential hindrances to the work of mission, factors such as expectations, perceptions of gendered normative behavior, and role divisions were mentioned. There were also numerous references to pervasive male leadership in certain denominations, churches, and mission organizations and its potential to curtail and undermine the involvement of women in mission. Mission researchers concur. For example, Patrick Johnstone observed and asked,

> In many fields, experience and maturity are more likely to be found among the longer-serving single female missionaries. How can missions and ministries better recognize this reality and capitalize on it? (Johnstone, 2011, 227)

We are conscious that any discussion around gender issues is likely to be thorny. A concept such as racism is much more likely to be universally recognized as something undesirable among Christians (at least as a concept), whereas sexism—prejudicial beliefs and discrimination against members of the opposite sex (historically, male against female)—is far less explicitly understood in those terms or recognized as something destructive in human relationships.

Simply put, for some Christians the concept of *complimentarianism* is simply biblical, for others, it is sexist, or there may be a level of indifference to the issues.[1] As we have emphasized several times, the nature of the current study allowed for open-ended responses to certain thematic questions because we were interested in exploring the dimensions of mission motivation wherever that would lead. We would be remiss if we ignored or

---

1   We will assume an understanding of *complimentarian* theology here and not develop it further in our text. In short, it is a view drawn from a particular interpretation of Scripture that men and women have different but complimentary roles and responsibilities in their marriages and families, ministries, and other realms. A popular contention is that this view can result in an expectation that women's roles and responsibilities are meant to be subordinate in any relationship involving men. Subordination need not denote inferiority, but it does present certain power/influence inequalities.

deliberately omitted any of the most prominent themes. We were not commissioned to look specifically at the implications of gender relations with regard to mission motivation, but the data points to potential areas of difficulty and even conflict that are impossible for us to brush aside.

Before highlighting more concrete findings of gender difference as retardant to mission involvement, we think it is appropriate to note the pervasive *androcentrism* (male centeredness) present throughout our data in the perceptions, experiences, and language of many of our respondents. Generic male linguistic designations were often used in everyday speech to denote the person of the Christian worker. While the use of the terms *man* or *men* is thought to be generic, which by default should include *woman* and *women*, social research has suggested that a generalized perception of maleness develops, reinforcing the figure of the male as predominant and ultimately excluding that of the woman.[2]

Using male-oriented pronouns generically may not provoke too much of a reaction from our readers, but it implies the exclusion of women, emphasizing men as central and visible while, whether intentional or not, the woman is made invisible. If *maleness* is linguistically the norm in mission then to be female is to be *other,* and by implication, less valued. As a result, "The (he) prescriptive affects females' life options and feelings of well-being" (L. Richardson, 1988, 19). If women feel this effect, it has great potential to diminish their mission service and therefore the objectives of mission in general. This will be developed more by the voices that follow.

If *maleness* is linguistically the norm in mission then to be female is to be *other* and, by implication, less valued.

We must be careful to reiterate that it is not our place to make value judgments in our presentation of the data. Rather, for this topic we are simply pointing out that a gender distinction exists, that subordination is evident, and some respondents felt that negatively. This may well not be an issue for women who are very comfortable with the situation, but in the context of the interviews many of our female voices did not agree with it. This will become apparent in the examples we have chosen to publish that are merely representative of a much larger data collection.

---

2   For a useful summary on what she terms the generic myth, see Linda Lindsey's chapter four in her book *Gender Roles: A Sociological Perspective.* She writes,

"The generic use of he is presumed to include all the shes it linguistically encompasses. It is quite apparent from research, however, that this is not the case. People develop masculine imagery for presumed neutral words, a pattern that is firmly in place by preadolescence. That pattern cuts across race, ethnicity, and social class, but males in all of these categories adopt the pattern more than females. Generics are supposed to be neutral, but children and adults report primarily male, sex-specific imagery when hearing generic terms. People visualize male and interpret the reference as male rather than male and female." (Lindsey, 2005, 76)

Women as Ancillary

A number of interviews illustrated the experience of women in marriage partnerships as subsidiary to that of the husband who is positioned in the lead. A pervasive Christian view is that wives are destined to be *helpmeets* to their husbands. This often manifests with married women being seen as ancillary, providing back-up support to the husband who is, by inference, primary. In many references to mission activity involving husbands and wives, tasks and responsibilities tended to coincide with traditionally perceived conceptions of male role importance. Ministry conducted by the female partner was generally focused on other women and children. A missionary from the United Kingdom shared with us what her main responsibilities were while serving at a college in her ministry location.

> While we were at *(college name)* (my husband) was teaching in the Missions Department and I taught on a course for the wives of the students. Many of the students who had come to study at *(college name)* were mature students; married, had families. And it's a residential course between two to four years depending on what course they choose. Families come with them, so to give the wives some opportunity to get training for ministry I was involved in an informal course for them. They have families so they don't have the time to study on a full-time course. Many of them don't have the educational background anyway to do a degree in theology and not everybody wants to do a degree in theology anyway. That really was my main ministry, if you like.

Also from the United Kingdom, this woman told us that while she and her husband were aboard a mission ship she,

> Got involved and had a number of little jobs on the ship. I looked after the kid's library. I looked after the Sunday school program for the kids on board. I got involved in the ladies' meetings and took some of the meetings; spoke at one or two.

Later in her interview, she provided an example of the ancillary role of women in mission.

> We were doing church-planting, but it was mostly guys on the teams and the girls' ministry really was in the office really, on a support basis.

While the above respondents seemed quite content with their roles and various tasks, our next contributor encountered difficulties when *officially* recognized as an equal partner to her husband in mission. Although she does not equate these difficulties as specifically related to issues of gender, her account illustrates the classic *second shift* syndrome experienced by many women who are expected to balance both domestic and occupational responsibilities—working a full day, then tending to the household at night.

> When (my husband) first applied to be a mission partner, it was very much (him) applying. By the time we got to college, during the process of application to be mission partners, I was told I could go to lectures as a spouse and there would be

preparation things about going and living overseas. It was very light, nothing very theological; nothing very heavy for me. By the time we actually got to college they had just started a new course and they actually changed things in that even though I was a spouse I wasn't going out doing any specific job, I was also considered to be a mission partner in recognition of the support you give and the background work the partner thinks you do. So I was to be seen as a mission partner as well, and I was to receive a salary. Because of that I also needed to go through the courses at college which I ended up doing three terms of, a couple of lectures and weekly assignments, at the end of which I received the college diploma in mission studies. Which was fine, but the lectures always started before I got back from the (children's) school run in the morning. I always had to leave (a lecture) to go and get one child from nursery. I always had to leave to get children from school in the afternoon, particularly fitting around (my husband's) lectures. So, although the expectations of me were to be in college, they weren't also child flexible. It was quite tough for me to do a weekly assignment because obviously my evenings were spent looking after the children. It was quite a shock to get to college and find that it's gone from something light to something quite heavy, theologically. Also, the half-term week was not (my children's) school's half-term week, so it meant I missed a whole week of lectures, and because of that I was given extra work to do to make up for it. Otherwise I wouldn't get the diploma. Through college I did all that was expected of me and we were both commissioned.

The expectations that arise from *default* gender role divisions may seem normal to many, but as expressed in this extended example the additional tasks mission activities require of mothers are quite obviously uniquely challenging for them.

Gender Dynamics

In contrast to the accounts above that indicated no strong recognition (on the part of the respondents) of a particularly negative form of gender dynamic in their experiences, other respondents seemed very aware of issues pertaining to the expectations and norms within gender relations, and the implications of these in their lives and work. For a missionary from South America a transition of status occurred upon her marriage to a man who was also in missionary service. She articulated a common perception in many societies that upon marriage women are *taken care of* (financially) by the husband; the assumption being that men should be/are the chief provider for the family. Not only did she feel this view was in error but it also had very practical implications regarding the financial support of them as a missionary couple.

It is usual that when a single missionary woman gets married in the missionary field, supporters tend to think that they no longer have a financial responsibility. It is a pity that the support is not considered a ministry in itself, and that it is not discussed clearly before making financial decisions based on assumptions that are not true. I got married with a missionary that had less financial support than I did.

We never lacked of anything, but the offerings from (*sending nation*) disappeared for some time.

Accounts from other women in our study also spoke of potential barriers to engaging in service because of the dominant *androcentricism* of their churches and cultures. From Eastern Europe, one female missionary shared her experience of discrimination.

It's hard in (*country name*) because we're still, we're still in the period where we've only just begun, it's pioneering in prayer. Especially for a girl. You know how it is—I don't know if you know in (*country name*), we have a lot of theologians, we like theology and if you don't speak super-theologically, and generally it's the boys who speak—so as a girl, to go to the front (of the church), the expectations are very high. "Ok, you're a girl, let's see what you can say." And if you don't speak to their standards there's great discouragement.

> Accounts from other women in our study also spoke of potential barriers to engaging in service because of the dominant *androcentricism* of their churches and cultures.

A mission mobilizer working in Eastern Europe identified gender expectations as a clear obstacle for many women. Specifically referring to single women interested in mission, they described the normative values of some of the churches there.

Also, sometimes the churches that see it as, would rather maybe not see young single ladies going into missions. They'd say what is she doing in missions? She should just stay home and find herself a nice husband and get some kids, and you know, why does she have to go to Indonesia or Ghana or whatever? So yeah, there's a number of things that, you know, that people could see or have in their way as they consider something like this.

Remaining in Eastern Europe, this missionary articulated a level of insecurity as well as the potential obstacles she faced on her journey to being involved in ministry. She also made reference to the expectations of the local church and their misgivings.

Then there was the problem, that I was a girl and in a church where girls didn't minister, except for reciting poems or singing, they weren't leaders. Those from the church were also a bit reticent at the beginning. They thought it would be hard for me to go, a girl, alone.

While there may be considerable reticence expressed by a local church or mission organization over the viability of male candidates, nowhere in our data does the simple fact of *being male* present it as such. Despite potential barriers, she did see her ministry come to fruition, and yet a final comment from her revealed something interesting.

The conference was in (*city name*) and I stayed for a few days after the conference to get to know the student movement there. And the students from there asked me to speak at their leaders' meeting, to share a message there. I didn't quite know what that meant, but I told them, "in (*country name*) women don't speak from the front." Coming from the context I was from, I told them I couldn't speak, that I didn't know how, that I have no experience. And this lady from Germany encouraged me a lot. She told me that, "God has worked through you, maybe think about something God has taught you and that you think would be useful to them. And don't think that you are preaching but just that you are sharing something with them. And use what God has put on your heart." She encouraged me a lot.

Although in practice women do minister, there is a stumbling block apparent in recognizing and valuing it; a stumbling block that does not exist for men.

Although seemingly capable and qualified to *preach* in a student leaders meeting, and told as much from a colleague; internally, this woman's ministry was veiled. Although she did speak to the student body, in doing so she could not allow herself to think of it as preaching. This is a specifically gendered phenomenon. Although in practice women do minister, there is a stumbling block apparent in recognizing and valuing it; a stumbling block that does not exist for men.

Leadership and Gender

While female involvement in missions is significant throughout the world, as we noted early from Patrick Johnstone, they are disproportionately underrepresented in positions of leadership and authority. In many ways, Christian work mirrors that of secular occupations with regard to the placement of women. If women in secular corporations and businesses at some point hit the *glass ceiling*, a position above which they cannot go, then the Christian missionary endeavor certainly has its equivalent.

When this respondent from Oceania was looking to become involved in mission work, she noticed something during her interview in North America with the mission organization in which she is now a senior leader.

The fact that there was one woman in the room who seemed very much a token woman, who didn't ask me any questions, that was *not* encouraging at that point.

She went on to say how she pursued the issue of male leadership in the interview.

The second question I asked is, "What about women in leadership? Do you have women in leadership, do you intend to have women in leadership, where are we?" And (*the mission director*) answered that question because he was in the room. And he was very honest. He said, "We are struggling in this area, we are committed to it, but we haven't quite figured out the socialization of that issue. But we are committed to it." Which was, I appreciated the fact that he was honest, and it sort of gave me a sense of, there was movement on some of these things; that, at least there was an openness to it.

While the staff at the mission organization appeared somewhat aware of the issue of disparity in male/female leadership, we can only speculate as to how this particular organization (and many others facing the same problem) continued to respond.

Some data illustrated an overt male gender preference with regard to leadership and ability (and, by extension, an undermining tendency regarding females in leadership roles). This we see as a simple extension of perceived gender roles and the entrenched expectations and norms associated with men and women that we discussed earlier. For the current study, if gendered division of labor applies to missionary service in general then it is magnified in the area of leadership and authority. A female missionary in India spoke about this.

> Interviewer: Are women accepted by men, to be taught by them?
>
> Respondent: No! In very few circles. In (*organization name*) I was given tremendous opportunities to teach and preach. In my church, maybe on woman's Sunday there is an opportunity given to preach. I requested them to let me present a paper on the role of women in Christian ministry and mission from an Indian context. It was well appreciated by them, but no pastor or anyone did anything after that, so that's the thing.
>
> Interviewer: So in a way you are getting a lot of historical opposition from within the church?
>
> Respondent: Yeah, some they don't express, but it is there very much in their minds. Some they encourage but majority, they don't encourage women or take them seriously.

From North America, a mission leader's discussion of recruiting practices was telling with regard to understanding male and female roles in mission from his mobilizing perspective. Motivated by the desire to recruit a particular kind of *leader* and with reference to the work of women in the organization, he confessed,

> These women are good but they are not apostolic. They're never going to recruit apostolic leaders. That is, the apostle Paul would not be interested in being recruited by my wife or yours. Paul is going to be challenged by another apostolic leader.

The implication here is that prospective mission workers (of a particular high caliber) could only be ministered to and in this case, recruited by men. During the same interview, this view was reinforced by a comment that "like attracts like," and further by this statement.

> So what we ended up doing was getting a lot of people that were second, but we would say, second lieutenants, co-captains of the teams, but not really the people with the form to go to new places and go to difficult places. So they ended up sitting around the room, talking about it and praying about, rather than doing it. Our women could go out and say all the right stuff, but they didn't say it as an apostolic leader, they said it as a person that loves people and a gift of encouragement and help. That's different I think.

Another of our mobilizer respondents, this time from Oceania, emphasized perceived notions of gender distinction, not from the perspective of spiritual gifting or perceived lack of authority, but from a more biologically determined rationale. Note here, his use of the term *emasculation*.

> And I think that's a cultural thing for us—that going back twenty, thirty years, the *pioneering* spirit, the *can do* spirit was very much there. Tell me I can't do something and I'll go and do it. I think there's been a real emasculation going on in our society in the last twenty, twenty-five years. We see it in all sorts of ways, whether it's that boys did poorly at school, girls did well because the system has changed and it suits girls better than boys. This whole thing, the need for men to go and chase things, you know the whole testosterone driven thing is seen as bad in our society and that's the lessons people get told, especially men. It's a surprise to get taught to be assertive, chase after your dreams. We even have rugby games amongst little kids now where the goal is to make a draw so nobody wins, because someone might get hurt feelings if they lose. What I've really seen happen is this loss of get up and go. I call that emasculation that's happening, and part of our role is, or my role is, to try and reverse the effects of that.

In the context of the interview he was clearly appealing for more men to engage in mission and the "loss of get up and go" equated to inertia in mission service from men.

Although there is a much larger context to this response, this comment reveals a particular logic developed (probably unconsciously) by an underlying assumption of gender difference even if the motivation for such a strong position is ambiguous. In the context of the interview he was clearly appealing for more men to engage in mission and the "loss of get up and go" equated to inertia in mission service from men. He observed that this was happening because of a diminishing masculinity (emasculation) in his context. However, we cannot say if that was because more women are answering *the call* than men or because he only wants to recruit men. The reality of gender balance in mission leads us to assume the former. If it is the latter, then what place do women have in mission at all?

The question of leadership is significant because to a large extent the leaders set policy; they are understood to be the source of spiritual and biblical authority and as such exert tremendous influence on their followers. Our findings indicate that for many women, leaders have the potential to be the gatekeepers in matters of service. As we have noted, a significant number of women are attracted to mission and the potential for more is great. A South American minister would agree and mentioned the desire of many young women to contribute in mission.

> Generally, they are girls. So, if you look at it, there are more girls willing to go into missions long term, to sacrifice comfort, than boys or couples. They do exist as well, but not so many. That is something that is specifically true here and now, at least in our experience.

This final observation brings us back to the observation we made at the beginning of this section—more women than men are, and remain, involved in mission, but our data and other statistical research reveals that far more men are in mission leadership than women. We note this as a hindrance to mission involvement because the phenomenon has potential to reduce the recruiting and effectiveness of the largest representative gender in mission. It leads us to wonder how much more could be possible in mission if women were accepted as truly equal co-workers for the gospel, without limit on role or authority? What difference would it make to mission strategies if more women were appointed to senior leadership positions in mission? Are we retarding mission potential because of a particular theological perspective, and does it really have to be this way?

How much more could be possible in mission if women were accepted as truly equal co-workers for the gospel, without limit on role or authority?

SENDING CONTEXT

In mission service there are discouragements enough without adding gender bias to the mix, that is assuming you make it into mission service. Discouragement from the church, represented by its leaders and fellow Christians, is something those called to mission least expect, yet it happens too often. We can understand how easy it might be for some to doubt the conviction of those called to mission. Something like an inquisition can ensue, testing the authenticity of the personal revelation. We would like to think that that is the responsibility of our communities of faith to test the validity of our call, but it is rarely so straightforward. Assuming the call is indeed true, those commissioned to mission need to hold on to their faith and persevere in order to see the fulfillment of their calling, as our respondents did.

It is miraculous that people receive a call at all. The globalized context in which we live today presents many new obstacles against the recruitment of laborers for the Lord's harvest fields. "The pattern of this world" (Romans 12:2) resists it, making it difficult for Christians to consider a call. Among our global voices we detected four parts of our globalized world's pattern that particularly hinder mission involvement. These are factors similar to those Bosch identified as contributing to a crisis in mission. We see the parts interrelated, and although we mention them only briefly they represent significant obstacles to the gospel and mission.

> Assuming the call is indeed true, those commissioned to mission need to hold on to their faith and persevere in order to see the fulfillment of their calling.

Before we address the stuff of *this world*, we will first consider the discouragements arising from challenges much closer to home, in the church.

Church Discouragement

The missionary road can be a very lonely one, especially starting out. As we heard in our chapter on vocation from respondents who experienced some sort of clear call, the realization that God has a grand purpose for your life in some far-flung ministry can be quite ecstatic. What a comedown it is if there is no one else around who understands the significance of that encounter. Discouragement can set in. Even worse, church leaders or other Christians can be prone to figuratively kick you while you are down.

A missionary from the United Kingdom shared this example with us from their experience.

> The church of which I was a member until my teenage years was not helpful in my missionary calling, actually they thought it was something bad!

We could *spin* that comment into a great marketing campaign to attract radical Christian youth for mission service, "Mission: it's bad." Or not. Sadly, from a South American missionary we heard a similar tragic story.

> My biggest hindrances (were) the mature pastors and Christian leaders who did not see the importance of missions. They thought that it was a waste that we would not prefer some ministry in our country. Consistent with their theology, they tried to discourage us.

Mission-oriented innovation was also frowned upon in the experience of this mission leader in India who trained a lawyer wanting to step out into some creative local mission involvement using their law training. Apparently discouragement is consistent with this church's theology too.

> Some years ago we trained a lawyer; at the end of the seminar he wrote of his goals and one of his goals was he wanted to start a free legal aid service for people under trial—those who were awaiting trial, charged with a crime; in India, you get to a hearing, it may be many years, but this is our legal system in India. And unfortunately a lot of poor people can't afford fancy lawyers and so on, so that was his vision, to use the occasion to share the love of Christ, because Christ has talked about prisoners and so on. After about a month, he comes back and says, "Why don't you advise me? My pastor says that what I'm doing is not ministry at all; it's work, my ministry is in the church." It's this, instead of embracing this guy and encouraging him and using his testimony to encourage others in the church, here is discouragement because of his understanding of what missions is all about.

From Eastern Europe a missionary told a similar story. Apparently they were considered to be "not really a Christian" enough to be considered seriously for mission service.

> Yes, too few (say) that what I am doing is good and they rejoice. Too few. They tell me, you're not really a Christian, you need to grow, you're not allowed, you're still at the beginning. It's happened to me.

A fellow missionary from Eastern Europe echoed this from their experience.

> I think for me one of the greatest obstacles is the lack of encouragement. And the lack of encouragement from people who could say, "Even if you make mistakes, we will be with you." And I think this is one of the biggest things that would make you give up, I mean when you don't have it. And it's very hard to find people to encourage you. Very hard to find people to encourage you. Especially in this area.

Secularism

We now turn from voices that represented respondents who experienced discouragement from the Christian community in their sending context to wider societal contexts and some of those issues that David Bosch identified as influencing his crisis. We will only touch on them briefly to bring them to your attention. It is important to note that they were not solely Western issues; they are global and in the church.

A church leader in the United Kingdom spoke of how the influence of secularism has become a retardant to mission involvement.

> I think one of the reasons why in the West we went down the league so far in sending missionaries is because our society's becoming more and more secular, more and more ungodly; there is no Christian influence and frankly at the moment there are laws that actively hinder. So, I think we have an awful lot of work yet to do as far as evangelism and gospel preaching is concerned and looking to how we can bring the gospel out into our community again and get the gospel message across. I think if you have a burden for souls, that will naturally transfer itself into mission and you will naturally want to hear what's going on and what's happening in Asia, you know, and go out once a year or so. I think one of the main things would be, "Where's your gospel heart?" Where's the gospel heart—because I think that feeds every mission. If they've no gospel heart, well why pray for mission? Why pray for missionaries? Why pray for souls? So I think that's important. I think we're losing that a wee bit today. We've become very insular and if people come to us that's great, but don't ask us to go out to people. And then when we do go out it's sometimes with a confusing message that's not clear-cut, and we may have to revise our evangelistic motivation.

> *Where's the gospel heart— because I think that feeds every mission. If they've no gospel heart, well why pray for mission? Why pray for missionaries? Why pray for souls?*

Depending on your perception of mission, this leader could be inferring that secularism is creating a mission-*receiving* environment as much as a mission sending one. It certainly creates opportunities for evangelism and other local ministry. The point they make about a person's "gospel heart" is particularly important. It relates to how interest in mission can be fostered. Applied from the perspective of mission retardants, this leader would see the lack of a gospel heart as a factor that hinders mission involvement.

This sense is born out in a completely different context. A church member in East Asia observed that Christians there were being seduced by secularism and they associated that with a lack of involvement in mission.

> I think secularism is the main culprit. Church today is very secularized. Christians are seeking what the world is seeking—something trendy and new. To acquire it they need more money, so they work harder and thus have no time to serve the Lord, no money to spend for missions.

This church member very insightfully touches on three by-products of our globalized reality that are interrelated with secularism and each other, so we will briefly explore them next: individualism, prosperity, and time.

Individualism

The interrelationship of the effects of globalization appears again from this Eastern European mission mobilizer's perspective. They contended that the chief retardant of mission involvement is the greater freedoms and financial blessings that enable an individual to focus on one's own well-being.

> I think that one of the challenges that (*nation name*) is facing right now is things are starting to go better economically, so people have all these possibilities of getting a better life here or going to Western Europe; they're free to travel anywhere they want to. And so I think that one of the dangers, not only for missions but for churches in general, is this increasing individualism and prosperity that can take people's attention off God's kingdom and get them to focus on their own well-being.

A church leader from East Asia spoke of the effects on mission strategy of an individualistic mind-set in their churches.

> Even though the worldwide church tends to evaluate very highly the (*nation name*) church's potential, I as an insider feel that we are seriously hampered by an individual approach to missions.

Another minister in East Asia shared similarly, and their response expanded on the implications of individualism at a church-wide level for mission.

> I think the (*nation name*) church's individualistic tendency has contributed to competitive missions but at the expense of sound direction. As its dysfunctional result there has been competitive drive for church growth. The kingdom of God is expanded through partnership of various individuals and churches. In that sense, the (*nation name*) church has not contributed but is detrimental to furthering of God's kingdom.

Individualism affects the potential for partnership, which negatively affects an authentic extension of the kingdom of God.

In their view individualism affects the potential for partnership, which negatively affects an authentic extension of the kingdom of God.

A mobilizer in the United Kingdom sees individualistic effects in their context too, limiting an emphasis on reaching out which, as suggested by their compatriot church leader in our secularism segment, has negative implications for mission.

> So all the emphasis is on our Sunday services, all the emphasis is on our home groups, and very little emphasis on what we are doing within our workplace or

within the church in terms of linking it with the community—in evangelism, in social action, or whatever it is. That's the major barrier, people are not being taught. There is a very selfish and very individualistic understanding of Christianity and that's where I go back to the original teaching I had in that church which was very counter-cultural at the time.

This person seemed to believe that better education could curb the influence of selfish individualism, but combined with the other elements of globalization identified here it has a very captivating allure.

Prosperity

In a similar vein to the East European voice that introduced us to individualism, this East African mission leader recognized the dark side of the kind of freedom that financial prosperity can bring and the individualistic, self-centered perspectives it can foster.

> I think sometimes one of the things that keeps coming out is the role-modeling that is taking place where there seems to be a conspiracy towards living well. Health, wealth, pursuing your career, making money, living well in a certain class. And therefore any involvement in Christian or God's work is not seen as fitting within that framework because there seems to be understanding that Christian work or God's work is not where money is—and if Christian work brings money, then somebody is commercializing God's work. The whole issue of personal comfort, and that may sound a very reductionist perspective, but I think personal comfort plays a very central role. Where I feel this is what I should do, but when I try to think what it will mean to me, I see I am not ready to pay the cost, particularly in relation to Christian ministry.

A conspiracy towards living well is emerging as a significant hindrance to mission involvement.

In this chapter "a conspiracy towards living well" is emerging as a significant hindrance to mission involvement. This leader drives right to the heart of the matter: seeking after individual comfort at the expense of obedience to God retards mission.

A mission-supporting church member in East Asia commented on the diaspora of their nation's people living in the United States and observed a phenomenon where mission interest declines as prosperity increases with each new generation.

> I think it is the worldly greed of (*nation name*) immigrants. Many second-generation (*East Asian*)-Americans are smart, doing well at college. And their parents want them to be successful in the world. I think most 1.5 and 2nd generation (*East Asian*)-Americans are not interested in mission primarily because of their parents' desire for them to achieve the American Dream, for which they have emigrated to America.

This is an instance where family can hinder mission involvement by the choices parents make for their children. The choices are decided according to certain priorities. The priority of a "better life" can be a powerful motivator and the expectations of prosperity can weigh heavy on the children for generations.

Time

Individual and financial well-being are not the only influencers of priorities. There are many more that hinder the cause of mission. We will mention only one other influence that appeared regularly in our responses—time. The curious thing about time is that we all have the same amount of it (not counting the length of years) but we so easily complain that we do not have enough of it. However, the issue is not time itself, it is what we decide to do with the time we have. It is an issue of *prioritization*. Keep that in mind as we listen to this recording of our final voices for this chapter, all mission mobilizers.

> We so easily complain that we do not have enough of it. However, the issue is not time itself, it is what we decide to do with the time we have. It is an issue of *prioritization*.

The first two mobilizers to comment were in South America and they said almost identical things (which is why we included them both).

> Pastors are involved in many activities so it is difficult for them to agree to something else, mostly if it is missions.

> The challenge is to be able to involve pastors, for they are loaded with activities and sometimes they prevent the work from having continuity.

The expectation here is that mission involvement would be accelerated if ministers were able to be involved. But demands on their time prohibit them from doing so. The first mobilizer hints that busyness could be being used as an excuse, as this next mobilizer from the United Kingdom also seemed to suggest.

> One of the challenges is that people seem to be so busy. For many churches, what we are going in to ask them to do requires time investment—in relationships, in individuals. It's not about being able to invest in say, twenty students who come along; but there are maybe five that the Lord seems to be working on and they could invest in them. But that's, again, very difficult because people tend to find, broadly, they have no time for *in depth* involvement.

If it is an issue of prioritization and not in fact time, then we can interpret the mobilizer's response as indicating that the people they're trying to mobilize would rather *choose* to spend their time elsewhere. Society and the workplace and family expectations may dictate our use of time to some degree but it is still a choice, and when it comes to avoiding mission involvement, it can be a convenient choice.

The prioritization quandary is not limited to church leaders or church members either. Many a mobilizer reading this book will likely resonate with this mobilizer in Oceania.

There are so many things we can do to promote mission and so much time and energy required to "make that work," so "where do we invest time wisely and well?"

> I think the biggest challenge for all of us is finding the time to do (effective mobilization). And that to me is a serious issue that I need to get my head around. Because there's so much, especially when we are talking about collaboration and working together, there's a lot of energy and time that is needed to make that work, just simply because relationships are high maintenance … And so where do we invest time wisely and well? And I think for mobilization it's a huge issue.

From the fuller context of this response this mobilizer was discussing the cost of collaborating with other mobilizers to present a unified perspective of mission to the church in their nation. As admirable as that may be, it clearly presented challenges to this mobilizer who was also concerned about their responsibilities to their own mission organization.

Throughout this entire section investigating mission retardants that emerged from our data we have presented far more problems than solutions, but sometimes identifying the problems can bring us a considerably closer to determining appropriate solutions.

To all mobilizers, mission organization recruiters, mission leaders, missionaries, church leaders, church mission committee members, mission supporters, and mission-interested church members everywhere, we sincerely hope the information in this book will help you to number your days, understand your times, and discern the most appropriate way for you to prioritize your resources for the extension of Christ's kingdom and God's glory over all the earth (cf. Psalm 39:4, 1 Chronicles 12:32 and Psalm 57:5).

The workplace and family expectations may dictate our use of time to some degree but it is still a choice, and when it comes to avoiding mission involvement, it can be a convenient choice.

While the opposition to mission can seem overwhelming, the patterns of this world are not impervious to the Spirit of God. As we have heard testified, the Spirit can indeed penetrate and transform from within, calling more laborers out. But the enemy is not content to allow that to happen unchallenged. The *powers* will do all they can to thwart the mission of God.

CHAPTER 22

SPIRITUAL OPPOSITION

Our final theme to explore concerning issues that retard mission involvement is more of an epilogue than a chapter, but we felt the subject matter deserved focused attention. In this case, the fact that it was not mentioned a great deal reflects limitations in our line of questioning more than it being an insignificant factor in the life of missionaries and the work of mission. Our representation of voices may be few, but it is appropriate that we end our section on retardants with the acknowledgment that mission involvement is a spiritual vocation that seeks to advance a kingdom—God's. It is the front line of a cosmic battle well described in the Bible for which we already know the outcome—our God reigns!

> *How beautiful on the mountains*
> *are the feet of those who bring good news,*
> *who proclaim peace,*
> *who bring good tidings,*
> *who proclaim salvation,*
> *who say to Zion,*
> *"Your God reigns!" (Isaiah 52:7)*

We have explored the complexities of funding and financial policies, the hindering limitations of mission organizations and their staff, the powers at play within gender differences, and the discouragement and deceptive seductions of sending contexts. All of these *realms* and much more—everything that would hinder people from bringing good news, proclaiming peace, good tidings, and salvation—can be part of a campaign by powers that struggle to resist change to the status quo of *this* world.

Theological differences interpret the influence of darkness in various ways, but the Scriptures indicate that the ruler of the realms of this world (Matthew 4:8–10, John 12:31, Ephesians 2:2 and 6:12, etc.) is working against the encroaching kingdom of God.

A popular spiritual warfare analogy is that of a *fifth* column, a traitorous group applying subversive tactics that seek to undermine the morale of an enemy from within. Our spiritual enemy is thought to influence us from within as well, with demoralizing thoughts and discouragement. Peter refers to the devil as an enemy "prowling around like a roaring lion looking for someone to devour." (1 Peter 5:8). He knew better than most, so what was Peter's solution? Be self-controlled, alert, and resist the devil, standing firm in our faith (strong convictions and beliefs) because of our solidarity with the ever-growing population of Christians the world over who are contending for the faith in similar ways (1 Peter 5:8–9, cf. Jude 1:3–4).

A mission organization staff member in East Africa illustrated this point when they shared with us what starting out in mission service meant for them.

> There was a spiritual battle in the biblical sense of the word, you know? That is, I think that when you start a new stage of life, the devil doesn't like it at all. And he starts reminding you of all kinds of things from the past, to make you disqualify yourself in your own eyes; to say you aren't worthy, you aren't good, you aren't suitable, there are others, you're the wrong age, you haven't got the training, you haven't; no, I couldn't say that I didn't have training, but the devil comes with all of these, you know?

A missionary from South America knows.

> For me, in the beginning, the obstacles were lies. Lies of the evil one. In my mind. I mean, I was thinking for others. What others might say—maybe they weren't saying it to my face but there were lies, or they might have a seed of truth.

All of these *realms* and much more—everything that would hinder people from bringing good news, proclaiming peace, good tidings, and salvation—can be part of a campaign by powers that struggle to resist change to the status quo of *this* world.

Oh the cunning stratagems of the devil! The enemy has a way of using us against ourselves and each other, taking seeds of truth and corrupting them. Like Peter, Paul encourages to take a firm stand against the devil's schemes, against the powers of this dark world, and against the spiritual forces of evil in the heavenly realms (Ephesians 6:11ff). The enemy comes against all of us, but missionaries are particularly vulnerable because after all, mission is by its very nature the taking of "enemy territory."

An East African church member we interviewed saw mission's relationship to spiritual warfare as plain as day. The solution was as obvious to them as it seemed to be to Peter and Paul.

> I think mission work is very serious and involves a lot of spiritual warfare, which is one thing that I have realized that many missionaries are not trained in. They get a lot of attacks, which to me are very obvious; it's just a simple prayer! I mean, how hard can it be? But since you don't understand the whole concept of spiritual warfare they begin and continue to live in suffering. And I have seen it. So what I did is that I had a book and I gave it to some of the missionaries so that they got to learn what spiritual warfare was in the first place, and now they are able to use the weapons. And I believe also each organization that is doing this missionary work should always have a prayer team that are covering them with prayer and just basically putting a ring of fire around them.

If you want to know the antidote to factors that retard mission's flame in the hearts of believers, here it is. It is basic. Just cover them with prayer and pray "a ring of fire around them." "Ask the Lord of the harvest, therefore, to send out workers into his harvest field" (Luke 10:2) and watch the fire spread.

PART FIVE: SUMMARY

It is a wonder that the kingdom of God advances at all when those who are entrusted with leading it are the cause of holding it back. At this end of the section on factors that retard mission, we can identify a similar common denominator with those factors that accelerate mission awareness—people. God's people hold potential to influence positively or negatively. Then again, very few things in mission do not involve people because the kingdom advances by people, one surrendered life at a time.

To consider people a *resource* for mission can be devaluing, yet we remain the critical component in God's plan. Through people God extends his dominion over darkness. Through God's people the light of life shines and society is salted with righteousness and justice. God has also invested in us the authority to control domains through our choices and the imposition of our will. In this, mission can become a bit *hit and miss*. No more do we see that than in the human mechanisms that control the flow of resources.

Through people God extends his dominion over darkness. Through God's people the light of life shines and society is salted with righteousness and justice. God has also invested in us the authority to control domains through our choices and the imposition of our will.

There is a reason the missionary Paul held that "the love of money is a root of all kinds of evil" (1 Timothy 6:10a). He was echoing Jesus' warning that we cannot serve two masters (cf. Matthew 6:24, Luke 16:13). The thirst for and pursuit of wealth seduces and too easily corrupts. In our experience many missionaries would say they do not have a problem with money. If anything, their struggle is to trust for supply of their basic human needs. That is, until they actually have surplus funds; then it can be a different story.

In chapter eighteen we saw some dramatic contrasts between churches that were generous toward mission, churches whose generosity was thought to be misapplied, and churches that wrestled with the challenge of deciding what need received the funds available. The voices that spoke to these issues indicated that the people who were in control of the funds were doing the best they could with the tough decisions they faced, yet we are left to wonder about the systems of control that can determine so much that happens (or does not happen) in mission due to how funding is directed.

Educating Christians about the wise use of funds and the place of money in God's kingdom helped put things in perspective for some respondents. For those who spoke encouragingly about some educational programs, these helped them to reprioritize their giving. Their choice of where their investment in mission would be directed presupposed the knowledge of a need. In contrast, other respondents felt led to *not* make their needs known at all, but would rather trust God alone for supply. Did such silence hinder would-be donors from directing their funds toward the unknown need? We cannot say. There was no direct correlation between keeping silent on need and being desperately short on supply, but some of our respondents spoke of times when their faith was certainly stretched. For whatever reason we can say that the perception of limited supply and low levels of income within mission service was deemed to be a significant retardant to mission interest from a mobilization perspective.

Whether the finances were flowing freely or hardly at all, they still needed to be managed. Churches wrestled with this in one way and mission organizations in another. Some voices spoke of tough decisions made at an organizational level that were hurtful to the missionaries in the field. In light of the current global economic crisis we cannot imagine it getting better any time soon. But God is not limited by our imagination. We chose to conclude the retardant theme of finance with a declaration of hope. God does provide. It was wonderfully refreshing to hear testimonies of God's faithful provision, even through those who had little to give. A widow's mite is a grand investment in God's kingdom (cf. Luke 21: 1–4).

We cannot imagine it getting better any time soon. But God is not limited by our imagination.

Our buoyancy was short lived as we moved into chapter nineteen. Where mission organizations were discussed in terms of their financial control in the previous chapter, in chapter nineteen the critique widened to other aspects of mission organizations that constricted mission interest. Application requirements were seen to be unnecessarily cumbersome, potentially discouraging people from attempting to join an organization. Organizations' ethos, their policies, procedures, and practices were seen to repel some people too. We viewed this issue from the perspective of the inquirer, and the point was made that some organizations would suit some people more than others.

We encouraged mission recruiters to remain aware of this for the sake of the inquirers and the mission organization itself. Nothing undermines the morale of a mission organization (and therefore retards the advance of mission) more than a cacophony of dissenting voices within an organization. This can be avoided at the point of application and orientation, with recruiters and agency mission coaches working with people to ensure the organization was going to be a good fit *for the inquirer*. We advise against seeing it the other way around. God's people are precious and selection processes for mission organizations need to honor those applying. If there are reasons an applicant would not suit an organization, denying membership must be done in a way that maintains the dignity of the applicant. Another mission might resonate better with their values and preferences. That is, assuming other organizations exist in the context.

Continuing our thesis that people both help and a hinder mission, we found that people working for mission organizations could too easily deter mission interest. This was a particularly frustrating reality for some of our respondents from new sending nations. The other frustration from that cohort of our global voices was the polar opposite of what has been discussed regarding mission structures. For those from new sending nations, the biggest issue with mission organizations was their absence, or at least the support structures mission organizations could be expected to provide. We suggested that somewhere between too much infrastructure and not enough there is balance to be found: a fulcrum point which tips more toward helping than hindering mission involvement.

One final tendency of mission organizations that was critically observed from a variety of locations was the perceived commercialization of mission. The business of selling mission seemed unnecessary to many and distasteful to most. In this regard we detected an underlying influence of *this world's* economic philosophies affecting mission organizations. The principles of free-market business were seen to be leeching in, dictating how mission organizations assess their success. We noted how far from biblical norms that seemed to many of our respondents and how close it seemed to resonate with those indicted in the Bible for being seduced by wealth; which, we add, need not be limited to money, it includes *serving* other *metrics* of success as well.

Arguably our most difficult chapter to write was chapter twenty where we were encouraged by our global voices to expose discrimination against women in mission. That is a very blunt way of putting it, but some of our respondents pulled no punches. We worked hard to walk a non-judgmental line in the presentation of all our data, but we could be seen to be pushing our own agenda with the gender issue. Rest assured that we only represented what was very evident from our global voices. Regardless of theological persuasion or sociological norms, the lesson to be learned from this chapter is that we need to be very aware of power disparities in mission. That is not limited to gender issues. It includes cultural, socioeconomic, linguistic, and educational biases, among others as well. It would do the cause of mission a great deal of good if we were able to love one another, bear with one another, live out the gift of reconciliation, and work hard to keep the unity of the Spirit through the bond peace—also known as shalom, harmony, or balance (cf. Ephesians 4:2–6). This is the ethos of the kingdom of God.

> It would do the cause of mission a great deal of good if we were able to love one another, bear with one another, live out the gift of reconciliation, and work hard to keep the unity of the Spirit through the bond peace—also known as shalom, harmony, or balance.

It is not like the pattern of this world, but all too often Christians forget that. Chapter twenty-one opens in a discouraging way in this regard. Missionary respondents reported that those they expected to help them most with their missionary call encouraged them the least. In the worst examples, ministers and Christians actively discouraged mission involvement. Admittedly, extenuating factors may be involved beyond our knowledge, but the impact on the missionary respondents was evident as they recalled these experiences; and it was untenable.

You could expect discouragement from the unbelieving world around us but from within the family of faith we live to a higher standard. A discussion about the effects of general society made up the bulk of the rest of chapter twenty-one, and it had quite the global reach. The topics spanned the influence of secularism, individualism, prosperity, and time prioritization on mission involvement. Each of these interacted with the others and some of our respondents clustered several together with the same breath. Taken as a whole, they were exposed as things that seductively woo Christians away from kingdom-oriented activities in general and mission involvement in particular, by promising peace and plenty. Ironically, we also saw the outcome of these self-centered pursuits: busyness. Even when pursuits were ministry oriented they seemed to be a convenient retardant to mission. The cost of mission can seem extreme when set against whatever perceived benefits this world offers, but our global voices would testify to a person that there really is no cost in the end. After all,

> What do you benefit if you gain the whole world but lose your own soul? Is anything worth more than your soul? For the Son of Man will come with his angels in the glory of his Father and will judge all people according to their deeds. (Matthew 16:25–26 NLT)

This promise of Jesus puts so much into perspective and our section concluded with a short chapter on that very issue. For chapter twenty-two, it was important for us to step back from the gloomy look at retardants to see them for what they are, machinations of the powers of this world seeking to resist the advance of the kingdom of God. When we are in a crisis, wrestling against the imposed will of others or being disadvantaged by the context around us, we can feel very impotent and alone. In this final chapter we heard voices reminding us that we have an enemy that seeks to undermine our calling, causing us to lose confidence in our faith. As we will expound in our final chapter we need to realize that we are contenders in a spiritual battle, and we should regularly take a step back and assess the powers at work in any given situation. Then, as the writer to the Hebrews encourages us, we need to press on with our purpose, the role we have been called to play, to see God glorified in all nations.

> *Let us hold tightly without wavering to the hope we affirm, for God can be trusted to keep his promise. Let us think of ways to motivate one another to acts of love and good works. (Hebrews 10:23–24 NLT)*

Questions for Reflection

1. Why don't you just give up now? What keeps you pressing on in spite of the obstacles that you face? How can you encourage others to press on?
2. If you have or are contemplating ceasing your active participation in God's global cause, what has influenced your decision?
3. Recall a time (or times) when God proved himself faithful to you. What did it feel like to experience that breakthrough? Do you tell others about God's deliverance? When thinking about your present struggles, can you believe for God to do it again? Are you asking God to do that?

4. How have you worked through the hurt that you have experienced from other Christians on your mission journey? Are you able to come to a place of forgiveness? Can you believe God to redeem those experiences? Have you asked God to do so?

5. Deep down do you sense that mission has cost you too much? What is it that you feel you lack or have lost? Is it in comparison with others, or is it something necessary for your basic survival? What can you ask God to do about that?

PART SIX: MOVING ON

By day the Lord went ahead of them in a pillar of cloud to guide them on their way and by night in a pillar of fire to give them light, so that they could travel by day or night. Neither the pillar of cloud by day nor the pillar of fire by night left its place in front of the people.
(Exodus 13:21–22)

In 2005 the Mission Mobilization Research Team of the World Evangelical Alliance Mission Commission set out on a quest to provide the evangelical missions community with tangible evidence of factors that help promote mission involvement. Along the way we realized that the very concept of mission was difficult to pin down and that assumptions about mission were in considerable flux. As a result, we coined the term *missional anomie*, recognizing it as a state of relative normlessness in mission. Unstable situations make people feel very vulnerable, but by placing differing perceptions of mission on continuums we aimed to help the evangelical missions community embrace the differences and affirm one another in a broader understanding of what God is working to achieve in the world.

The systems of this world throw up many barriers to thwart God's plan for it. David Bosch articulated some of those threats and we identified some more from our data. Bosch was buoyant in his belief that God's mission could not be stopped, so we were encouraged to press on to identify phenomena that our voices indicated as accelerants to that mission. Our research team's collective experience of mobilization led us to people willing and able to tell us their stories of mission, but it was not until we heard the harmony among our global voices that we were able to discern which activities helped and which hindered mission involvement.

> It was not until we heard the harmony among our global voices that we were able to discern which activities helped and which hindered mission involvement.

From that data we grouped together activities that were common to the concept of mobilization and we identified them as mobilization ideal-types. We heard some very strong opinions from mobilizers invested in one mobilization ideal-type or another, and we saw how they were all quite interrelated in philosophy and activity. Ultimately they all seek to influence a person toward greater involvement in God's mission, but none by themselves seemed any more effective than the others. Even together, integrated, they were limited means, models, methods, and mechanisms.

Each mobilization ideal-type contained certain accelerants identified from our data, so we turned from the devices used by mobilizers to the lived experience of our global voices to explore those elements that encouraged them to engage in mission service. We grouped the accelerants into three themes, but explored them as four categories in the *Accelerants* section of the book. The first accelerant theme, incorporating two categories, involved influential relationships. We first we separated out familial relationships as its own category before moving on to hear of other types of relationships that showed potential to advance mission involvement. In the second accelerant theme we noted the impact of various forms of education, observing that learning influenced mission involvement. But, according to our voices, neither of those themes, relational or educational, was strongly identified as that which *conceived* a commitment to mission involvement. Each category certainly supported and strengthened a commitment to mission but something else, something *other*, was credited with giving life to that commitment. Our voices experienced it as a calling, which became the climax of our research.

A supernatural sense of vocation, whether it was a sudden realization or a gradual awareness, was so compelling that it motivated our respondents to pursue God's purpose for their lives in the wider world regardless of the opposition; and many of those we interviewed spoke of significant opposition. These things we identified as retardants to mission service. There were not many dominant themes, but instead a lot of smaller categories. Little foxes that spoil the vine if you will (cf. Song of Songs 2:15 KJV); occurrences that hinder the voice of God. Financial concerns, controls, and policies were noticeable retardants. Mission organization principles, practices, and people could hinder as much as they have the potential to help. The ancient issue of gender was also identified as limiting the potential for mission, particularly the leadership potential of more than half the world's mission force. We then exposed some damaging influences within our sending contexts, even within sending churches.

Our section on retardants and our entire conversation with global voices concluded with the acknowledgment that mission activity is the leading edge of the global advance of the kingdom of God. That advance does not proceed without resistance. The enemy attacks from without and within, and we need to be aware of the powers and schemes that seek to undermine God's redemption of the world person-by-person, community-by-community, and environment-by-environment until the glorious return of our Lord.

> This is the narrative of mission, not in a triumphant or militaristic sense, but in a humble, compassionate, and reconciliatory one.

Jesus declared that from the time of John the baptizer the kingdom of heaven began advancing (Matthew 11:12). We have no cause to think it has since stopped. The very gates of hades will not keep it from advancing (Matthew 16:18). This is the narrative of mission, not in a triumphant or militaristic sense, but in a humble, compassionate, and reconciliatory one. We are still the people of God who wander through the wilderness of this world following God's Shekinah glory by a pillar of cloud when it is light and by fire when it is night. Wherever it settles, there we gather the harvest. Whenever it moves then we follow. So where do we go from here?

CHAPTER 23

FANNING THE FLAME

We mere mortals may be perplexed by the causes of Bosch's crisis and the missional anomie we identified earlier, but we were never called to be in charge anyway. We are called to be obedient. The Spirit of God is rightfully recognized as *the* Director of mission.[1] The Holy Spirit represents Jesus' presence with us even to the end of the age. This *paraclete* is the pillar that guides us. So how can we best fan that flame so we can follow it?

Our relationship with God is central to our discernment of God speaking to us by the Spirit. Our respondents' relationships with God are not made explicit throughout our presentation of analyzed data, but they are most certainly implicit. The very fact that our respondents were continuing to persevere in some form of mission service testifies to that.

If we dismantled all the scaffolding that mission leaders have erected to try and maintain mission today and peeled away the artificial cladding, we would find that the internal structure is quite robust because this dwelling has endured much worse throughout the history of the world than what we have identified. As another way of viewing the kingdom of God, the house of God is very resilient and it continues to grow room-by-room, community-by-community. We should not be surprised at this because Jesus said it was so (cf. John 14:2 and 23); and he said we would know the way to that place, his dwelling place, where we are destined to make our dwelling places. He is the way. He is both the path and the destination (cf. John 14:6–7). When we see the presence of God in this light, maintaining mission is easy. Of all the things, only one thing is needed, and Mary chose that which was better (Luke 10:42).

> If we dismantled all the scaffolding that mission leaders have erected to try and maintain mission today, and peeled away the artificial cladding, we would find that the internal structure is quite robust, because this dwelling has endured much worse throughout the history of the world than what we have identified.

We are not discounting the wonderful eschatological use of the metaphor of Jesus preparing a place for us in heaven, but instead we draw on the more immediate application of Jesus' words of comfort to the disciples, because they comfort us too and they are fuel for mission's flame. His promise to be with us to the end of the age (Matthew 28:20b)

---

1   In his exploration of Luke's missionary paradigm, Bosch notes,
    "Moreover, the Spirit not only *initiates* mission, he also *guides* the missionaries about where they should go and how they should proceed. The missionaries are not to execute their own plans but have to wait on the Spirit to direct them" (Bosch, 1991, 114).

is echoed in John 14 by Jesus. His presence with us (which we now know is via the Holy Spirit) is a critical accelerant of God's mission and always has been. What is mission, what is extending God's kingdom, if it is not going into a habitation of people to create a habitation of Christ? Not just by simply turning up there. No, missionaries go there to collect living stones so that a new room (a community of Christ-followers we commonly call *church*) can be built in God's house in which the Father and the Son will dwell, and where the Holy Spirit makes God manifest in the world through the witness of this growing community of the people of God. That and that alone sets mission apart from every other good work that looks like mission.

Why do we insist on making mission more complex than it needs to be, as if God's plans are dependent on the success of our latest ideas? Are we mission Marthas, too frantic busying ourselves *for* the Lord that we neglect our priority to be *with* the Lord? If that is the case, it would behoove us to heed the warnings of Matthew 7:21–23 and the whole of Matthew 25; stories that tell of those entrusted with kingdom responsibilities *missing the point*. The supernaturalists were speaking and driving and performing yet did not know the Lord enough to *do his will*, the foolish virgins were not ready *for the groom*, the lazy servant did not invest wisely *for the master*, and the goats were not interested in attending *to the Son of Man's needs*. What is the common denominator in these stories? The accused were concerned about a lot of things, but not the one thing.

Our point is this, if the flame of mission is dim, spending time with the Lord of the harvest will ignite even the coolest of embers. Not necessarily reading time or conference time or worship time or learning time, although those things can help. One-on-one relationship interaction with God is needed in order for you and your community to hear the One Voice that matters saying, "This is the way, walk in it" (Isaiah 30:21). We agree with our wise friend from East Africa, "I mean, how hard can it be?"

At the conclusion of our research the most productive encouragement we can give is to emphasize that mission service is a response to the voice of God, to a call that speaks out of presence, and that presence needs to be fostered. Once that is established then all manner of accelerants will help that calling become reality. In this final chapter we briefly suggest some ways you can start to apply what has been learned from the analysis of our research project. These are by no means exhaustive, and we do not give any of them the justice they deserve. Here, we take the liberty to venture more into the realm of opinion, but even as opinion it remains rooted in our research. So consider these next few closing paragraphs tiny sparks, embers floating in the darkness. Our hope is that they will land on some tinder and ignite a new flame that will advance God's glory among that nations.

Engaging

The most potent accelerant we identified was the influence of mission-interested people engaging with others. Family was very significant and then various other relationships of influence followed. Creating familial influence is somewhat tricky for Christians because there are only three ways you can become part of a family that has some mission interest.[2] You are either born into one, adopted in, or you can marry into one. We saw evidence of family of origin and marriage as accelerants in our data. But it is not one that is easily replicated. Although, with romantic interests and spouses having potential to be influential, if we consider the disproportionately high number of single females in mission...

Outside of family it was the impact of other people carrying a mission flame that most heavily influenced our respondents' understanding of mission; and either preparing the ground for or further developing the call of God on their lives. We identified mission-interested individuals, missionaries, and ministers as personal categories, along with networks and mission organizations as influential groups, but the common element was just people engaging with people. The point we take from that is that some sort of interaction has to take place. This gives credence to activities that create spaces for mission-related interaction. Our second dominant theme, education, speaks to that because opportunities for learning are great spaces for interpersonal interaction. We will go there in moment.

> Friendship is the best way for individuals to influence as an accelerant of mission interest.

One of the issues we identified in passing was, "How do you attract people to interact so that mission can be discussed?" The question is much broader than simply getting people along to a course regularly, it is related to the issue of persuasion, which we identified as a core concern for mobilizers. In their book *Influencer*, Kerry Patterson, et al., investigate the dynamics of leading change. One critical element they recognized through their research was,

> No resource is more powerful and accessible than the persuasion of the people who make up our social network. (Patterson, Grenny, Maxfield, Ron, and Switzler, 2008, 138)

They are not referring to our Facebook friends or WhatsApp groups; they mean people you interact with on a regular basis, your real friends. They go on to explain,

> These friends provide us with access to their brain, give us the strength of their hands, and even allow us to make use of their many other personal resources. In effect they provide us with social capital. (Patterson et al., 2008, 174)

The main takeaway we will leave with you is that friendship is the best way for individuals to influence as an accelerant of mission interest. If you are passionate about mission, be a friend. Invite people to participate in what you are interested in and offer them something to do to help you. Then reciprocate; go help them with something they're interested in. This creates interaction-space in a very natural and organic way. Of course, this assumes

---

2   We add the "Christian" clarifier because for some cultures family is defined quite differently than what we have assumed throughout our research, and anthropologists will be aware that there can be many more ways to become part of an extended family (for example, through ritual or rite), other than via birth, marriage or adoption.

you have the time to engage in more friendships. Sometimes we are just too busy doing mission. In which case, perhaps you are best to focus on being a missionary influencer.

Missionaries were shown to make an impact in a very short amount of time. One speaking engagement, a night hosted in a home, a *bring and share* mission-oriented dinner—whatever the occasion, in our research the Lord seemed to use missionary testimonies in powerful ways. Without a relationship with God and a deep conviction of the Spirit's leading, no one can sustain the rigors of missionary life for long. It is no wonder many of our respondents spoke of being impressed and influenced by the caliber and call of other missionaries. The light of their faith shone brightly even in their stories of hardship. Not, we suggest, because of any merit of theirs, but because of their testimony of God's faithfulness in their lives. That is compelling. What growing disciple would not want that kind of faith?

Missionaries are not usually people who are in the pulpit week after week. Many of them have not trained to be eloquent teachers or Bible expositors or motivational preachers. In these days of high expectations from the stage, missionaries are not likely to come across nearly as dynamic as the charismatic circuit speaker. So we should not put them in a position to disappoint. Our takeaway tip for missionary influencers is to be true to who God made you to be and to speak of what the Spirit of God is doing in you and through you and teaching you in your context. Personal authenticity and concern for the glory of God are key elements. God will not be upstaged. If the glory of the Lord remains the foremost aim, mission will be promoted and people will be impacted. Our global voices testified to this. The role for mission organizations and mobilizers in this regard is to manage peoples' expectations and arrange venues that will maximize the testimony of the missionary. We are long past the wow factor of exotic ethnic encounters and photographic slides. But you do not need to compete. If reality TV has shown us anything, it is how compelling someone else's real life experience can be. So missionaries, be yourself and just tell of the wonderful things the Lord has done. Can we get a witness?! Praise the Lord. Amen.

> If reality TV has shown us anything, it is how compelling someone else's real life experience can be. So missionaries, be yourself and just tell of the wonderful things the Lord has done.

Ministers on the other hand have a different opportunity than most. They can utilize the stage to engage and influence the worldview of their congregation toward mission service. However, the most powerful contribution ministers seemed to have on our respondents was encouragement. One of our missionaries longed for a minister to come alongside them and affirm them in their call with a "you can do it." Others shared how they did "do it" because a minister had encouraged them to pursue mission involvement. A minister usually enjoys a certain level of ascribed influence because of their role or status. Some self-deprecating ministers may play this down, but people do listen to them. They can have the power to bind or loose mission interest in their church so our obvious recommendation to ministers is to do all you can to loose it and let the Lord lead you and your flock wherever the Spirit will.

The social capital mentioned above is magnified if you belong to a formal network. The beauty of networks is that their collaboration can pool resources, creating a synergistic effect where the potential for influence is greater than the sum of the network's constituent parts. The ability for networks to influence for mission can be diminished by the need to belong to the network in the first place to access the resources. Nevertheless, networks still have a role to play over all. Networks are particularly helpful as places of support and encouragement to which individuals, missionaries, and ministers can point people. If you are involved in a network that is open to new members then the obvious takeaway here is to promote the network's existence so people get to know about and can engage with it. National missionary alliances can be particularly helpful in this regard. They are often a hub around which mission in, from, or to their nation connects. We commend such associations to you if you do not already participate in one.

People can access missionary associations or networks in different ways. A common way to access resources from a national missionary alliance is through a mission organization's membership. If the organization is a member often those who belong to that organization can also access the member-restricted resources of a network. These days a lot resource is freely available on network's websites. Mission organizations and their websites can be an obvious starting point for mission information too. Websites are particularly helpful because you can usually access the resource anonymously if they know where to look. As we heard from one respondent, people can be reluctant to contact a mission organization directly for fear they might be committing themselves to something they cannot easily get out of.

The sending offices of mission organizations can be great incubators for mission interest once people feel safe relating to the organization. That often depends on the organization's staff. Promoting mission involvement is the *bread and butter* of mission organizations so we need say no more about that. The lesson for organizations to learn from our research is to work hard on *personalizing* your presentation of mission. Our respondents were quite critical of organizations *commercializing* their presentation so be warned. By personalizing we don't mean laser-etch an inquirer's name on to a giveaway pen or USB drive, we mean maximize the potential of interpersonal interaction. We realize that takes a considerable amount of talented people power, but that is something we recommend you build into your philosophy of mobilization. It should also go without saying that it is in a mission organization's best interests to ALWAYS AFFIRM an inquirer's mission interest. They may not be the best fit for your organization, but that does not give you the right to suggest they are not fit for mission. Mission history bears witness to the fact that God does great things with peculiar people.

The lesson for organizations to learn from our research is to work hard on *personalizing* your presentation of mission.

From our research we conclude that every person with a heart for mission can be an influencer for mission. Although we have noted elsewhere the absence of references to prayer in our analysis, it remains a critical piece of the puzzle. Mission has traditionally been supported by dedicated prayer groups that also acted as incubators for mission. In our experience we have seen a decline in those groups and the decline is accelerating as the dedicated pray-ers age. In his *Handbook for Great Commission Ministries* (Shaw, 2016), Ryan Shaw seeks to address this challenge with his encouragement to start Global Prayer Teams. This is one of *Four Core Components for Mobilizing Ministries* recommended by Shaw, the other three being: Great Commission Bible Studies, Mission Forums, and his GO Declaration. Shaw expresses some wonderful aspirations and gives some very practical and helpful guidelines, but the lack of younger people engaging in dedicated groups for prayer or mission awareness is not for the want of more programs. It is related to what we discussed in our *Sending Context* chapter. Lives have become more pressured and priorities have shifted.

Nevertheless, as we implied while introducing this chapter, if we cease asking the Lord of the harvest to send out workers how can we expect them to hear the call? We can all pray as individuals but there is a dynamic to prayer that manifests if even only two or three gather in Jesus' name. He promises to be present. Furthermore, if those gathered agree about what they ask for, it will be done for them (Matthew 18:18–20). And remember, immediately after Jesus encouraged the disciples to pray for workers to be sent out *they* were sent out. Whether as part of a preset program or a more casually gathered group, we agree with Shaw,

> If we cease asking the Lord of the harvest to send out workers how can we expect them to hear the call?

> It is not by greater mobilizing appeals or conferences alone that Message Bearers for the unreached and unengaged will be raised. Jesus emphasizes the method of mobilizing them through focused and sustained prayer. (Shaw, 2016, 83)

Engaging in prayer for harvest laborers is mobilization like nothing else.

Educating

Shaw's *Handbook* is the latest in a long line of publications available to encourage people to reflect on the relevance of mission for them. A lot of mission resource has gone into developing educational tools to promote mission, and for good reason. Many of our respondents were influenced toward mission involvement because of educational resources that exposed them to aspects of mission involvement. The efficacy of education for mission mobilization should be apparent from our exploration of education as an accelerant. We need not explore each element separately here.

We think the main takeaway from the education theme is the issue of *relevance*. Many of our respondents spoke of education as an influence on their mission journey when they were able to identify something in mission that they could participate in, something they could contribute. For some it was the apparent need in the world and they were impacted when they realized they could be a part of meeting an aspect of that need. For others it was a specific opportunity for which their marketable skills were uniquely suited. Still others were drawn to the way aspects of mission service appealed to a latent desire they had long carried, or the education resource helped awaken a yearning they did not know was there. Whatever the unique impact, a mission-oriented educational process can create an opportunity for the Spirit of God to speak to people about their purpose in God's world—if you can get them there. For that, you would do well to review our previous point regarding interpersonal engagement.

Educators really cannot hope to determine personalized outcomes or effects *en masse*; the individual nature of each person's unique potential in mission sets a bar far too high for any educational influencer to hurdle. The positive mission-related outcomes of education of which our voices spoke were more to do with the Holy Spirit's impact on each person than the course material as such. Mission educators can, however, provide room for the Holy Spirit to inspire. Aside from that, we believe that making courses and curriculum *relevant to the context* of the student will go a long way toward attracting their attention. Most of us on the research team are involved in some form of education, so we can appreciate what we are recommending here. Redesigning curricula is no small feat, but many of our respondents seemed to indicate that mission education is well overdue for a reboot.

> What students need is inspiration, motivational guidance as to how best to *apply their sense of purpose* to the information available.

It is not about providing up-to-date information either. We now live in an information age. Information is readily available to anyone with the means of participating in mission beyond their borders (whatever those borders represent). Assuming information is available, what students need is inspiration, motivational guidance as to how best to *apply their sense of purpose* to the information available. Courses and curricula are traditionally constructed to layer information from basic or foundational to help the student understand incrementally more advanced or more complex aspects of a subject toward desired outcomes. This can be quite linear and fragmented and irrelevant and boring.

Mission courses and books attempting to promote involvement in mission can struggle to attract a hearing because they are pitched as something Christians *ought* to know, rather than something a Christian *wants* to know. The difference is the perception of relevance. A guiding principle is to start where *they* are, rather than where *you* are. That includes being prepared to answer their question, "What's in it for me?" That is a question of relevance. Platitudes and propositions will not suffice as answers. Hammering home scriptural absolutes about mission, the horrors of hell awaiting those who haven't heard, the dire needs of those in darkness, or any other means to motivate via a *push* mechanism no longer holds sway. Mission educators would do well to genuinely hold the prospective student's best interests at heart and *pull* them toward God's purposes. Motivational mission courses and books need to become personalized and speak to issues of significance and purpose. Yes, we realize this plays right in to the dominant philosophies of "Generation Me" (Twenge, 2014), which, because of our information age, is an increasingly global phenomenon; but that is precisely our point. If we are to attract successively globalized and increasingly connected generations to mission service we need to start where they are and help them hear the voice of God *for them* in their context. And… forty years after

Lausanne '74, we need to start letting a new generation set the agenda for mission into the next forty or more years of the twenty-first century.[3] That will be some reboot.

The type of education desired by the information generation is much more along the lines of discipling (mentoring and coaching) than lecturing. In the early '90s educationalist Alison King coined the phrase, "From sage on the stage to guide on the side" (King, 1993). The side-guide approach is likely to result in much more effective mission education. The interpersonal influences we identified earlier as accelerants suggest as much. But most of our education programs are still oriented around the sage on the stage, even if that sage speaks from a book or on a screen, via an online learning course. Commentators researching generational change note that the generation that started to come of age at the turn of the century expect a great deal more personalized support than previous generations (Elmore, 2010), which, in our experience, is being felt acutely by mission organizations. You can thank their parents for that (Strauss and Howe, 1991). Personal support is another way of saying guidance, which is another way of saying coaching or mentoring. Either way, it is a personnel intensive exercise, but we feel it will be worth the commitment of people, time, and money.

Ruth Wall, a WEA Mission Commission Associate and chair of the International Mission Training Network, is advocating for a more transformative learning approach in mission training. Her PhD thesis resonates with what we are encouraging here (Wall, 2014). In her chapter in the book, *Reflecting on and Equipping for Christian Mission*, edited by Stephen Bevans et al. (Wall, 2015b), Wall makes a comment that sums up what we are expressing here, "Mission educators must critically reflect and understand the underlying assumptions that underpin their practice."[4] In an online mission trainer's forum, she expressed concern for mission training to be much more learner focused, which reinforces our point.

> If you seek a transformative approach then this will start with the learners and ask different questions. For example, who are the learners? What are their concerns and questions? What is their context? How will they use (apply) this knowledge after the course? How will this course enable them to become lifelong learners? How will this course help them to relate better to God, to themselves, to others, to the world? (Wall, 2015a)

We are not educational theorists, and it is beyond the scope of this book to develop these idea-sparks further; but following the example of Ruth Wall we hope others will be inspired to cultivate them toward a major paradigm shift in mission education at all levels of training.

---

3   At times throughout the book we have marked Lausanne '74 as a major turning point in modern mission history, for indeed it was. The significance we have laid on that being forty years ago is related to the mentions of forty years in the Bible, which was often shorthand for a societal generation. Cf. Numbers 32:13, Judges 8:28 and 13:1, 1 Samuel 4:18, 2 Samuel 5:4, 2 Kings 12:1, Hebrews 3:9. We are acknowledging a generation shift in mission from that Lausanne event.

4   We took this quote from the first page of Wall's chapter in *Reflecting on and Equipping for Christian Mission* which provided for us by her in PDF format.

Before we leave the subject of education completely, we want to highlight the power of story. Storytelling was implicit throughout our data and broke through especially when books and missionary testimonies were mentioned. Storytelling is an ancient medium that should not be quickly dismissed. Combine the lived missionary experience that we identified as an accelerant with mission education and you have a powerful point of influence.

Elisabeth Elliot's *Through The Gates of Splendor*, Don Richardon's *Peace Child*, Brother Andrew's *God's Smuggler*, Bruce Olson's *Bruchko* (For This Cross I'll Kill You), Jackie Pullinger's *Chasing the Dragon*, Brother Yun's *Heavenly Man*, Heidi Baker's *There Is Always Enough*, and so many more well-written contemporary true stories of mission have inspired thousands to believe God for more from their lives. Where are the next compelling stories going to come from? Who is going to write them? We do not mean the blow-by-blow accounts from a missionary's journal; we mean tales of daring faith where God shines through to save the day. No, it probably does not represent ninty-nine percent of mission reality but we are talking about inspiration not replication. We need to get a new generation dreaming of how they can "expect great things from God and attempt great things for God" (William Carey).

With the exception of personally lived experience, a well-crafted narrative has the potential to educate like little else. Living someone else's experience vicariously through its retelling is an age-old method of inspiration. Human beings seem to be hardwired to put ourselves into the narratives of others, to feel what they felt and find elements of their story that resonate with our story to learn from them. Our thinking reflects something like this, "If they could do that (and survive to tell about it, or glorify God powerfully if they did not survive) maybe I could do (this)." The story of God through the stories of others is what the Bible contains. It is made up of testimonies, or Testaments if you will, compiled for our education (cf. 2 Timothy 4:16).

> Human beings seem to be hardwired to put ourselves into the narratives of others, to feel what they felt and find elements of their story that resonate with our story to learn from them.

Janet Litherland in her book *Storytelling from the Bible* wrote,

> Stories have power. They delight, enchant, touch, teach, recall, inspire, motivate, challenge. They help us understand. They imprint a picture on our minds. (Cavanaugh, 1998, ix)

If you have a gift of storytelling you can do mission no better service than to search out missionaries and help them tell their story of God at work. Generations will thank you for it.

Energizing

The easiest way to put out a fire is to starve it of oxygen, but you can also remove the fuel or reduce the heat. Those three elements are required for a fire to exist and influencing any one can affect the flame event. Quenching the Spirit (1 Thessalonians 5:19 KJV) is often debated as being one particular thing or another, but Paul does not specify and it comes in the middle of quite a substantial list of instructions, so it could be any manner of things. In part five of the book we identified a number of mission-flame retardants and we close out our exploration of mission in motion with a brief recommendation about how best to counteract those obstacles that hinder mission's movement. Whether seen as an object in motion or a fire, the same effect is sought—acceleration.

To neutralize the retardants, we need only to *energize* the flame. The issues we highlighted as retardants need no further explanation. They were obvious from the descriptions and illustrations we provided. As you read through the chapters you may well have formulated some solutions of your own. Rather than talk at length about each hindrance again we will instead *flip the script* to close. If the way to retard a fire is to starve, remove, or reduce, then the way to accelerate it is to feed, add, and increase. To neutralize the retardants we need only to *energize* the flame.

Lest we be seduced into a frenzy of doing more to generate friction in the hope that sparks will ignite, we remind you that our struggle is not of this world (cf. Ephesians 6:12).

- If the Christian community appears to be stemming the flow of funds into mission, believe that God will supply (cf. Philippians 4:19), pray against the powers that seek to interrupt it, and *give*.
- If the mission organization or church is acting in a way that is restricting your perception of God's will in mission, believe that, "In all things God works for the good of those who love him, who have been called according to his purpose." (Romans 8:28), pray against the powers that seek to frustrate God's will, and *forgive*.
- If anyone is devalued or their potential is diminished within the missions community, believe that in Christ there are no distinctions that privilege anyone over others (cf. Galatians 3:28), pray against the powers of division, and *love one another*.
- If those around you are discouraging and your context provides little fuel for the fire of mission, believe that Jesus has overcome the world and take heart (John 16:33), pray against the powers of doubt, and *be at peace*.

For the fire of mission
God's Spirit is flame
prayer is oxygen
actions are fuel
influence is felt.

If you remain in me and my words remain in you, ask whatever you wish, and it will be given you. This is to my Father's glory, that you bear much fruit, showing yourselves to be my disciples.
(John 15:7—8)

REFERENCES

Anderson, G.H. 1961. *The Theology of the Christian Mission.* First ed. New York, NY: McGraw-Hill.

Anderson, G.H., J.M. Phillips, and R.T. Coote. 1993. *Toward the Twenty-first Century in Christian Mission: Essays in Honor of Gerald H. Anderson.* Grand Rapids, MI: Eerdmans.

Besnard, P. 2003. *Études Durkheimiennes.* Geneve: Libraairie Droz.

Bessenecker, S. 2014. *Overturning Tables: Freeing Mission from the Christian-Industrial Complex.* Downers Grove, IL: Intervarsity Press Books.

Bosch, D.J. 1991. *Transforming Mission: Paradigm Shifts in Theology of Mission.* Maryknoll, NY: Orbis Books.

————. 1995. *Believing in the Future: Toward a Missiology of Western Culture.* Valley Forge, PA: Trinity Press International.

Carey, W. 1792. *An Enquiry into the Obligations of Christians to Use Means for the Conversion of the Heathens. In Which the Religious State of the Different Nations of the World, the Success of Former Undertakings, and the Practicability of Further Undertakings Are Considered.* Leicester: Ann Ireland.

Case, J.R. 2012. *An Unpredictable Gospel: American Evangelicals and World Christianity, 1812–1920.* New York, NY: Oxford University Press.

Cavanaugh, B. 1998. *Sower's Seeds of Encouragement: Fifth Planting.* New York, NY: Paulist Press.

Chee, E.J. 2014. *Changing Pathways in Confirming a Long-Term Missionary "Call": Some Implications for Missionary Recruitment.* (DMin) Kings University: Kings University.

Coffey, A., and P. Atkinson, 1996. *Making Sense of Qualitative Data: Complementary Research Strategies.* London: Sage.

Corbett, S., and B. Fikkert. 2009. *When Helping Hurts: How to Alleviate Poverty Without Hurting the Poor, and Yourself.* Chicago, IL: Moody Publishers.

Dewerse, R. 2013. *Breaking Calabashes: Becoming an Intercultural Community.* Unley, Australia: MediaCom Education Inc.

Douglas, J.D. 1975. *Let the Earth Hear His Voice: Official Reference Volume, Papers and Responses.* Minneapolis. MN: World Wide Publications.

———. 1982. *The New Bible Dictionary.* Leicester: Universities and Colleges Christian Fellowship.

Durkheim, É., and R. Buss. 2006. *On Suicide.* London: Penguin.

Durkheim, É., and G. Simpson. 1933. *[On the] Division of Labour in Society: Being a Trans. of His De la Division du Travail Social with an Estimate of His Work.* New York, NY: Macmillan.

Elmore, T. 2010. *Generation iY.* Atlanta, GA: Poet Gardener Publishing.

Esterberg, K.G. 2002. *Qualitative Methods in Social Research.* London: McGraw Hill.

Frost, M. 2011. *The Road to Missional: Journey to the Center of the Church.* Grand Rapids, MI: Baker Books.

Frost, M., and A. Hirsch. 2003. *The Shaping of Things to Come: Innovation and Mission for the Twenty-first Century Church.* Peabody, MS: Hendrickson Publishers.

Geertz, C. 2000. *Available Light: Anthropological Reflections on Philosophical Topics.* Princeton, NJ: Princeton University Press.

Giddens, A. 1989. *Sociology.* Cambridge: Polity Press.

Gold, M. 2003. *The Hybridization of an Assembly of God Church: Proselytism, Retention, and Reaffiliation.* Lewiston, N.Y. : Edwin Mellon Press.

Guder, D.L., and L. Barrett. 1998. *Missional Church: A Vision for the Sending of the Church in North America.* Grand Rapids, MI: W.B. Eerdmans Pub.

Guinness, M.G., and M.G. Taylor. 1894. *The Story of the China Inland Mission.* Third Edition. London: Morgan and Scott.

Guyau, J.M. 1885. *Esquisse d'une Morale sans Obligation ni Sanction.* Paris.

Hammond, P., R.P. Stevens, and T. Svanoe. 2002. *The Marketplace Annotated Bibliography: A Christian Guide to Books on Work, Business and Vocation.* Downers Grove, IL: Intervarsity Press.

Hay, R.,et al. 2007. *Worth Keeping: Global Perspectives on Best Practice in Missionary Retention.* Pasadena, CA: William Carey Library.

Hibbert, R., E. Hibbert, and T. Silberman. 2015. The Journey Towards Long-term Missionary Service: How Australian Missionaries Are Being Called and Choose Mission Agencies. *Missiology: An International Review.* 43(4), 469–482.

Honderich, T. 1995. *The Oxford Companion to Philosophy.* Oxford: Oxford University Press.

Howell, B.M. 2012. *Short-term Mission: An Ethnography of Christian Travel Narrative and Experience*. Downers Grove, IL: IVP Academic.

Janssens, A. 1993. *Family and Social Change: The Household as a Process in an Industrializing Community*. Cambridge: Cambridge University Press.

Jenkins, P. 2002. *The Next Christendom: The Coming of Global Christianity*. Oxford: Oxford University Press.

Jennings, B. 1979. *A New Forward Thrust for World Missions*. Retrieved from http://www.missionfrontiers.org/issue/article/a-new-forward-thrust-for-world-missions

Johnson, T.M., G.A. Bellofatto, A.W. Hickman, and B.A. Coon. 2013. Christianity in its Global Context, 1970–2020. *Society, Religion, and Mission*. June 2013.

Johnstone, P.J.S.G. 1979. *Operation World: A Handbook for World Intercession*. 2nd British ed. Bromley: STL Publications.

————. 1993. *Operation World: Day-to-Day Guide to Praying for the World*. 5th rev.ed.. Carlisle: OM Publishing.

————. 2011. *The Future of the Global Church: History, Trends, and Possibilities*. Colorado Springs, CO: Biblica; WEC International.

Johnstone, P.J.S.G., J. Mandryk, and R. Johnstone. 2001. *Operation World*. 6th ed. Carlisle: Paternoster Lifestyle.

King, A. 1993. Sage on the Stage: From Sage on the Stage to Guide on the Side. *College Teaching*, 41.

Kollman, P.V. 2011. At the Origins of Mission and Missiology: A Study in the Dynamics of Religious Language. *Journal of the American Academy of Religion*, 79(2), 425–458.

Koyama, K. 1980. *Three Mile an Hour God: Biblical Reflections*. Maryknoll, NY: Orbis Books.

Kuhn, T.S. 1970. *The Structure of Scientific Revolutions*. 2nd ed. Chicago, IL: University of Chicago Press.

Küng, H. 1987. *Theologie im Aufbruch: Eine ökumenische Grundlegung*. Munich: Piper Verlag.

Lane, J.F. 2000. *Pierre Bourdieu: A Critical Introduction*. Sterling, VA: Pluto Press.

Lausanne Movement. 1974. *The Lausanne Covenant*. Retrieved from https://www.lausanne.org/content/covenant/lausanne-covenant

Lindsey, L.L. 2005. *Gender Roles: A Sociological Perspective*. 4th ed. Upper Saddle River: Pearson Prentice Hall.

Livermore, D.A. 2013. *Serving with Eyes Wide Open: Doing Short-term Missions with Cultural Intelligence*. Updated ed. Grand Rapids, MI: Baker Books.

Livesey, C. 2010. *Sociology Central Teaching Notes: Introduction to Sociology*. Retrieved from http://www.sociology.org.uk/AS_Introductory.pdf

Martin, R.P. 2007. *Philippians: An Introduction and Commentary*. Downers Grove, IL: Intervarsity Press.

McVay, J., and D. Parrott. 2015. *Mobilizing More Missionaries: Insights from Surveys of Long-termers and Prospective Missionaries*. Retrieved from Launch Survey website: www.launchsurvey.wordpress.com.

Merton, R.K. 1968. *Social Theory and Social Structure*. 1968 enl. ed. New York, NY: Free Press.

Northouse, P.G. 2013. *Leadership: Theory and Practice*. 6th ed. London: SAGE.

Patterson, K., J. Grenny, D. Maxfield, M. Ron, and A. Switzler. 2008. *Influencer: The Power to Change Anything*. London: McGraw-Hill.

Reese, R. 2014. John Gatu and the Moratorium on Missionaries. *Missiology: An International Review*. 42(3), 245–256.

Richardson, L. 1988. *The Dynamics of Sex and Gender: A Sociological Perspective*. 3rd ed. New York, NY: Harper and Row.

Richardson, R. 2013. Emerging Adults and the Future of Missions. *International Bulletin of Missionary Research*. Vol. 37(No. 3), 79–84.

Rutherford, S. 1648. *Survey of the Spiritual Antichrist*.

Sanneh, L. 1987. Christian Missions and the Western Guilt Complex. *The Christian Century*. April 8, 1987.

Shadrach, S. 2015. *The Key To World Evangelization: Mobilization*. Retrieved from http://www.thetravelingteam.org/articles/mobilization.

Shaw, R. 2006. *Waking the Giant: The Resurging Student Mission Movement*. Pasadena, CA: William Carey Library.

———. 2014. *Spiritual Equipping for Mission: Thriving as God's Message Bearers*. Downers Grove, IL: Intervarsity Press Books, an imprint of Intervarsity Press.

———. 2016. *The Handbook for Great Commission Ministries*. Chiang Mai, Thailand: Ignite Media.

Skreslet, S.H. 2012. *Comprehending Mission: The Questions, Methods, Themes, Problems, and Prospects of Missiology*. Maryknoll, NY: Orbis Books.

Strauss, W., and N. Howe. 1991. *Generations: The History of America's Future, 1584 to 2069*. First ed. New York, NY: Morrow.

Suttle, T. 2015. Walter Brueggemann: *Faith and Culture Conference Lecture 01, detailed Notes*. Retrieved from http://www.patheos.com/blogs/paperbacktheology/2015/ 04/ walter-brueggemann-at-faith-culture-conference-2015-lecture-01-detailed-notes. html

Taylor, W.D. 1997. *Too Valuable to Lose: Exploring the Causes and Cures of Missionary Attrition*. Pasadena, CA: William Carey Library.

Thomas, W.I., and D.S.T. Thomas. 1928. *The Child in America: Behavior Problems and Programs*. New York, NY: A.A. Knopf.

Twenge, J.M. 2014. *Generation Me: Why Today's Young Americans Are More Confident, Assertive, Entitled—and More Miserable than Ever Before*. First Atria paperback ed. New York, NY: Atria Paperback.

Wall, R. 2014. *Prepaing Adults for Crossing Cultures: A Transformative Approach to Christian Mission Training*. PhD, University College Institute of Education, London.

————. 2015a. Equipping The Whole Person. Retrieved from http://www.mission-arytraining.org/mt/index.php/forum/bulletin-no-1-equipping-the-whole-person/3-equipping-the-whole-person?start=6

————. 2015b. A Transformative Model of Mission Training. In S.B. Bevans, T. Chai, J.N. Jennings, K. Jorgensen, and D. Werner, eds. *Reflecting on and Equipping for Christian Mission*. Oxford: Regnum Books.

Walls, A.F. 1996. *The Missionary Movement in Christian History: Studies in the Transmission of Faith*. New York, NY: Orbis Books.

Weber, M. 1949. *The Methodology of the Social Sciences*. New York, NY: Free Press.

Winter, R.D., and S.C. Hawthorne. 1981. *Perspectives on the World Christian Movement: Reader*. Pasadena, CA: William Carey Library.

————. 2009. *Perspectives on the World Christian Movement*. 4th ed. Pasadena, CA: William Carey Library.

Woodberry, R.D. 2012. Missionary Roots of Liberal Democracy. *American Political Science Review*. 106(2).

Wright, C.J.H. 2006. *The Mission of God: Unlocking the Bible's Grand Narrative*. Nottingham: Intervarsity Press.